Understanding
Middle School
Math

Understanding
Middle School
Math

Cool Problems

to Get Students

Thinking and

Connecting

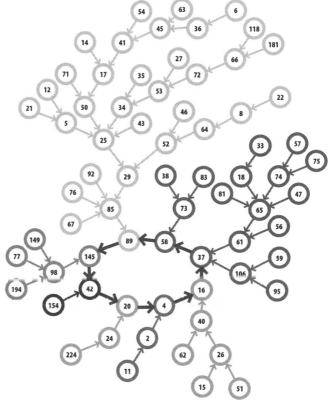

Arthur Hyde

with Susan Friedlander, Cheryl Heck, and Lynn Pittner

Foreword by Judith Zawojewski

HEINEMANN

Portsmouth, NH

Heinemann
361 Hanover Street
Portsmouth, NH 03801–3912
www.heinemann.com

Offices and agents throughout the world

The author and publisher wish to thank those who have generously given permission to reprint borrowed material:

"A weighty matter" by Lauren Cabell and Phil Geib from *Chicago Tribune*, 2/1/2002. Copyright © 2002 by *Chicago Tribune*. Used by permission and protected by the Copyright Laws of the United States. The printing, copying, redistribution, or retransmission of the Material without express written permission is prohibited. All rights reserved.

Library of Congress Cataloging-in-Publication Data
Hyde, Arthur A.
    Understanding middle school math : cool problems to get students thinking and connecting / Arthur Hyde ; with Susan Friedlander, Cheryl Heck, and Lynn Pittner.
        p. cm.
    Includes bibliographical references and index.
    ISBN-13: 978-0-325-01386-2
    ISBN-10: 0-325-01386-1
    1. Mathematics—Study and teaching (Middle school). 2. Creative teaching. I. Title.
QA135.6.H93 2009
510.71'2—dc22   2008047625

Editor: Emily Michie Birch
Production: Lynne Costa
Cover design: Night & Day Design
Typesetter: Val Levy, Drawing Board Studios
Manufacturing: Steve Bernier

Printed in the United States of America on acid-free paper
13 12   VP   2 3 4 5

CONTENTS

CHAPTER 6: GEOMETRY AND MEASUREMENT 182

CHAPTER 7: DATA ANALYSIS AND PROBABILITY 220

Foreword

A book of cool problems for middle school mathematics classrooms—
does it get any better? Yes, it does. Art Hyde and his colleagues, three
middle school math teachers, go far beyond providing a collection of
problems. They address big ideas, make connections, nurture the use of
varied representations, and provide vivid accounts of actual classroom
implementation all through the lens of the author-created Braid Model,
a coherent model of learning that links language, cognition, and mathematics through problem solving.

The middle school mathematics classroom has traditionally been a
place to review and polish some set of basic skills—primarily arithmetic—to prepare for the journey through high school algebra, geometry,
advanced algebra, and trigonometry. Although some innovative programs
have been designed that engage middle school students in the development of concepts and intuitions about algebra, linear and exponential
growth, spatial relationship and geometric properties, statistics, and
probability, these programs are not found in the majority of American
classrooms.

I taught from traditional textbooks for nine years as a teacher of
sixth-, seventh-, and eighth-grade mathematics. Along with many of my
peers, I was always on the search for ideas, activities, lessons, and units
that would enrich the experience for *all* of my students—experiences that
would challenge, engage, stretch, and open my students' minds to the
wonder, beauty, and application of mathematics. I ended up with two file
cabinets full of replacement lessons, ideas for units of study, collections
of problems, and various articles from the teaching journals. Every year,
I recreated my sixth-, seventh-, and eighth-grade plans to meet the needs
of the students I had that particular year, and assimilated new and innovative ideas that I found during the year. What a resource *Understanding
Middle School Math* would have been for me!

Art Hyde and colleagues, in their quest for cool problems that teach
concepts in deep ways, help teachers make the connections between their
classroom needs and the resources provided in this book. *Understanding*

Middle School Math acts as a lesson study, with its conversational style and its vivid illustrations from teachers' classrooms. As a result, teachers obtain concrete ideas for differentiating challenges for students who bring varied talents to the table. They help facilitate students' evolution in the use of various representations, from initial visual and verbal representations to abstract generalizations and symbols. Mathematics comes alive as students engage in varying contexts, from applied situations, to games, to explorations of mathematical environments for their own sake. Throughout the book, the problems help teachers develop the problem-solving aspect of a model curriculum—making connections within and across problems, using rich mathematical problems as a means to enhance students' learning, and using problems as a basis for serious discussion and to encourage conceptual dialogue.

The chapters in this book are connected by the KWC method for scoping out a problem—What do I *Know* for sure? What do I *Want* to find out? Are there any special *Conditions*?—and a view of mathematics learning and teaching that braids together language, cognition, and the domain of mathematics. In particular, students are viewed as actively developing their conceptual understanding in the context of mathematical problem solving. This approach is consistent with research (Lesh and Zawojewski 2006) that reveals that higher problem-solving performance is associated with breadth and depth of mathematical knowledge.

No compelling evidence exists that links direct instruction in *isolated problem-solving strategies* (for example, draw a picture, make a table, consider a similar problem) to *improved problem-solving performance*. Rather, problem solving needs to be thought of as a means for learning mathematics. Simultaneously, mathematical knowledge is a launch for more sophisticated problem solving, and students can use problem-solving strategies as they engage in problem-solving activities. The authors of *Understanding Middle School Math* show that students' development of solutions to mathematical problems goes hand in hand with students' acquisition of deep conceptual understanding.

The role of *representation* and the development of *representational fluency* is foundational to the cool problems in *Understanding Middle School Math*. Most important in middle school mathematics education is that instead of teaching representation simply as a skill for its own sake, teachers must link representation to a function or purpose that is compelling for students. For example, in Chapter 5, when reflecting back on the Chocolate Algebra problem, a boy said, "I liked the tables the best for figuring out the patterns and equations, but I liked the graphs the best for making predictions" (158–59). Such insight on the part of students can only be accomplished when teachers explicitly establish reasons for engaging students in the production and analysis of a new representation. Throughout *Understanding Middle School Math*, the authors traverse the representational landscape from visual and verbal to general and symbolic by connecting each form to purposes and functions that are immediately apparent to the students.

With each set of cool problems, the authors provide vivid classroom narratives, which help teachers make connections to significant mathematical content. Further, the narratives provide ideas for organizing students for small-group work and clues for diagnosing and assessing what relevant knowledge students possess. Organized around number, proportional reasoning, algebra, geometry, data analysis, and probability, the collection of problems in *Understanding Middle School Math* ranges from reworked standards to new or unique problem situations, all the while making connections across mathematics topics within each chapter.

Understanding Middle School Math provides teachers with sound problems to augment any middle school mathematics textbook series, as replacement lessons, enrichment activities, and replacement units. Most importantly, the book is written in a way that helps middle school teachers implement the problems with *all* students, using flexible grouping that is responsive to students' ongoing individual needs.

Understanding Middle School Math can also be used in professional development settings, especially lesson study—which was also the origin of the narratives for this book. In lesson study, teachers read activities, plan common lessons, and then implement those activities while observing each other or making videos for later study. The follow-up reflection session provides opportunities for teachers to discuss what happened, to explore what modifications might be made to the planning and the implementation, and to think about how the problems empower students' problem-solving and learning abilities. Equally as important, *Understanding Middle School Math* empowers middle school mathematics teachers to become professionals who create challenging and exciting mathematical environments for *all* students.

—*Judith S. Zawojewski*
Department of Mathematics
and Science Education
Illinois Institute of Technology, Chicago

INTRODUCTION

As I think back on the way I first imagined this book about six years ago, I really have to laugh. What was I thinking? I don't consider myself a compulsive person, though I suspect others might. I see myself as thorough, comprehensive.

My vision of *Understanding Middle School Math* was to empty my filing cabinets and share the unusual manipulatives, activities, and problems I have created over the nearly forty years I have been teaching mathematics. I had indexed and coded my files (the Hyde Decimal System) to make them easily accessible for teaching. When I began to plan this book, I just kept adding more and more until I finally realized that subconsciously I was trying to build my own middle school mathematics curriculum, complete with relational database for more than five hundred problems and their concepts.

I went back to the drawing board. I decided that a book for middle school math teachers should have the insights of current, experienced middle school math teachers who had taken my ideas and run with them. I asked three excellent teachers, all of whom have taken multiple courses with me and have incorporated many of my problems into their repertoire, to create this resource with me.

Susan Friedlander, Cheryl Heck, and Lynn Pittner are with the same students day after day, and their planning and teaching must reflect the continuity of experiences they want their students to have. In contrast, I am all over the Illinois map doing my own idiosyncratic version of lesson study. I pose problems and activities in dozens of very different schools and at many different grade levels, constantly tinkering with the activities and trying to get more from students. More *what*? More excitement, more engagement, more buy-in, more awareness of their own thinking, and ultimately more understanding of mathematical concepts.

The four of us decided to select problems and activities that could readily replace bland traditional textbook content. Susan, Cheryl, and Lynn added richness to the problems by sharing the work of their students. We wrote many of the classroom descriptions collaboratively, some individually. I created almost all the problems, but we also modified in novel ways others we encountered over the years.

The more we dug into challenging, cool problems, the more we realized that *Understanding Middle School Math* could not just be about curriculum. We needed to show how we interacted with our students, helped them build connections of all kinds, and helped them think.

What are criteria for *cool*? Cool problems and activities

- are set in easily imaginable, real-world situations;
- are set in intriguing contexts or have inherently interesting, motivating premises that provoke students to think; and
- contain rich, deep, meaningful mathematics, big ideas, and important concepts that can be understood and connected to related concepts.

In our experience, the textbooks and programs school districts purchase do not always provide the best ways to build students' understanding because they

- do not address all the concepts we want to hit;
- do not go into sufficient depth on concepts;
- do not make the necessary connections among concepts;
- do not use the approach to thinking about the concepts that students ought to use;
- do not have enough examples of good problems for the students to practice;
- have a narrow definition of problem solving; and
- are more concerned with memorizing procedures than with understanding concepts.

Even though we love creating our own materials, problems, and activities, we are on a constant quest for cool problems. No single textbook can do all the things that our students need—we can use cool problems to replace drab, contrived, and ineffectual textbook problems, or we can use cool problems as extensions to textbook problems. (See the Problem Index, page 255, or refer to our website, www.braidedmath.com, for color versions and extensions of many of the problems in this book.)

In *Understanding Middle School Math* we include story problems, hands-on math activities, and worthwhile mathematical tasks. We also consider other factors when creating supplemental problems:

- When we know that learning the procedures in the next chapter of the textbook depends on true understanding of a particular concept (whether or not that is acknowledged in the chapter), we look for a really good problem that could unlock the understanding we seek before moving on to those procedures.
- Students develop their understanding of concepts by working on and solving mathematically rich problems. *Problem solving is not an application of what they have already learned: it is a major vehicle for building new meaning.*

- Surprising things happen along the way. Results are unexpected or counterintuitive.

Teachers easily can extend and differentiate the problems and activities in *Understanding Middle School Math* by

- preparing problems, questions, or activities with three levels of difficulty, from least challenging to most challenging;
- encouraging students to create their own representations—objects, language, actions, pictures, lists, tables, graphs, and equations—that vary in abstractness, sensory modalities, or information-processing channels, from concrete to increasingly abstract; and
- considering the extent to which some students may be working in unfamiliar contexts.

Our particular approach to problem solving is designed to get the most productive thinking from our students. We call it the Braid Model (see Chapter 2) because it braids language, cognition, and mathematics. The Braid Model is a major feature of *Comprehending Math* (Hyde 2006), to which this book is a companion.

A major feature of the Braid Model is KWC, an adaptation of a reading comprehension strategy that the teacher models for the whole class. She shows students how to ask themselves three questions that will *focus their attention on the most important parts of the math problem* or task:

What do I *k*now for sure?
What do I *w*ant to know?
Are there any special *c*onditions?

We fully examine how to use this approach, incorporating all the math content and process standards. Rarely will a KWC solve the problem, but it will help students clarify what is happening and what is being asked of them. It will help them understand the problem. It is a great metacognitive prompt that students can use naturally as a habit of mind. Please, get some scratch paper and try this problem with us:

A Checkerboard of Squares

How many squares are on a standard 8-by-8 checkerboard?

This deceptively simple classic problem has been used in classrooms and possibly at dinner tables across the country to get people to think. Whenever I have used this problem with students and adults, I find that they complete the *K* and the *W* of their KWC quickly, many with a grin of smugness.

Despite my students' confidence, as I walk around the classroom I begin to smile and eagerly await the incredible, teachable moment. This is precisely *the* moment where students must pay attention to *C*, the special conditions of the problem.

To get my students to derive the special conditions, I distribute standard-sized checkerboards and ask them to carefully look back at the *K* of their KWC. See Figure I-1.

In the *K*, I bring their attention back to what they knew for sure about squares. Given what my students knew for sure about squares, four congruent sides and four right angles, I prompt them with the following question: "Is there more than one way to describe a square, in terms of

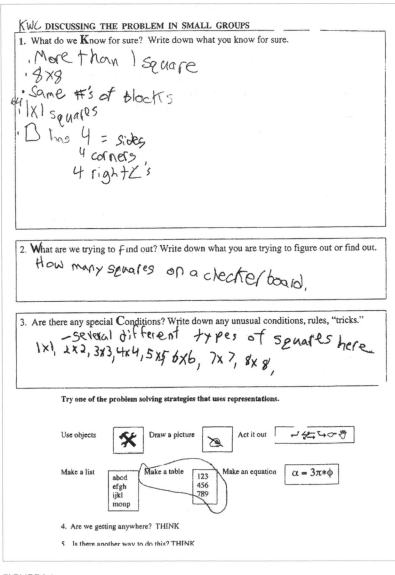

KWC DISCUSSING THE PROBLEM IN SMALL GROUPS

1. What do we **K**now for sure? Write down what you know for sure.

· More than 1 square
· 8x8
· Same #'s of blocks
64 1x1 squares
· ▢ has 4 = sides
       4 corners
       4 right∠'s

2. **W**hat are we trying to **f**ind out? Write down what you are trying to figure out or find out.

How many squares on a checkerboard.

3. Are there any special **C**onditions? Write down any unusual conditions, rules, "tricks."

-several different types of squares here
1x1, 2x2, 3x3, 4x4, 5x5 6x6, 7x7, 8x8,

Try one of the problem solving strategies that uses representations.

Use objects | Draw a picture | Act it out

Make a list | Make a table | Make an equation $\alpha = 3\pi * \phi$
abcd | 123
efgh | 456
ijkl | 789
monp

4. Are we getting anywhere? THINK

5. Is there another way to do this? THINK

FIGURE I-1

its dimensions, on this checkerboard?" Several moments of group collaboration pass by, and the students generate a list of eight different sizes of squares they see on the checkerboard. See the special conditions in Figure I-1.

Once the students fully wrap their minds around the problem and truly understand it, I have them continue working in groups to determine the total number of squares on a checkerboard. Depending on the amount of scaffolding needed, and the visual-spatial reasoning abilities of my students, I provide them with square cutouts that resemble the 7-by-7, the 6-by-6, 5-by-5, 4-by-4, 3-by-3, 2-by-2, and 1-by-1. The students use these cutouts to cover certain portions of the checkerboard to complete a tab record of their findings. See Figures I-2 and I-3.

FIGURE I-2

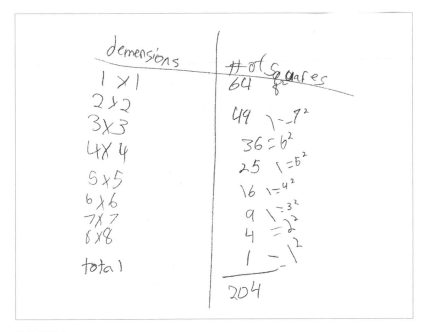

FIGURE I-3

Dimensions	Number of Squares	
1 * 1	64	8^2
2 * 2	49	7^2
3 * 3	36	6^2
4 * 4	25	5^2
5 * 5	16	4^2
6 * 6	9	3^2
7 * 7	4	2^2
8 * 8	1	1^2

FIGURE I-4

In our debriefing of this activity, my students were quick to recognize that their totals for each type of square were square numbers. Most also saw a pattern in the data table that they called a "mirror-reflection." Figure I-4 shows a cleaned-up table of Figure 3 so you can more readily see this pattern. We would probably refer to this pattern as *inverting* because the values on the left column are the same as the right column except they are in reverse order.

The students also demonstrated their newfound understanding and appreciation for the *C* in their KWC. Because I use A Checkerboard of Squares as one of my students' initial exposures to the power of KWC, I typically follow this activity with a ceremonial placing of the right hand on their math books to solemnly promise to always pay special attention to detail when completing the *C* of future KWCs.

Understanding Middle School Math is filled with problems and activities that we have used with our students, ranging from regular fifth graders to eighth graders taking honors algebra. Some of the problems are so critical to help students build understanding that we refer to them as *anchor problems* or *anchor lessons*. Anchor lessons are those that provide strong and deep conceptual understanding; teachers can refer back to anchor lessons time and again during the year and students will remember the connection. We've modified the cool problems in different ways to make them effective for different kinds of learners.

Even though there is a clear need in our schools for solid, supplemental mathematics problems, ones that are easy to implement in classrooms and that are beneficial to students and their math comprehension, a whole new curriculum is not necessary. Teachers can make good use of cool problems to intrigue and engage students, help them understand concepts that never made sense to them, or get them to make connections both inside and outside the classroom. That's what you will find here.

1 | What You Teach and How You Teach It

Let's be candid. By the time they get to middle school, the majority of the students in your classrooms dislike math. They really hate story problems. They'd rather grab any two numbers they see tucked away somewhere in the problem and just guess which operation to perform (appendectomy, tonsillectomy, lobotomy?) than read the problem. "Wait. Do ya mean I gotta like actually *read* all those words? Last year Mrs. Jones didn't make us read. She said we could just look for the key word that would tell us which thing to do. Ya know, like if it had *altogether*, you're supposed to add up all the numbers. Or if it says *product* somewhere, you *times* the two numbers."

Misconception

Many students and teachers still adhere to the myth about the value of *key words* or *cue words*, which is a tragic mistake. Experts (Harvey and Goudvis 2007, Keene and Zimmermann 2007) in reading comprehension—the in-depth understanding of meaning in the written word—agree that while context cues can help build meaning of a passage, they are no substitute for reading the full text and using powerful reading comprehension strategies such as:

- making connections
- visualizing
- determining importance
- metacognitive monitoring
- asking questions
- inferring and predicting
- synthesizing

THE POWER OF KWC: AN ALTERNATIVE TO KEY WORDS

As we can see in the Checkerboard problem, the KWC provides a structure for thinking. For the kids who are lost, it gives them a place to start (and more). If you have heard "I don't know what to do. Where do I begin?" more than 1,000 times in your career, you can use the KWC with authority and say, "Everyone in your group should ask yourselves the three questions that are on the poster for the KWC." For your talented yet impulsive students who don't read the problem carefully, this structure (especially asking for the special conditions) forces them to slow down and think about the real constraints inherent in the problem situation.

The Tall Tale of the Two Texas Ranches

At the Longhorn Saloon many years ago, two Texas ranchers were overheard having the following argument.

Rancher 1: I don't know where you got your information, mister, but I've been told I have the largest ranch in this here county.

Rancher 2: Well, I just reckon you've been told wrong. My ranch is the biggest in the county. Why, my Triangle T Ranch is so big, it takes 48 miles of barbed wire to go all the way around it!

Rancher 1: Well, ain't that somethin'. It takes 48 miles of barbed wire to go all the way around my ranch, too. My Wright Triangle Ranch is in the shape of a triangle and the 3 sides are 12 miles, 16 miles, and 20 miles.

Rancher 2: My Triangle T Ranch is shaped like a triangle, too. Its sides are 10 miles, 17 miles, and 21 miles. Well, I guess our ranches are the same size, then.

Rancher 1: No, I still think mine is bigger.

Are the two ranches the same size or is one bigger than the other?

If we are working with a class of thirty students to demonstrate a KWC using this problem, before sharing the problem we tell them the title—in this case, *The Tall Tale of the Two Texas Ranches*—and ask them to guess what the problem is about. The brainstorming students do is not off-task; it is time well spent because they are warming up their imagination engines. Brainstorming helps motivate students to try to understand the problem. It helps to counteract years of not reading the problem, making wild guesses, and giving up.

We share the problem with students and begin the KWC process. They read one sentence at a time and imagine the situation being described. (If students had no prior experience with a KWC, we would first put the problem on an overhead and reveal only one sentence at a time.) We ask, What are the basic facts here? What do we *know* for sure? and keep track of students' answers on the board. See typical student responses in the box below. At some point, we explicitly ask, Can you visualize the two ranches?

There are two ranchers who think they have big ranches.

They both think they have the biggest ranch in the county.

The Triangle T Ranch has 48 miles of barbed wire around it.

The Wright Triangle Ranch also has 48 miles of barbed wire around it.

The Wright Triangle Ranch is in the shape of a triangle with sides 12, 16, and 20 miles long.

The Triangle T Ranch is also in the shape of a triangle with sides 10, 17, and 21 miles long.

Next, we ask the students to think through the *W* in the KWC, What do we *want* to find out? A student may ask, for example, "Are the two ranches the same size or is one bigger than the other?" We also keep track of students' responses on the board.

Last, we address the *C* in the KWC, Are there any special *conditions*, anything strange that we need to take into consideration? Students' observations may include:

- It sounds like the two ranches have the same perimeter.
- Does that mean they are the same size?
- What does the problem mean when it says *size*?

We find that the *C* questions often provoke students to make powerful connections. In the example above, one student *inferred* that the ranchers were talking about perimeter, although she did not *literally* use that term. The distinction between literal meaning and inferential meaning is important in reading for understanding and is worth clarifying for the students. We usually ask students, "Does it actually say *perimeter*? Is that literally the exact word used in the problem?" When they say no, we ask, "What did the problem say that led you to *infer* that perimeter was involved?" We explain to students that it is fine to make inferences, but in mathematics it is important when making an inference to check to be certain that the inference is accurate.

Returning to the ranch problem, we can see that it literally says that 48 miles of barbed wire surrounds each ranch. Since perimeter is a distance around an object, the inference seems justified.

The two other responses to the *C* question lead us to consider what is meant by *size*. Experience has shown us that many students assume *equal in size* could mean *the same distance around*, and in fact this is true of circles and regular polygons. For instance, if an equilateral triangle has a perimeter of 48 (miles, inches, and so on), we know that each side is 16. If both ranchers had said that their ranches were in the shape of an equilateral triangle with a perimeter of 48 miles, we would know the two triangles must be congruent.

Most students readily infer that *size*, in relation to triangles, means a two-dimensional space that they would measure as area. Some middle school students, however, continue to confuse area and perimeter, concepts worth addressing.

Using KWC to Tap Prior Knowledge

In the initial phases of looking at a story problem, students essentially are trying to *understand* the problem. In the understanding phase, we explicitly ask students to try to imagine the situation presented in the problem. KWC is a potent way for students to bring to the surface of their minds relevant prior knowledge about the situation, the context, and math concepts (also referred to as *activating relevant schemata* by reading specialists).

After we ask students to imagine the situation in the story problem, we ask them to create a *language representation*, oral or written, of how they *conceive* the situation or problem. Once students have sufficiently imagined the situation and described it, we encourage them to choose another *representational* math problem-solving strategy. For instance:

> Please try drawing a picture of the two ranches. It does not have to be to scale. Drawing a free-hand picture to help you see what is going on or to help you imagine the situation is very different from making a scale drawing, where you need to be precise in your visual representation.

In scale drawings the students' focus is split between attending to the accuracy of the graph paper drawing and the mathematical concepts in the problem. We prefer that they sketch a picture at first and then refine the picture to be more accurate later. Students can rethink, revise, and redraw pictures many times as their conceptions of the problem change.

Let's draw a picture that considers what we know about the ranch problem situation. See Figure 1.1.

Most students now correctly think that the problem is about determining which ranch (triangle) has the *greater* area or whether or not the triangles are *equal* in area. Most also immediately want to use the formula $A = \frac{1}{2}bh$. At some point we have to ask students why they could use the

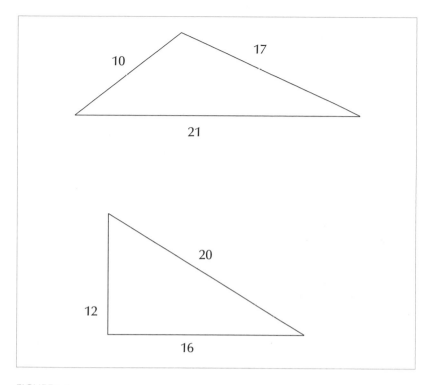

FIGURE 1.1

formula for one triangle but not the other, and we usually hear that they "know the height of one but not the other." We then feign ignorance and ask students how they know the height, and they respond, "because it is a right triangle." Then we ask, "but how you do *know* that?"

As we mentioned earlier, we want students to check their inferences. The Pythagorean Theorem tells us that in any right triangle, the sum of the squares of the two short sides equals the square of the long side (the hypotenuse). However, that presupposes that one knows the triangle has a right angle. We have found it necessary on numerous occasions to re-mind students that the converse of the theorem can help us here: *If the sum of the squares of the two short sides equals the square of the long side (the hypotenuse), then it must be a right triangle.* In this case, does $12^2 + 16^2 = 20^2$? Yes, 144 + 256 = 400. Therefore, the shape is a right triangle with a height of 12 and a base of 16. Its area is then $A = \frac{1}{2}(12)(16)$, or 96 square miles.

When we ask students what can we say about the other triangle (ranch), they are unsure how to proceed. We ask more questions:

- Let's go back to the W. What are you trying to figure out?
- Basically, do the triangles have the same area or is one bigger than the other?
- What would have to be true for them to be equal?

Almost all students realize that the 10, 17, 21 triangle also would have an area of 96 square units, so we ask, "What would cause that triangle to have an area of 96?" Some realize that its height would have to be "just right" for a base of 21, so then we ask, "And what would that be?"

$$96 = \frac{1}{2}(21)\,h \qquad h = 96 * \frac{2}{21} \qquad h = 9\frac{1}{7}$$

We know the students are on the right path, so we continue: "Is it possible that the height of this triangle is a little more than 9?" Most of the students are not sure, but every class seems to have at least one who has good spatial visualization and says,

> *If you take that side of 10 and hold it tight at the top while you swing the bottom of that side to the right and make it perpendicular to the 21 side, it will hang down a lot. More than just 1 unit, I bet. So its height is probably less than 9. See Figure 1.2.*

Other times a student will mention using a compass to draw an arc of a circle with radius 10 and center at the vertex formed by sides 10 and 17. Therefore, the students have reason to believe that the right triangle is the larger of the two. (Note that this is not proof. We will look at that later in this chapter.)

Using KWC to Structure Group Learning

The language used in the math classroom is vital to everyone's success, students and teachers alike. When a teacher arranges students into small groups of three or four so they can discuss the problem, he or she must provide scaffolding, the supporting structures necessary for students to accomplish challenging tasks. As with painting or plastering, a scaffold enables a person to do the work. A scaffold does not do the work, nor does it provide clues, hints, or insider-trading information.

KWC is a structure for discussions and thinking. It gives students a good place to start their deliberations. A few years ago, I conducted a series of staff development sessions with the entire mathematics department of a high school in a working-class suburb of Chicago. When I suggested to teachers that they have their students work in groups, I heard groans worthy of a Greek chorus:

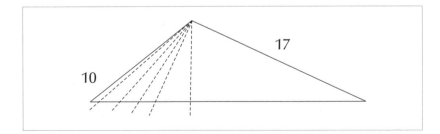

FIGURE 1.2

"I tried it and it doesn't work."

"They just fool around."

"They are totally off-task all the time."

"When they take quizzes and tests they are not going to work in groups, so why should I do it now?"

"I put them in groups, but they don't know what to do."

In response to this last statement, I asked, "Why don't you show them what to do?" One teacher immediately, and somewhat indignantly, blurted out, "That's not my job. That should be done by the junior high school teachers."

My colleagues and I disagree. Our students need to learn *how to learn,* and part of our job as teachers is to help them do just that, whether they are kindergarteners, middle schoolers, or graduate students.

So, I took a deep breath and described to the high school teachers some of my experiences with students working in pairs and threes and occasionally in fours, as well as some specific ways to make it work. The key to consider is: If teachers model the three questions of the KWC for the whole class and explain their thinking along the way, students will be able to practice the KWC process in small groups. Teachers can then encourage students to use KWC in testing situations. When we see students taking a test muttering, "What do I know for sure?" we are fairly certain they have internalized the KWC structure.

Using KWC to Deepen Connections

Let's go back and figure out the actual area of the 10, 17, 21 triangle. If a student draws a perpendicular dashed line signifying height, she can reason that the dashed line divides the 10, 17, 21 triangle into two right triangles, with 10 and 17 as hypotenuses. We label the height as variable h. See Figure 1.3.

The two right triangles have a common side of length h, and their three sides are made from partitioning the base of 21 into two lengths, which we can label x and $(21 - x)$.

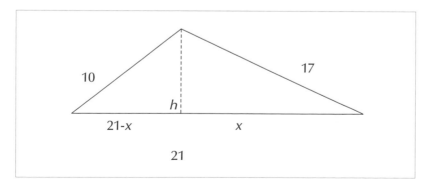

FIGURE 1.3

Misconception

Textbooks and teachers often demonstrate partitioning and labeling so quickly that many students get lost. They have no idea what was done, why it is legal (in at least thirty-one of the fifty United States). What is their misconception? It's magic. And when students are shown that they could do it another way, they are *really* convinced it's magic. See Figure 1.4. Another nail is driven into the coffin. Math makes no sense. But of course it should and it can.

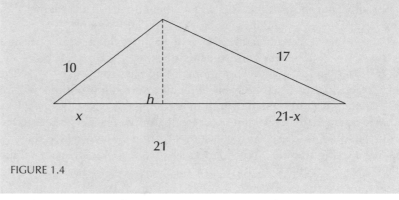

FIGURE 1.4

We can do another cycle of KWC, which takes about two minutes, on our picture in Figure 1.4:

What do I know for sure?
- I have a triangle with sides of length 10, 17, 21.
- I don't know what the height is.
- My picture has two variables, h and x.

What do I want to find out?
- What is the height of the triangle?

Why?
- So I can calculate its area and compare it to the other triangle.

Are there any special conditions? Any things to watch out for?
- That $21 - x$ looks like trouble.

Ideally, next we would ask students to work on the problem individually or in small groups, and then in the debriefing we would explore different ways they solved the problem (see below) with the intention of helping them experience the necessary logical reasoning. Note that this debriefing is not a lecture—we take what students have done and model for them how to think about each step in the process.

After groups or individual students report how they solved the problem, we begin:

Art: Sally, tell us what you did first. And how do you know it's okay to do that?

Sally: I wrote $h^2 + x^2 = 10^2 = 100$. I knew I could do this because I can use the Pythagorean Theorem with the right triangles.

Art: Okay, this tells us a basic relationship between h and x. What's next?

Billy: I just did the same thing with the other right triangle:

$h^2 + (21 - x)^2 = 17^2 = 289.$

Art: What would we do next?

Billy: Let's try clearing out the parentheses and combining the things that go together:

$h^2 + 441 - 42x + x^2 = 289.$

Art: Yes, this looks kind of yucky—but what do you see that's like what happened when we used Pythagoras with the other triangle? Both have h^2 and x^2, so we can do some substitution:

$h^2 + x^2 = 42x - 152$ and $h^2 + x^2 = 100$

$100 = 42x - 152 \quad 42x = 252 \quad x = 6 \quad 21 - x = 15$

$h^2 + x^2 = 100 \quad h^2 + 6^2 = 100 \quad h^2 + 36 = 100 \quad h^2 = 64 \quad h = 8$

Determining the height and area of the scalene triangle is good for students to work on because it reveals how beautifully substitution of equivalent quantities can quickly simplify a system of equations. What at first looked like messy quadratics became quite manageable—the height of the triangle is 8 and its base is 21, therefore $A = \frac{1}{2}bh$ or $A = \frac{1}{2}(21)(8) = 84$ square miles, making it definitely smaller than the 12, 16, 20 right triangle (area = 96 square miles), despite identical perimeters of 48 miles.

We like the ranch problem because, by using KWC, prior knowledge, inference, language, and scaffolding, teachers can help students see connections that deepen their understanding of geometric concepts and of algebraic equations representing geometric relationships (formulas). Teachers can differentiate the ranch problem easily by:

1. backtracking to make connections for those students whose knowledge is not well developed; for example, partitioning and part-whole relations in concrete form and expressed algebraically;
2. creating more examples at the same level of difficulty; for example, there are many scalene triangles like 10, 17, 21, composed of two Pythagorean triangles, where students would have to find the heights (altitudes); and
3. challenging those few students who can profit from going way beyond; for example, saying,

You don't need to find the height of a scalene triangle, or any kind of triangle, to calculate its area because if you know the three side lengths (a, b, and c), you can find its area by this formula:

$$A = \tfrac{1}{4} \sqrt{(a+b+c)(a+b-c)(a-b+c)(b-a+c)}$$

This is a version of Heron's formula. Can you see the triangle sum theorem hidden within this equation? Look at the four expressions under the square root sign. The first (a + b + c) is the perimeter. The other three expressions check to see if the sum of two sides is greater than the third side. If not, it is not a triangle.

Extensions

The following modification can be made for early middle school students who are learning about perimeter and area, but have not yet been introduced to the Pythagorean Theorem.

The Even Taller Tale of the Two Texas Ranches

At the Longhorn Saloon many years ago, two Texas ranchers were overheard having the following argument.

Rancher 1: I don't know where you got your information, mister, but I've been told I have the largest ranch in this here county.

Rancher 2: Well, I just reckon you've been told wrong. My ranch is the biggest in the county. Why, my Rectangle R Ranch is so big, it takes 48 miles of barbed wire to go all the way around it!

Rancher 1: Well, ain't that somethin'. It takes 48 miles of barbed wire to all the way around my ranch, too. My Wright Triangle Ranch is in the shape of a right triangle, and the lengths of the 3 sides are 12 miles, 16 miles, and 20 miles.

Rancher 2: My rectangular-shaped ranch must be larger, because it is 19 miles long!

Are the two ranches the same size or is one bigger than the other?

Despite the modification to the problem, students are still required to use their understanding of both perimeter and area to calculate which ranch is larger—the rectangular ranch or the right triangle ranch. The results may be counterintuitive to many young math students because the rectangular ranch has an area of 95 square miles (19 * 5), but the right triangle ranch has an area of 96 square miles. Students might initially believe the rectangle would have the larger area.

In another modification, the students work with messier numbers to calculate the area of a circular-shaped ranch with a circumference of 48 miles.

Rancher 3

Just as Rancher 2 sadly realizes Rancher 1 has the larger ranch, a stranger enters the Longhorn Saloon and says, "I'm new to this here county. I just purchased 48 miles of barbed wire to fence in my circle-shaped ranch." Does Rancher 1 still have the largest ranch in the county? See Figure 1.5

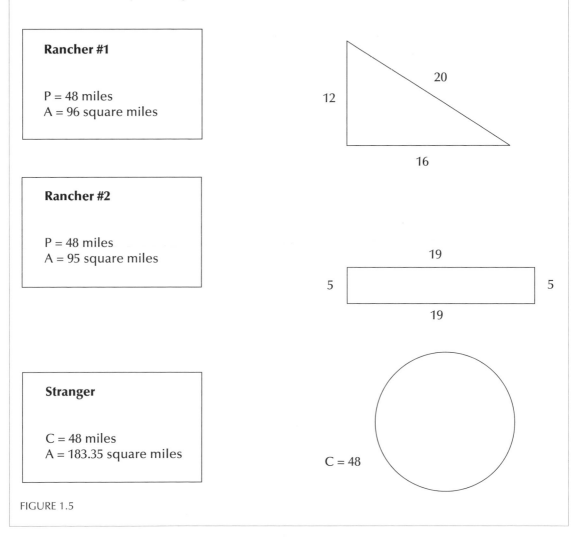

Rancher #1

P = 48 miles
A = 96 square miles

Rancher #2

P = 48 miles
A = 95 square miles

Stranger

C = 48 miles
A = 183.35 square miles

FIGURE 1.5

This extension has fascinating connections—note that the circle has almost twice the area of the other figures. How would students attack this problem?

A circle with circumference of 48 units would equal the diameter times pi:

$$\frac{C}{D} = \pi \qquad C = D * \pi \qquad D = C / \pi$$

$$D = \frac{48}{3.14159} = 15.2789$$

and the radius [r] is half the diameter (r = 7.64). The area of the circle must be

$$A = (3.14159) \, r^2 = (3.14159) * (7.64)^2 = 183.35.$$

This fact is fairly counterintuitive because it makes a circle with the same distance around almost twice the area of the others. Drawing the three figures on graph paper will help students see the relationship. See Figure 1.6.

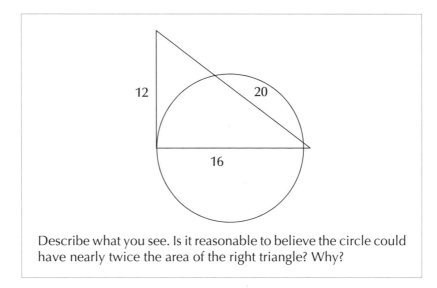

Describe what you see. Is it reasonable to believe the circle could have nearly twice the area of the right triangle? Why?

FIGURE 1.6

2 | SIX BIG IDEAS

THE RESEARCH ON MATHEMATICAL LEARNING AND TEACHING

In our teaching practice, we *braid* together language, thinking, and mathematics in order to develop a better and deeper understanding of mathematical concepts and to help us teach mathematics more effectively.

Throughout *Understanding Middle School Math*, we refer to six big ideas derived from extensive research on human cognition, learning, and development. Two volumes in particular, from the National Research Council (NRC), *How People Learn: Brain, Mind, Experience, and School* (Bransford, Brown, and Cocking 2000) and *How Students Learn: History, Mathematics, and Science in the Classroom* (Donovan and Bransford 2005), have added immensely to our knowledge of how students learn mathematics with understanding. Trying to summarize all the research findings is daunting—all we can do here is give a strong taste of what the research says. Donovan and Bransford (2005), in particular, use three overarching principles to organize and explain mathematical learning.

Principle 1: Engaging Prior Understanding

Students build new knowledge and understanding on what they already know and believe. Pioneering cognitive psychologist David Ausubel once stated, "The most important single factor influencing learning is what the learner already knows" (1978). It sounds obvious now, but it wasn't forty years ago. Ausubel focused on people who were engaged in meaningful verbal learning at a time when most psychologists who "studied learning" ran rats through mazes or had college sophomores try to memorize nonsense syllables for later recall.

In the mid-1980s, a few mathematics educators realized the value of cognitive psychology. Yet even today, forty years after Ausubel introduced ideas such as *advanced organizer*, *ideational scaffolding*, and *subsumption* (relating new ideas to one's existing cognitive structures), most mathematics educators do not have a deep knowledge of cognition. According to Ausubel, meaningful learning and conceptual understanding occur when the learner consciously and explicitly ties new knowledge to relevant concepts in his or her schemata. Consequently, conceptual learning is idiosyncratic and requires personal recognition of links among concepts.

We have now come to understand that learners formulate new knowledge by modifying and refining their current concepts and by *adding new concepts* to what they already know. Piaget helped us see that sometimes students can readily *assimilate* new knowledge into their prior knowledge, elaborating on what they already know. For instance, if a student has a reasonably good working knowledge of fractions, he or she may be able to grasp that $\frac{1}{10}$ and .1 symbolize the same relationship. However, a student with only a marginal understanding of fractions will not be able to do so. A reorganization of the student's cognitive structures may be necessary in order for him or her to *accommodate* the new relationship . . . and *decimal equivalent* won't sound more like the name of a rock group.

Research on conceptual change shows that students change their ideas when they find that their prior knowledge does not sufficiently explain a task. For instance, after a long series of calculations, perhaps using a calculator, a student thinks about the answer shown on the little screen and realizes that the number cannot possibly be correct. Now comes a key moment in the life of this budding mathematician: Does she consciously think through alternatives? Is there an error in her calculations? Did she choose the wrong formula? Is she thinking about this problem the wrong way? Is she using the right concepts?

It is important that teachers determine the nature and extent of their students' prior knowledge in order to plan effectively for the problems, tasks, and questions most likely to activate the best schema for particular students. In this way, teachers can practice *differentiation*.

Principle 2: The Essential Role of Factual Knowledge and Conceptual Frameworks

Although knowing facts is important, understanding mathematics is much more than knowing facts and procedures. Success in mathematics requires that factual knowledge be understood within a *conceptual framework* where mathematics is seen as a coherent set of interconnected ideas. When students' math knowledge is organized, it is readily remembered and appropriately applied. When students learn with understanding, they are more able to apply knowledge (also referred to as *transfer of learning*) to new situations than when they merely memorize things they don't understand,

In order to use what they learn, students must achieve an *initial threshold of knowledge, practice using the knowledge in a variety of contexts*, and then get feedback (formative assessment) on how well they did. Students need to acquire extensive knowledge and know how to organize, represent, and interpret new information. It is essential for learners to develop a sense of *when*, or *the conditions in which*, knowledge can be used; this is called *conditionalized knowledge*. Sometimes just to make a point, for example, I ask students to get into groups of four, add their phone numbers together, and divide the number by four in order to get the group's average phone number. Some laugh, others dutifully calculate an answer. The procedure may be done correctly, but it is inappropriate and the answer itself is meaningless. We simply must teach concepts and ensure that they are understood.

Principle 3: The Importance of Self-Monitoring

As with the previous two principles, this one covers a lot of ground. It refers to metacognition, which for many educators involves both:

1. the awareness of one's capabilities, propensities, strengths, and weakness in a given area; and
2. the ability to step back and assess one's own work, including:
   • monitoring one's own progress; and
   • realizing when an avenue being pursued is not working.

Some math educators refer to metacognition as executive control. Other math educators discount metacognition as simply a part of cognition, which may account for significantly less research on metacognition in mathematics than in reading.

Effective learning requires that students take responsibility for their own learning. Students can be taught how to recognize when they understand and when they need more information. They need to be able and to know when to ask themselves, "Is what I am doing actually working? Am I on the right track?" Reading educators talk about the "gradual release of responsibility," a systematic way of encouraging and helping students to make decisions about their learning, acting upon their decisions, and being responsible for them.

Metacognitive processes are not generic across subject areas and should not be taught as general thinking skills or strategies. In *Comprehending Math: Adapting Reading Strategies to Teach Mathematics, K–6* (2006), I emphasized the need to modify and adapt reading strategies for math rather than use the exact same strategies, which will not work. Reading experts are oriented toward processes and although they do address big concepts such as *figures of speech*, which subsume smaller concepts such as *metaphor, simile, personification, metonymy*, and so on, their focus is not on conceptual knowledge. Mathematicians and math educators are definitely oriented toward conceptual knowledge, but they must have a *combined* focus of conceptual knowledge and processes. The National Council of Teachers of Mathematics publishes guidelines for both content standards (algebra, geometry, measurement, number and operations, and data analysis) and process standards (problem solving, making connections, creating representations, reasoning, and communication), all of which require attention for effective teaching (NCTM 2000).

SIX BIG IDEAS: BUILDING ON MATHEMATICAL RESEARCH AND PRINCIPLES

Students rarely build new knowledge alone; research indicates (Lesh and Doerr 2003) that students benefit from interactive opportunities to articulate their own and challenge each others' ideas, and, in doing so, reconstruct their own ideas.

Our own six big ideas, detailed below, build on mathematical research and principles in order to help teachers put them into practice in the classroom. The six big ideas overlap, interact, mutually support one another, and provide the foundation of our teaching:

1. Teachers broaden their view of *problem solving* to move beyond the traditional story problem to building mathematical models of situations and phenomena.
2. Students make *connections*—tap into their prior knowledge—among the problem they are working on and their lives, the world around them, and the mathematical concepts they know.
3. Students create their own meaningful *representations* (language, objects, pictures, actions, lists, tables, graphs, equations) of increasing abstraction.
4. Students solve problems involving the same concept in multiple different *contexts* to build a generalized understanding of the concept.
5. Teachers use cognitively-based *planning* for language, connections, contexts, and representations.
6. Teachers put all the above together in the *Braid Model* of problem solving.

Big Idea 1: Teachers Broaden Their View of Problem Solving

In the past, problem solving referred to how students applied *what they had been taught*. Today, most mathematics educators view problem solving as *teaching*, a powerful vehicle for building understanding of mathematical concepts. When students are presented with well-constructed problems and worthwhile mathematical tasks, and they use good strategies and good mathematical thinking to solve them, they begin to build concept meaning.

Educators realize that problem solving should be more like the work of mathematicians and less like the computations of the clerk in a general store in the 1800s. ("Let's see, Ma'am. That's five and seven-eighths yards of calico at seventy-two cents per yard. That'll be four dollars and sixty-three cents.") Students should be creating *mathematical models* of situations, phenomena, and so on, rather than one- and two-step drill exercises not so cleverly disguised as story problems (for example $5\frac{7}{8} * 72 = ?$).

The traditional approach to problem solving has consisted of encouraging students to:

- acquire the mathematical knowledge needed;
- acquire the problem-solving strategies needed to make decisions about what already-known procedure to try;
- acquire the metacognitive strategies needed to trigger the appropriate use of problem-solving strategies and mathematical knowledge; and
- unlearn beliefs and dispositions that prevent effective use of problem-solving and metacognitive strategies, while also developing productive beliefs.

Misconception

Research has *not* shown this traditional approach to be consistently effective, despite how logical and sequential it may sound, for the following reasons:

1. Problem solving is placed *after* learning the knowledge, rather than using a good problem-solving process to *build* knowledge.
2. Some curricula and textbooks unwittingly lead teachers to believe that:

   - problem-solving strategies are like procedures and can be "mastered," as if their acquisition is an end or goal in itself;
   - each problem-solving strategy can function in a similar way independent of content, across diverse sets of tasks, situations, and concepts.
   (Lesh and Doerr 2003)

Types of Problem-Solving Strategies

A number of recent textbooks are cutting back on the time and space afforded strategies in prior editions. That is a mistake. We have found that students become successful problem solvers when their teachers make several specific modifications in the way the students approach problem solving and the various strategies. First, teachers choose problems for their conceptual richness and use the problem-solving process to *examine the concepts*. This keeps the focus on the concepts. Second, they make explicit to the students that there are different types of problem-solving strategies. We see three very different kinds of strategies: meta-strategies, representational strategies, and supplementary strategies.

Metastrategies　Metastrategies are not really strategies in the same sense as the others. If you conceive of a strategy as a method of operating on something that you consciously choose to use or not to use with any given problem, then there are two that don't fit those criteria. They are so clearly part of what mathematics *is* that they should *always* be used in problem solving.

- Look for a pattern (Mathematics is the science of patterns.)
- Use logical reasoning (What is the alternative?)

Every branch of mathematics has its characteristic patterns. What is the pattern in the problem of the Two Ranches from the previous chapter? The pattern comes from right triangles. One triangle is found to be a right triangle, by applying the converse of the Pythagorean Theorem. The other triangle is a non-right scalene, which is then partitioned into two right triangles.

Students need many experiences with different kinds of reasoning: inductive, deductive, analyzing, synthesizing, discerning, and interpreting patterns. Students also need to be aware of the language of reasoning and to understand the differences and the nuances of words such as: *compare, contrast, infer, predict, interpret,* and *conclude.*

Humans are pattern-seeking, meaning-making creatures. We have experiences. We encounter people, events, phenomena, circumstances, thoughts, ideas, symbol music, art, emotions. And what do we do with these things? We classify, organize, sort, group, pull apart, look at little pieces, grab a whole handful of pieces and put them back together. We even look for the pattern in tea leaves, ashes, and chicken bones. We see faces, animals, and many strange shapes in clouds.

Perceiving patterns is essentially an *inductive* (moving from the particular to the general) process: the person examines a bunch of particular examples and derives a pattern. These perceptions can't be forced. Pure induction can be amazingly challenging and motivating, if the example or the context is conceivable for the student. Some students love to intellectually struggle with this pure induction. However, many students become frustrated and anxious with a "pure induction" process: a bunch of examples and very little feedback on students' hunches or hypotheses, especially when no real-life context has been provided.

Conversely, can you remember your math teachers who gave brilliant lectures, explaining the rules, the principles, and the concepts? They'd explain the rules, the formulas, the theorems and then expect us to apply them, using *deductive* (moving from the general to the particular) reasoning. The problem with pure deductive teaching is that most of the time an explanation of the principles does not *connect* to anything in kids' heads because most of the time, most humans need examples. In most cases of mathematics in the middle school, *simply telling* does not work.

Teachers need to encourage their students to look for patterns and to provide their students with a mixture of logical *examples* and *explanations* that make sense to them. We all need examples to build the meaning of the concept, principle, theorem, or rule. Examples can clarify what the explanation meant.

Representational Strategies   Representational strategies are based on
five different ways humans process information:

- Discussing the problem in small groups (language representations using *auditory* sense)
- Using manipulatives (concrete, physical representations using *tactile* sense)
- Acting it out (representations of sequential actions using bodily *kinesthetic* sense)
- Drawing a picture, diagram, or graph (pictorial representations using *visual* sense)
- Making a list or table (*symbolic* representations often using abstract reasoning that can lead to creating equations)

Each strategy employs a different sensory modality and a different way that humans process information, making cognitive differentiation readily available for the teacher. Through this creation, the students are *constructing meaning* that can be used to develop one's initial understanding of the problem itself. Teachers encourage students to create their own representations that gradually become increasingly more *abstract*. We refer to the dynamic flow from concrete representations to more abstract representations: *language, object, picture, action* → *list, table, graph, equation*. The first four do not rely on symbols. Of course, language has a special communicative function in these other representations and is used throughout. Language may be very concrete (as in a very literal description of an object or very abstract such as discussing stellated versus truncated polyhedra).

Supplementary Strategies   Students cannot use supplementary strategies until they understand a problem. This is really a critical point. Understanding the situation, the question, the task, is the first order of business in problem solving. Supplementary strategies can only work when you know enough about the situation to use them. They are:

- Work backward
- Choose a simpler problem
- Guess and check

Using Strategies

We start by working with the whole class, modeling for them our thinking and self-questioning out loud. We ask them to visualize the situation, to break down the story with the KWC to activate their prior relevant knowledge with connecting questions, and to check the accuracy of their inferences. All these questions may imply a lot of time and suggest a tedious process, but we make it more like a brainstorming and keep a good pace. After they have practiced this strategy with the whole class, they need to practice it in small groups. When they have thoroughly discussed the problem and believe they understand the situation and what the problem requires, then we encourage them to *represent* their conception of the problem using one of the representational strategies. Sometimes, we strongly encourage or even require that they use a particular strategy.

If the teacher knows the strengths and weaknesses of the students in the class she/he might *differentiate* right at the start of the activity and make sure that the students who have some difficulty drawing have manipulatives that will make it possible for these students to build a physical model. For example, in our ranch problem in Chapter 1, both ranches had the same perimeter (48 miles). We might encourage the students to model these ranches, letting one inch in the model represent one mile. They'd get two pieces of string, both 52 inches long, and for each piece they must tie its two ends together, giving them about 48 inches (miles) of fence. With a yardstick, six pushpins, and a bulletin board, they can set two of the pushpins as the vertices of one of the sides. The placement of the third pushpin can be determined by a little experimenting with the yardstick to get the other two sides the right lengths.

But the real power of the push pins in the bulletin board comes in seeing that even though two perimeters are the same, their respective areas may not be. We can readily help them see this by putting two pushpins in the corkboard two inches apart and then pulling the 48 inch perimeter of string with a third pushpin (vertex of the triangle) almost perpendicular

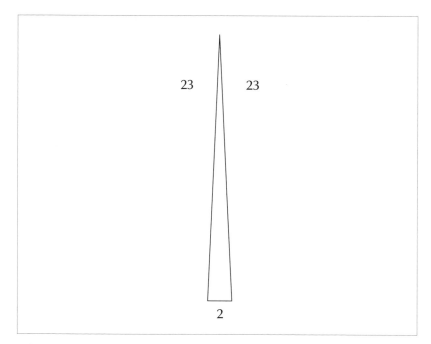

FIGURE 2.1

to the side formed by the other two pushpins and as far away from them as possible. This will create a tall skinny isosceles triangle of 2, 23, 23 (see Figure 2.1) with very little area enclosed (22.978 sq. in.), far smaller than the two Texas ranches. The fancy way mathematicians express this idea would be: *You can hold the perimeter constant and still vary the area.*

Students who could handle a challenge could investigate what happens to the area of isosceles triangles of perimeter 48, as they increase the length of the base by 2. Why 2 and not 1? After making a few triangles with the three pushpins and the 48-inch string, some students switch to paper and pencil drawings or a table (or just jot down the answers from a procedure they have discovered—such as the Pythagorean Theorem). See Figure 2.2 for a table that shows the areas of the various isosceles with integral base and side length.

Most students are surprised that the areas increase up to a base of 16 and then begin to decrease. Why? Many inquiries by students have been launched from this simple table.

This process is called "translating between representations." In this example, there were five different representations:

- the written description of the actual situation,
- the oral language descriptions as the students discussed the mental images evoked by the different written language representations,

Areas of isosceles triangles

Interger sides & perimeter of 48

Base	Equal Sides	Area
2	23	22.978
4	22	43.818
6	21	62.353
8	20	78.384
10	19	91.652
12	18	101.851
14	17	108.444
16	16	110.851
18	15	108.000
20	14	97.980
22	13	76.210
24	12	0.000

FIGURE 2.2

- the concrete, physical scale model with string and pushpins,
- the various drawings (visual, pictorial representations), and the data tables.

Creating multiple representations and translating between them smoothly with no big jumps is a critical part of successful problem solving.

We mentioned mathematical models and their creation a few pages ago. In essence, a representation is a model. Probably it would seem more like a "mathematical model" if the relationships being described were expressed as an equation or a formula. We can modify Heron's formula from the previous chapter. The base is still b but now we can use $a = c$.

$$A = \tfrac{1}{4} \sqrt{(a + b + c)(a + b - c)(a - b + c)(b - a + c)}$$

$$A = \tfrac{1}{4} \sqrt{(2a + b)(b)(2a - b)(b)}$$

$$A = \tfrac{1}{4} \sqrt{b^2(2a + b)(2a - b)}$$

$$A = \tfrac{b}{4} \sqrt{(2a + b)(2a - b)}$$

$$A = \tfrac{b}{4} \sqrt{(4a^2 - b^2)}$$

Extension

Use the data from the table (Figure 2.2) and make a graph. See Figure 2.3.

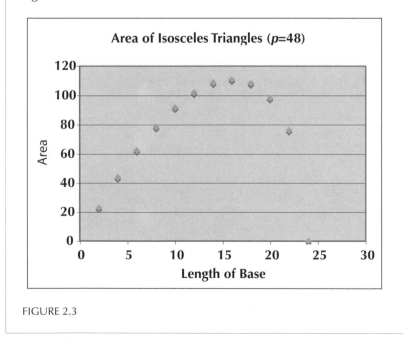

FIGURE 2.3

Doing this extension, students experience a non linear relationship via several different representations. As they become comfortable with these representations and explore strategies, problem solving is no longer a scary, hit-or-miss ritual for students. It is an adventure, an exploration that allows each student to investigate the world with a new perspective.

Some math educators use a perspective referred to as "modeling" or "creating models" in which problem solving serves primarily to *interpret* the problem. This approach to problem solving emphasizes the need for interpretation, description, elaboration, and explanation of the nature of the problem, recognizing the importance of the context, content, and the concepts of the problem. The solution to problems is often the building of a model using particular concepts that are still being developed by the students. In this view, the purpose of the strategies is to help students refine, revise, and to extend their ideas, especially through interaction with others.

In the next section Susan describes how she incorporates model-eliciting activities for problem solving.

Problem Solving for Modeling

Problem-solving strategies should be developed with students in a variety of dimensions—rather than just as an unnatural break from the normal routine in math class when the textbook decides to incorporate the problem-solving strategy *de jour*. These dimensions should include multiple contexts and representations that promote what Lesh and his colleagues (Lesh and Doerr 2003; Lesh and Zawojewski 2006) refer to as *cycles of reconceptualization*. Their research shows that middle school students working on "model-eliciting activities" can progress beyond "initially incorrect or overly simplistic interpretations" of problems when allowed to take their prior knowledge, create a variety of representations, and refine them repeatedly (cyclically). Neither textbook problems, nor our teaching of them encourages such reconceptualization. But it is critical to building meaningful, long-lasting mathematical understandings.

So, the question remains, what would an activity that promotes cycles of reconceptualization look like in my classroom? What do I plan for? To inspire my students to use models during their conceptual development process, I try to create problems that *naturally* demand a revision or check for comprehension. Ironically, when I honestly analyze my lesson plans, I have found that sometimes it is the problem itself that requires constant revision.

In previous years, I had implemented an activity in sixth-grade math, called the Extreme Classroom Makeover that would connect operations in the rational number system to area, perimeter, scale, and customary measurements in a real-world situation. Right off the bat, I knew my catchy title would intrigue several students who were die-hard fans of ABC's "Extreme Makeover—Home Edition" television show. In addition to connecting the math concepts and exciting my students with a

Ty-Pennington-themed assignment, I made the objective of this activity clear from the beginning: *To discover how perimeter and area are used when replacing the flooring in our classroom.* The students were also given the following task description:

Extreme Classroom Makeover

Your teacher is replacing the flooring in her classroom. She wants you to "order" the materials for the floors. For this classroom, the materials consist of a floor covering and a type of baseboard. Carpet, hardwood, and laminate flooring are all great choices for floor covering in her classroom and chestnut or natural wood are her options for the baseboard. Your teacher has $3000 to spend on flooring materials for the entire classroom. Using your measuring tools and your knowledge of area and perimeter, present a professional proposal for three different flooring renovation ideas to your favorite math teacher, Mrs. Friedlander.

In the past, I assigned this activity at the beginning of the school year, and my sixth graders only had experience working in cooperative groups on short-term activities. The Extreme Classroom Makeover was to be their first long-term group activity. As a result, I chunked this activity into four different parts—measuring, Internet researching, calculating, and proposing, and I gave the students due dates for each part as they were initially introduced. This activity required the students to create an accurate scale drawing of our classroom (which was fairly rectangular) using customary measurements. Once the students had successfully created their drawings, which would take them about two class periods, they would use the Internet to find prices of various baseboards and flooring to use in a hypothetical classroom renovation. The students would then write a persuasive essay convincing me, with mathematical evidence, which option for baseboard and flooring renovations would be the best choice for our classroom.

This activity certainly had its strong points—active student engagement, cooperative grouping, authentic tasks disguised in a math story problem, technology integration—but it did not in any way help my students to reorganize their thinking or understanding of the math concepts I had wanted them to fully develop. In fact, as I looked closer into the proposals my kids presented and the original task I designed for them, I noticed that not only did the activity *not* inspire any insight into *why* and *how* area and perimeter were to be used, but my activity sheet actually required minimal thinking because I had explicitly written in the calculation section that the floor covering dealt with area and the baseboard dealt with perimeter.

I observed that most students had gotten so frustrated with researching baseboard and flooring prices at various home improvement stores that they neglected to make time to differentiate and/or demonstrate their understanding of the difference between area and perimeter and how baseboards and flooring fit into each of those calculations. Only now was it obvious to me that I did not give them any reason to take time to understand why they were using area and perimeter—it was already written down for them!

I had to stop and think, not only about the assumptions I made about my students' understanding area and perimeter and the benefit of improving my students' learning, but also how I could improve my ability to create activities that inspired students to construct their own knowledge. It was difficult for me to accept that an activity I had spent a great deal of time refining and improving looked really good on paper, but not in practice. To step outside my own "hidden assumptions" about understandings my students would naturally form, to determine whether my activity really would reach the intended objectives required me to engage in a deeply personal and reflective journey.

Instead of feeling guilty and hitting a dead-end for not recognizing the Extreme Classroom Makeover's flaws early on, my enthusiasm for continual improvement enabled me to take this as a chance to realize the disconnect between my activity's objectives and its outcomes. Had I just brushed this off as my students simply "not getting it," I would have missed an incredible opportunity to reflect on how important it is to ensure that not only are the objectives attainable within the constraints of the problem, but also the value in teaching where my students *are*, and not just where *I* am or where the book says they should be. Further, I realized that the intended revelations that I had hoped my students would make at various points in this activity appeared to have been clouded by their hasty jump to use the Internet for research in math class. Aside from not explicitly writing down area deals with flooring and perimeter deals with baseboard, I could not put my finger on exactly what else needed to change, but I knew that somehow this problem had to be focused differently to naturally derive meaningful understandings of area and perimeter.

I shared my original activity with Art, and he too agreed that there was a significant disconnect between the activity's objectives and tasks. Instead of specifically pointing out what needed to change in my activity, as usual he wanted me to construct my own understandings, so I could fully appreciate the value in the reflection and revision process. He pointed me in the direction of some research in problem-solving strategies done by Lesh and Doerr, in *Beyond Constructivism* (2003).

Richard Lesh has conducted research whose results suggest that "the most important purpose of most problem solving strategies and procedures is to help students refine, revise or extend ideas that they already have (which are initially in some primitive form)" (Lesh and Doerr 2003). This meant that in my classroom, I had to have a solid understanding of what my students understood (and misunderstood) about area and perimeter—well before I expected them to apply their knowledge of area and perimeter in the Extreme Classroom Makeover activity. After reading through chapters of *Beyond Constructivism*, I was immediately intrigued by the depth, and yet simplicity, of the Carpentry Problem (Zawojewski and Lesh 2003, 322)—the extent to which his students went through cycles of reconceptualization by reorganizing their knowledge about area and perimeter, questioning their understandings of the problem's constraints and testing their ability to visualize the problem they were solving—things that had clearly been missing from the Extreme Classroom Makeover activity I had used in previous years.

The Carpentry Problem has kids determine baseboard configurations—under a variety of given constraints—based upon a defined room size and baseboard length, and does not "explicitly ask students to produce a model, or some other type of conceptual tool as a final product . . . " (Zawojewski and Lesh 2003, 322). It simply gets students to think, and elicits their models naturally. What I found most interesting was the dialogue that had taken place between his students. This dialogue clearly revealed the revision process (something that was not naturally occurring in the Extreme Classroom Makeover problem). It specifically showed the role that a small group's (three or four) interaction played in moving from an initial understanding of what the problem was asking the students to find out about area or perimeter (they had to work through this to decide which one), to a more sophisticated understanding about *how* and *why* they knew this was a perimeter problem and *not* an area problem.

As a result of my research, I created a similar problem that has its roots deeply connected to the Carpentry Problem and the Extreme Classroom Makeover Problem. I called my problem, "A Dog-Gone Renovation":

A Dog-Gone Renovation

1. The Friedlanders are renovating their dog room into a recreation room. They currently have walls and flooring already installed. The problem is that their two teething terriers have chewed and destroyed a significant portion of the baseboard, and, thus they need to buy new baseboard to put along the walls. The room is 21 feet by 28 feet. The baseboards come in 10-foot and 16-foot lengths. How many of each kind should they buy?

2. If the Friedlanders want to have as few seams as possible, how many of each size baseboards should they buy? Also, suppose the cost per 10-foot baseboard is $7.97 and the cost per 16-foot baseboard is $14.97, what would be the total cost of supplies for this project?

3. If the Friedlanders want to have as little waste as possible, how many of each size baseboard should they buy? Also, suppose the cost per 10-foot baseboard is $7.97 and the cost

per 16-foot baseboard is $14.97, what would be the total cost of supplies for this project?

4. Compare and contrast your answers to question 1 and question 2. In what ways are they alike? In what ways are they different? How do you know? Which procedure would you recommend for the Friedlanders and why?

Immediately, you can see three main differences between the Dog-Gone Renovation Problem and the Extreme Classroom Makeover:

1. Students don't have to perform any Internet research (which most of my sixth-grade students were not immediately ready to do on their own);

2. A Dog-Gone Renovation deals only with perimeter, so differentiation between area and perimeter is key to solving the problem; and

3. Students do not have a picture of the problem in front of them, so concluding that my dog's room was rectangular and using the appropriate formulas is a key development in their problem-solving process.

In order to make A Dog-Gone Renovation successful, I began by showing photographs of what my dogs had sunk their teeth into (not photos of the room layout, however). Then, I asked students to complete a KWC. I expected to find that my students could define the givens and clear goals of the activity better than in previous years. With the Extreme Classroom Makeover problem, it was obvious that my students did not have a clear understanding of how they were to achieve the activity's main objectives—most thought it was just practice with measuring and Internet researching—which prevented them from fully developing deep understandings of the mathematical concepts.

Next, instead of jumping into measuring my classroom—a visual that was already in front of them—the Dog-Gone Renovation deliberately requires them to visualize, whether formally or informally, precisely what is going on in this problem and to communicate their visualizations while reading this problem. Just asking my students "What shape is the room described in the picture?" will help them critique their original drawings. "Pictures tend to be drawn for the purposes of communication" (Zawojewski and Lesh 2003, 327), and they are especially critical to inspiring cycles of reconceptualization. Even if original drawings aren't always used throughout all parts of the problem-solving process, they encourage kids to visualize and they help teachers, as faciliators, to understand that a true indication of their students' level of comprehension can be communicated verbally and visually in the pictures their kids draw. The hope, with time, is the students will create more advanced or detailed representations throughout the problem-solving process. The interaction of group members during the problem-solving process is also critical to the evolution of the solution because this interaction serves as a window to the group's thinking as their collaborative solution develops over the course of the problem-solving episode.

Finally, making A Dog-Gone Problem more focused allows my students to dissect the meaning of perimeter and area through a variety of teacher-directed comprehension check questions rather than quickly moving into an Internet research hoping that they've used the correct formula listed on their activity sheets. That is, because my students were originally heavily bombarded with the complexity of the desired outcomes, they did not have the ability to scrape away all of the "glitz and glamour" of the Internet to hone in on the true mathematics in this math problem—perimeter/baseboards and area/flooring—which I had clearly written out for them anyway!

Ultimately, you can also see how one's mastery of this problem, using the given baseboard prices and the prompt for cost analysis, along with Internet research assistance, could prepare them to have success with my original Extreme Classroom Makeover problem—an activity that I still desire my students to complete *after* the Dog-Gone Renovation problem. This problem could also be a great segue into future problems, such as Chocolate Algebra (see Chapter 5), by extending it to require students to examine and analyze different combinations of 10-foot and 16-foot baseboards to create the whole perimeter using the list of given constraints.

Big Idea 2: Making Connections Between the Problem and Their Lives

In general, the more connections of the right kind, the more examples in different but relevant contexts, the more elaborate the networks of ideas and relationships, the deeper, richer, more generalized our understanding of a concept will be. Making connections is at the heart of doing mathematics—from simple connections about how two things are related (for example .1 and $\frac{1}{10}$) to major breakthroughs in understanding (such as realizing that multiplication is not "making something bigger," but that it could mean having only part of a group, as in $.25 * 84$, or having multiple groups of an amount smaller than one, as in $84 * .25$).

How do we help students make good and accurate connections? It is folly to take an extreme position at either end of the spectrum—that connections are made by students only by discovery or only by direct instruction. Such extremes in teaching are successful only in unusual circumstances. Humans learn well when they encounter many examples and try to make sense of them, try to see a pattern. At some point in this work the students profit greatly from a good explanation that connects to their specific experiences and examples. The explanation enhances the meaning of the examples and helps organize them. Conversely, if students do not have some initial examples and experiences to draw on, then even the most cogent, brilliantly worded explanation does not connect to any prior knowledge.

For decades the mathematics curriculum has consisted of little, bite-sized chunks of mathematical knowledge. I am not speaking only of narrowly defined skills (as in skill and drill), although some still cling to the erroneous belief that if children crank out a gazillion math facts then they know how to do mathematics. I am concerned here with the fragmentation of concepts into isolated compartments that is contrary to the premise that students need to see that mathematics as a *coherent whole*. Many concepts are connected to a multitude of others. Even when teachers go after conceptual understanding, the curriculum treats that concept in isolation from its related and interconnected concepts.

The right connections can build conceptual understanding. The more and the stronger the connections are among related concepts, the deeper and richer the understanding of these concepts. There are dozens of different psychological theories concerning the connections that humans make and what it means to understand a concept. Rather than trying to summarize, compare, and contrast the different theories, I want to briefly address several ideas that are central to the approach we are using.

Concepts are abstract ideas organizing a lot of smaller bits of information (facts) in a somewhat hierarchical fashion. We can see a set of concepts, subsumed under a macro-concept (an even bigger idea). In mathematics, the science of patterns, we have branches devoted to the study of specific types of patterns such as *shape, dimension, change, uncertainty,* and *quantity*. These are certainly big ideas or macro-concepts that can organize a lot of information. Subordinate to quantity we'd find the concept of multiplication, one that subsumes a great many facts: *quantity* (macro-concept) → *multiplication* (concept) → *multiplication tables* (facts).

The concept of multiplication and its relationship to division, another concept, continues to grow more complex each year for about six years as the operation is performed with different kinds of numbers, then with variables, matrices, vectors, and so on. These concepts can grow richer and more elaborate and more abstract as you experience them in different contexts.

Conceptual understanding is not like an on-off light switch: you don't *understand* a concept in an all or nothing fashion. Initially we grasp some aspect of the concept and build on it, adding and elaborating our understanding. I like to think of it as building a snowman. First, you find some good snow for making a snowman—not too wet and slushy, not too dry and powdery. You make a snowball with your hands and roll it in some good snow. The ball gains size as more snow sticks to it. You do this to make a big sturdy ball of snow for the foundation. You repeat this process for other parts of the snowman. But you must continue to roll it in the right kind of snow; the wrong snow or worse, rolling it on grass, will not accumulate more snow. In general, more connections of the right kind, the more examples in different but relevant contexts, the more elaborate the networks of ideas and relationships—the deeper, richer, more generalized, and more abstract our understanding of a concept. A good rule of thumb for effective math teaching is to make sure that every symbol has concrete references and numerous tangible examples that you and the students can refer back to when dealing with abstract symbols. Bear in mind that our goal in teaching mathematics is *understanding*. Making connections, organizing knowledge, and understanding concepts are three things that fit together nicely.

Drawing from the reading folks and adapting it for math, we see three major kinds of math connections that teachers should make explicit to students and encourage them to make special note whenever they encounter examples of mathematics connecting to self, world, or math.

Math to Self: connecting to prior knowledge and experience; connecting to preconceptions and misconceptions

> What does this situation remind me of?
> Have I ever been in any situation like this?

Math to World: connecting to natural or created structures, events, environment, media

> Is this related to anything I've seen in social studies or science, the arts?
> Is this related to things I've seen anywhere?

Math to Math: connecting the math concepts to other math concepts (for example, big ideas), within and across strands of mathematics; to related procedures; within and across contexts and representations)

> What is the main idea from mathematics that is happening here?
> Where have I seen that idea before?
> What are some other math ideas that are related to this one?
> Can I use them to help me with this problem?

Local Concept Development

Students are motivated to think when the *context* of a problem appeals to them. Initially they are much more interested in the particular examples, the situation, and the context than they are in the mathematics. Working in a meaningful context can help students build an initial understanding of a concept. When the student considers a bunch of examples from a particular context, an inductive process is at work to create meaning, to derive a pattern and create a particular and perhaps context-specific version of a concept that describes or explains the pattern.

A number of educators use the term *internal model* to explain what is going on here. We humans interpret our new experiences by comparing them to internal models that are based on our past experiences. These internal models filter, construct, and create how we conceive of the new experiences. Students' knowledge is generally organized around their experiences, not around the abstract concepts of the discipline of mathematics. Similar experiences are grouped together in their internal models. Does this sound like schemata?

Students build up concepts gradually. First they come to understand the concept in a very specific context or situation (that is, "local"). They create a kind of model that explains a particular problem-solving situation. With more experience in somewhat similar situations and with facilitation by the teacher, more elaborate understandings can be built.

Students' initial understanding of a concept in mathematics is very much grounded in a set of examples in a specific context. Their understanding is local, particular to that situation or context, not global. It is built up by experience and inductively derived. Heavy doses of deductive explanations trying to get them to generalize across contexts and to think abstractly about the concept will not likely have much effect until they have had experience with those other contexts. We cannot do Mr. Spock's Vulcan mind meld and make a student conceive of a concept the way we do. It does not work that way.

Planning for Naturally Derived *"Right" Connections*

Forming the right connections in mathematics, regardless of the grade level, is crucial to establishing global conceptual development. Susan says, "Just *hoping* it will happen by chance does not serve our students—or our communities—any justice whatsoever. So, if we cannot rely simply on luck or shear force (sorry Mr. Spock) as a means to inspire students to form valuable math to world (MW), math to self (MS) and math to math (MM) connections, how do we plan to have kids *naturally* derive them?"

Susan continues, "Well, let's first think about what those moments look like. Visualize with me. You know, those *aha* moments when the usually quiet student exclaims, 'Wait a minute, this is just like...!' Or how about when the excitement felt after a genuine connection has been made in class continues to buzz through the hallways, well after class is over, into the lunchroom . . . where there's always at least one student, covered in spaghetti sauce, who still comes up to you to add to their new-found insights! I thrive on *those* moments. I am a middle school math teacher because of *those* moments."

Thinking deeply about those moments causes me to be able to identify a common thread woven throughout all of those lesson plans. They all incorporate with real-life, relevant and messy data. Data that was interesting and cool to students! (This is no longer your grandmother's math!—baking pies and crocheting aside.) Working with real-life data and problems make math come alive and is more interesting to students with the added bonus of increased student engagement.

Some educators resist messy real-life data. They say that students become too confused by the complexities of real-life situations; there are too many concepts impinging all at once on children. They feel that only after students have mastered the skills or understand the concepts from easier, simplified cases can they transfer their knowledge to other more complex ones and apply their new knowledge to real-life situations—a completely false idea. I have *seen* and *heard* my students form the right connections, and I have felt their true excitement when I give them opportunities to learn within a context filled with meaning and intrigue, where those seemingly messy numbers come alive and refer to comprehensible things. I remember one instance in particular—an activity that revolved around the soft drink data in the table below.

This data is a perfect example of how real-life math does not always present the question to the student, particularly information that is displayed in graphs or tables found on the news or in newspapers. Instead, it is up to the reader, and the teacher to show students how to plunge into the data, asking questions that help them to understand and interpret the data—just like they do in their science and social studies classes.

Having initially been exposed to this soft drink data as a graduate student in one of Art's courses, I had first-hand knowledge of what natural connections evolved and what connections I had to plan for in my classroom. So I would begin this activity with a simple, yet extremely

GALLONS OF SOFT DRINKS SOLD IN THE UNITED STATES IN ONE YEAR

	Gallons Per person		Gallons per person		Gallons per person		Gallons per person
Alabama	59.62	Indiana	46.66	Nebraska	53.30	S. Carolina	63.34
Alaska	47.79	Iowa	46.98	Nevada	55.89	South Dakota	41.31
Arizona	47.14	Kansas	58.16	New Hamp.	46.01	Tennessee	58.97
Arkansas	53.95	Kentucky	57.19	New Jersey	46.49	Texas	58.16
California	52.16	Louisiana	59.45	New Mexico	46.49	Utah	45.36
Colorado	48.60	Maine	47.30	New York	51.35	Vermont	43.09
Connecticut	50.71	Maryland	56.54	N. Carolina	64.64	Virginia	62.05
Delaware	52.65	Mass.	51.19	North Dakota	37.58	Wash. D.C.	58.32
Florida	64.31	Michigan	54.11	Ohio	55.24	Washington	40.66
Georgia	63.83	Minnesota	53.46	Oklahoma	50.22	West Virginia	55.40
Hawaii	50.71	Mississippi	61.88	Oregon	38.56	Wisconsin	46.66
Idaho	33.53	Missouri	58.97	Pennsylvania	42.93	Wyoming	33.37
Illinois	53.78	Montana	33.75	Rhode Island	46.17		

significant, question. Below each data set that I distributed to my students was the following question: *What are you thinking when you see this data?* Half of the page below the data was left blank for them to respond. Because my students had seen a question like this in previous activities, they were prepared with the idea that every table and graph has a message and it is up to them to "read" the story being told. I also asked this question because I wanted my students to quickly jot down their ideas, free of teacher-rigged hints, so they could work as though they were at a museum, where the soft drink data represented the exhibit they were to interpret. I use this metaphor frequently in class because many of my students have grown up going to museums—some even while in the womb—asking questions and naturally demanding to know more about a particular artifact. After a few moments of individual working time, I opened the class to a large-group discussion where my students responded in the following ways:

- Who got all this data?
- The number of soft drinks sold in each state for one year.
- The number of gallons of soft drinks for each person in a state.
- Is a soft drink, like, just soda pop?
- This can't be true, I'm not even allowed to drink soda!
- How many cans fit into a gallon?
- Who is this data for, nutritionists or parents?
- Just because soda is sold, doesn't mean it is drunk.
- How did they get this data, by asking each person in each state to keep track? I don't remember being asked.
- I can barely drink a whole gallon of milk by myself in one week, but this says 53,78 gallons for each person a year In Illinois. How is this possible?
- I think that the hotter it is, the more soda drank to keep those people cool. That's why we're (IL) in the middle. Not too hot, not too cold.

Even if the kids *don't* naturally ask these questions or make similar comments, still record what they say and treat it as valuable information, but you may want to use some teacher-directed questioning techniques to derive these thoughts.

As they responded, I recorded their questions and comments on large chart paper. My hand was on fire recording their responses. I was excited because embedded in these simple responses were valuable MW, MS, and MM connections. You may even want to color-code the connections or group them under specific chart headings to be even more explicit during the large-group discussion—connections that I had *not* shoved down their throats, but connections that they had naturally derived within the first five minutes of class!

We are bombarded daily with data tables, charts, diagrams, and graphs in newspapers and all forms of media. If ever there were a time in mathematics to "determine the author's purpose" or "interrogate the author"—the way it's done in language arts, social studies, and science class—this is it. The Internet has created an almost instant capability to gather electronically, truly vast amounts of data. The bait I had dangled in front of them, this soft drink data, was to be an incredible opportunity for them to understand and appreciate the value of data analysis in a real-world situation.

I knew that most of the questions they had come up with overlapped and had a variety of answers—a variety that was certainly about to explode into a (controlled) volcano of lively, student-centered debates. Yes, all it took was one little data table. As a result, before we moved on to drawing conclusions about the relationships between geographical location and amount of soft drinks sold (I thought that was an incredible insight), and the data analysis calculations, my students and I began to hash through the diverse questions and comments they had proposed so we could all really wrap our heads around our "artifact." Truthfully, no matter how many times I have seen a specific data set, even this one in particular, all it takes is a fresh pair of students' eyes to recognize something that mine may have overlooked.

So I decided that as a class we should take these questions and ruthlessly interrogate the author about the soft drink data. But who? How? The first step is the critical awareness of the need to ask these questions. They certainly accomplished this with their initial exercise. Next, students had to do some digging and combining of similar questions/comments.

What is a soft drink? Without the KWC, or some device to ask questions, students will not even think twice; they'll go charging ahead unwittingly assuming that soft drinks mean "soda pop." However, when asked, they will debate this question heatedly. Questions about sugar, carbonation, and sugar substitutes abound. They will discuss popular fruit drinks, boutique iced tea, and designer water. I had one student, whose father was a bartender, say simply that *soft drinks* are the opposite of *hard drinks*. Soft drinks are the liquids you put into mixed drinks with the hard liquor. And that is just about accurate for these data. While mostly consisting of soda pop, soft drink also includes carbonated water and quinine water.

What is the unit of data in the table? Gallons of soft drinks. But note that the table also says "sold" in the United States in one year. It does not say *consumed*. It also says "gallons per person." I ask the students, "What does that mean?" How did they (whomever *they* are) calculate the statistic of 53.78 gallons of soft drink per person sold in Illinois in one year? What unfolds is a great discussion about statistical concepts and procedures embedded in a real (and admittedly messy) context. Some students think that this must be from a survey. Perhaps a random sample of Illini. But who buys soft drinks by the gallon? Not individuals, except those who get the "Big Binge" at the local speedy-mart. The source of data was not a survey.

The unit of *gallons* is a clue to how the data was collected. It came from beverage distributors who obviously keep very accurate records of their sales. A trade periodical for beverage distributors compiled the raw data. With more discussion the students suggest that the magazine collected data from beverage distributors and added up all the people in the state: *gallons per person*. This measure of central tendency is actually the mean.

A student complains, "That isn't fair. I'm not allowed to drink soft drinks!" And then another says, "My baby brother doesn't drink any soft drinks and neither does my grandmother!" Another fascinating debate occurs among the students about the concept of *mean*, what it means in this context, and the procedure for calculating it. They realize that if some people neither buy nor drink soft drinks then there must be people who drink more than 53.78 gallons per year. Frequently two things emerge: the students decide to collect their own data on beverage consumption, and someone asks, "How many cans of soda pop is 53.789 gallons? Is that a lot for a year?" Just imagine their eyes when you place 54 empty gallon jugs in front them! Most students can somewhat conceive of consuming *that* much soft drink—until they see what it looks like!

Now imagine if I had asked my students to open their textbooks to page 114 and do problem 7, which read, "If the consumption of soft drinks in Illinois last year was 53.78 gallons per person, how many 12-ounce cans would that be?" Presented with this cold problem, most students would yawn. But in the context of the debates about the data, this question arose naturally and meaningfully. They are intensely motivated to figure out the answer.

It's valuable for students to make a reasonable estimate before doing somewhat complicated calculations. Some students reason that 53.78 gallons is about one gallon per week—a low estimate. Each gallon holds 128 ounces, which is about ten and a half of the 12-ounce cans per week. The daily rate would be $10.5 \div 7$ or 1.5 cans per day (a somewhat low estimate). The accurate calculation would use 128 ounces in a gallon; so, 53.78 gallons is 6,883.84 ounces, which when divided by 12 (12-ounce cans) is about 574 cans over a year, or between 1 and 2 cans per person per day! See Figure 2.4.

Is this the only story in this data—the only questions that derive true connections? Certainly not! Given accurate population data the students could compare the population to soft drink purchases and draw mathematically-based conclusions. What's more, given accurate land area data, the students could also compare the land area to soft drink purchases to draw even more mathematically-based conclusions. I think you know where I'm headed . . . population density! What an incredible opportunity this context has provided for the students to analyze the relationship between state population and land size and how they connect it to the number of gallons of soft drinks sold.

So far we have looked at the quantity aspect, but this might not be the most interesting part. Let's return to the chart paper with the kids' original

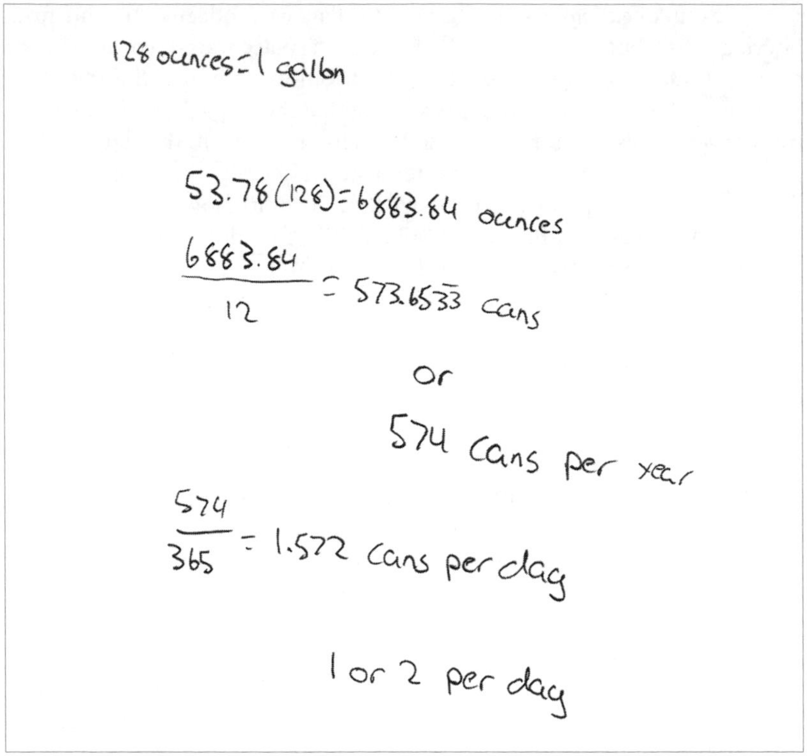

128 ounces = 1 gallon

53.78 (128) = 6883.84 ounces

$$\frac{6883.84}{12} = 573.65\overline{33} \text{ cans}$$

or

574 cans per year

$$\frac{574}{365} = 1.572 \text{ cans per day}$$

1 or 2 per day

FIGURE 2.4

thoughts and then to the table and look at the way the data is displayed. Students notice the alphabetical listing of the states, which makes answering the following questions cumbersome. *Which state has the highest consumption? Which state has the lowest consumption?* Students easily recognize the difficulty of answering an order question when the data is not displayed in that format—except for the one student mentioned earlier who predicted that there was some relationship between geographic location of each state and the number of gallons of soft drinks purchased. Some skeptical student suggests ordering the data from high to low because they don't quickly see the insight that the other student has seen.

Once the data is ordered, more students notice the highest sales occur in the southern states. We then have the students use a map to examine this connection. Students choose two color markers and color the highest eight states in one color and the seven lowest in another color. Have the students alternate coloring between the high and low states for an even more dramatic revelation. Color the highest state in red, then the lowest in blue. Next, color the second highest red and then the second lowest blue. Continue in this fashion until . . . ? How would you know when to stop? The eighth lowest state is not touching the other low ones See Figure 2.5.

The eight states with the highest soft drink sales are North Carolina, Florida, Georgia, South Carolina, Virginia, Mississippi, Alabama, and Louisiana. The seven states with the lowest sales are Wyoming, Idaho, North Dakota, Montana, Oregon, Washington, and South Dakota. What is the story here? Students are intrigued with the findings and quickly state possible reasons for this data clustering that concur with the insightful student's earlier prediction (meanwhile that student is grinning ear to ear!). Is more sold in the southern states because the weather is hotter? Does the presence of a distributor in a state increase sales? Would a hot beverage data display result in reverse findings? The students' curiosity is piqued, and they are excited about looking for possible answers to their questions, even approaching me after class, in the lunchroom with their insights! What a rich opportunity for discovering interdisciplinary connections—rich, right connections to the world, themselves and mathematics!

Big Idea 3: Creating Multiple Representations of Increasing Abstraction

Students need to create their own representations. This is where students express their conceptions of a problem, where they create something that represents the images in their minds. The students may work through several different representations before they truly "see" the important concept for which we chose this problem. They may need several different

FIGURE 2.5

representations of the same problem situation before they can grasp the relationship in question. The actual question asked by the problem is not yet answered, but they are moving in the right direction and closing in on an answer.

Types of Representations

Let's look at how students can incorporate representations into their problem solving. For example, if the teacher asked students to find *all* the triangles with integer sides that had a perimeter of 48 (a somewhat different question than the previous one in which students were asked to determine which triangle was larger), the students might try all of the representations that we mentioned earlier and others we've seen:

- *manipulatives*: pushpins, string, and rulers;
- *actions*: three students represent three vertices, pulling a 48-inch circle of rope while a fourth student measures;
- *pictorial*: drawing on graph paper with ruler and compass or free-hand sketching;
- *recording data* with symbols;
- *organizing data* into tables;
- *graphing data* on rectangular coordinates;
- *language* (oral and written) are used throughout.

Using Equations   In some problems, students will create equations to represent and model the data. Every time one manipulates the symbols of an equation to change its form, the new equation will show you a different aspect of the relationships or a new relationship entirely. We tell students, it's going to tell you a different story each time. For example, Heron's formula is traditionally presented as: $A = \sqrt{s(s-a)(s-b)(s-c)}$ where $s = (a + b + c)/2$, which is the semi-perimeter. In one sense, the formula is very simple and emphasizes the semi-perimeter, which introduces a fourth variable (s). The formula that we have been using $A = \frac{1}{4}\sqrt{(a + b + c)(a + b - c)(a - b + c)(-a + b + c)}$, which also requires multiplying four lengths together. We like it because we can help the students see that the formula uses the perimeter ($a + b + c$) and each of the other three terms can be seen as the way you'd check to see if you really had a legitimate triangle: the sum of any two sides must be greater than the third side (the triangle sum theorem).

Using Language   Language representations are notoriously tricky; words can be ambiguous or have multiple connotations. In general, teachers help students move from their natural language of the world to more precise and abstract mathematical terminology. But even this translation depends on language!

Students need many experiences with different language and communication modes: the language of reasoning, procedural language, descriptive language, reflective language, and the language of explanation. These modes characterize different functions or purposes and have different vocabulary and terminology. The exact wording of the question the teacher asks determines the kind of answer the students are supposed to give. For instance, "Analyze this quadrilateral in terms of its properties" calls for descriptive language. The question, "Are these two quadrilaterals similar?" may be answered with the language of reasoning or explanation.

Using Manipulatives   A wide variety of technology and tools are available to teachers to help their students learn mathematics. Each carries with it the promise of opening new windows of understanding as well as the challenge dealing with their impact on our representations. From tangrams to gram weights and balance scales, from geostrips to meter sticks, teachers use concrete objects (math manipulatives) to help students get started at the beginning of their investigations of concepts. *They are tools for thinking.*

There are also tools that are more technical in nature, for instance, the protractor, a calibrated instrument that gives fourth grade students trouble. When they are not certain in their knowledge of what an angle is, a protractor is virtually unintelligible to them.

We have an abundance of digital electronic technology the likes of which have never been seen in any prior generation: graphing calculators, palm pilots, CBL sensors, laptop computers with wireless connections to the Internet as an intellectual playground, software programs of a very high caliber (for example, Key Curriculum's Geometer's Sketch Pad and Fathom Dynamic Data, and Microsoft's Excel). The spreadsheet is a tool that in many ways eliminates the need for students to learn programming languages.

Metarepresentations

Researchers have begun studying representational fluency, also known as meta-representation, which is the capability a student has to construct, critique, and refine a variety of representational forms. It refers to a person creating a representation appropriate for a particular problem, mathematical task, or situation/context and not simply imposing a standard representation. Such highly appropriate representations are essentially models. Students need to be able to create with various representational systems so that their creations truly embody their internal images and conceptual systems. Representational fluency is especially valuable in communicating conceptions and in flexibly using them to develop solutions to real-life problems.

Researchers have found that with minimal intervention from a teacher, students can develop metarepresentational competence. Developing competence is enhanced by students talking with other students to test representations, getting feedback from peers. Through continual cycles of representing for a specific purpose, creating, producing, sharing, critiquing, and revising, students are able to improve their representations considerably. Copying a teacher's representation is not enough. Creating something of their own, something that they understand intimately, is far more important. Perhaps there is a certain amount of experience and knowledge about representations that needs to be in place, like a minimal threshold, that once attained, helps students really take off.

How Concrete Should We Be?

A key issue that I get hit with fairly frequently by middle school math teachers is my insistence that they begin new units with students using concrete representations. As soon as they realize that I am talking about language and objects, the complaints roll in. The most common are:

- Our students are eighth graders; they shouldn't need manipulatives now. (*Our response: Whenever a human of any age encounters a new, unfamiliar concept, he or she will learn best by beginning with concrete examples.*)
- Our students won't be allowed to use objects next year at the high school. They might as well get used to not having them now. (*Our response: If students need them now, use them now. Who knows what the high school is really doing?*)
- Our students think manipulatives are for babies. They resent using them. (*Our response: If teachers believe manipulatives are for babies, they will transfer that attitude to their middle school students.*)
- I tried using objects once, but my students just played with them and wouldn't do the assignment. (*Our response: Once? That's barely enough time for students to begin to get a "feel" for the tools.*)
- I tried using objects once, but my students just threw them at each other. (*Our response: If your students are throwing manipulatives, you've got a bigger classroom management problem to deal with!*)
- Manipulatives don't work. Our students can do the problem with manipulatives, but as soon as we switch over to paper and pencil, they can't. (*Our response: Manipulatives are generally the most concrete representation, and paper-and-pencil algorithms the most abstract. Rarely can anyone make that leap without intermediate steps.*)
- We don't have any manipulatives in our school. (*Our response: Lobby the school, the PTA, and the district to buy them. Or make some out of sturdy paper.*)

Teachers who express concerns about using objects in their math classroom reveal some real problems with their own teaching practice. While *objects* does include manipulatives, it's not limited to them. *Tools* is another term that includes a wide range of objects and manipulatives. Tools help students see relationships, patterns, and solutions—and help them *think*.

It is true that manipulatives can be used inappropriately, foolishly wasting precious class time; teachers must learn how to use all the tools properly. A carpenter won't cut a board with a chain saw, nor drive a finishing nail in with a sledgehammer. Below is a problem that illustrates how multiple representations can work.

Consider the following number pattern:

(1) (3, 5) (7, 9, 11) (13, 15, 17, 19) ?

What comes next?

If you are thinking that (21, 23, 25, 27, 29) comes next, you are correct. There is clearly a pattern to this symbolic notation, and although it is somewhat abstract, the only concept you need to know is odd numbers. You would have to discern that each set has one more element in it than the previous set and be aware that if you keep a cumulative total of the number of elements, you will have 1, 3, 6, 10, 15, which are the first five triangle numbers. Let's arrange the sets like a triangle. See Figure 2.6.

In number theory there are sets of numbers that were seen by the ancient Greeks to correspond to patterns that were like polygons. Most familiar are the *square* numbers: 1, 4, 9, 16, 25, and so on. The triangle numbers are one way of representing a fundamental pattern of growth, each successive number is added to the cumulative total. This summation is readily seen when objects are arranged in the shape of a triangle.

```
        O       O        O        O        O
                OO       OO       OO       OO
                         OOO      OOO      OOO
                                  OOOO     OOOO
                                           OOOOO
```

Cumulative Total	1	3	6	10	15

								1
							3	5
						7	9	11
					13	15	17	19
				21	23	25	27	29
			31	33	35	37	39	41
		43	45	47	49	51	53	55
	57	59	61	63	65	67	69	71
73	75	77	79	81	83	85	87	89

FIGURE 2.6

Each row of the triangle is composed of one of the sets in the number pattern. There are a total of nine rows, and the ninth row has nine numbers. (Note that a tenth row would generate three digit numbers.) What patterns do you see in the rows, besides the sets of number patterns mentioned above?

If you were to calculate the sum of each row you'd get the numbers shown going down the far right column. See Figure 2.7. If they look familiar, it's because they are the cubic numbers.

Because there are cubic numbers, it would be helpful at this point to get a large quantity of cubes, at least one hundred, preferably Multilink Cubes, Linker Cubes, or Snap Cubes. If you make the 2-by-2-by-2 cube, you'll see that it can be two layers of 2-by-2. The triangle in Figure 2.8 does not say, "make two layers of 2-by-2," however; it says only "(3, 5)." What does that mean? There are only two elements in the set (3, 5). Note that their sum is 8, a perfect cube (2 * 2 * 2). As we continue, we observe that all the rows sum to the cubic numbers, in order.

We usually have our students work directly with individual cubes. While they are busy building big cubes, we ask open-ended question such as:

- *Why* do a bunch of odd numbers add up to cubes?
- Think about layers. How is a layer of cubes related to what is in the table?
- Look at the ninth row (in Figure 2.8), which has nine elements in it. Look at the middle number in the row. It is 81. What does that tell you?
- The eighth row has eight elements, so it does not really have a middle number, but the seventh row does, 49. What are your ideas at this point about the patterns?

								1	**1**
							3	5	**8**
						7	9	11	**27**
					13	15	17	19	**64**
				21	23	25	27	29	**125**
			31	33	35	37	39	41	**216**
		43	45	47	49	51	53	55	**343**
	57	59	61	63	65	67	69	71	**512**
73	75	77	79	81	83	85	87	89	**729**

FIGURE 2.7

									1	$1 = 1^3$
								3	5	$8 = 2^3$
							7	9	11	$27 = 3^3$
						13	15	17	19	$64 = 4^3$
					21	23	25	27	29	$125 = 5^3$
				31	33	35	37	39	41	$216 = 6^3$
			43	45	47	49	51	53	55	$343 = 7^3$
		57	59	61	63	65	67	69	71	$512 = 8^3$
	73	75	77	79	81	83	85	87	89	$729 = 9^3$

FIGURE 2.8

- How does this new information relate to making a big cube and creating its layers?

Eventually, when we review the problem together as a class, we hand out a picture that shows why the sum of consecutive odd numbers are perfect cubes. See Figure 2.9. How do our students benefit from working with cubes to create layers and by analyzing the picture we hand out during class review?

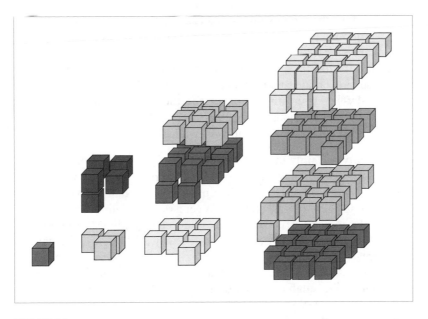

FIGURE 2.9

1. When students make the cubes 1, 27, 125, 343, and 729, using the triangle table (Figure 2.8) they can see that the middle number in the odd rows of the triangle is a square number and is the number of cubes needed for each layer of the big cube. For example, the third row has a middle number of 9 and its layer is a 3-by-3 square. Three layers of 3-by-3 cubes would be 27 total cubes. Similarly, the fifth row has a middle number of 25 and its layer is a 5-by-5 square. Five layers of 5-by-5 cubes would be 125 total cubes.

2. However, when students see the pictorial representation (Figure 2.9) of 7, 9, and 11 cubes, they realize that 7, 9, and 11 are not *initially* made up of three layers of 9 cubes. The 11 is a 3-by-3 square with 2 additional cubes attached to the bottom; 7 has 2 fewer cubes than 3-by-3; therefore, the extra 2 cubes used to make up the 11 fit nicely together with the 7—thereby creating three rows of 9 cubes.

3. Similarly, the numbers in the fifth row are 21, 23, 25, 27, 29, which are, respectively, 4 fewer than 25 (5-by-5), 2 fewer than 25, 25 exactly, 2 more than 5-by-5, and 4 more than 5-by-5. Although the cubes for the fifth row's layer are not pictured, can you visualize their symmetry? With the fifth row including the numbers 27 and 29, we can make a 5-by-5 square and then have extra 2 cubes and 4 cubes attached to the bottom of the 27 and the 29 arranged to fit right into the spaces left in the 23 and 21, which could not make the 5-by-5 by themselves.

4. When students make the cubes 8, 64, 216, and 512, using the triangle table they can see there are no middle numbers in the even rows. However, the unseen number between the two numbers nearest the center would be considered the middle number. For example, in the fourth row (13, 15, 17, 19), we would consider 16 to be the middle number. Sixteen is the number of cubes needed for the fourth row's layer of the big cube and its layer is a 4-by-4 square. Because there is no actual 16, we'd first make the 17 with a 4-by-4 square with 1 extra cube on the bottom, which fits together with the 15. Similarly, the 19 is a 4-by-4 square with 3 additional cubes on the bottom, which fits with the 13.

This activity certainly involved several varied symbolic representations in addition to language descriptions, concrete representations with the cubes and a picture of the manipulatives. Students wove back and forth among these representations to get a deeper understanding of the pattern. By making it with the cubes and color coding the number of cubes, they were able to get down to the *why*. Although this insight is not formal proof, it does show you what avenue a formal proof might take. Some mathematicians call this a "look-see" proof. Several excellent books are available on this topic that is also called "proof without words" (Nelson 1993).

Big Idea 4: Students Solving Problems: Same Concept, Multiple Contexts

Working with only one context with a limited number of examples may accomplish what is called *local conceptual development* (Lesh and Doerr 2003), but students rarely can generalize this understanding to other situations or contexts. They need to work with a concept in multiple contexts. Teachers build bridges across contexts to help students generalize their understanding.

Situated cognition refers to learning and problem solving in a particular context. There are many situations in real life where groups of people have developed significant types of mathematics to handle a specific need. These particular ways of thinking about the concepts and accompanying procedures make perfectly good sense to those who use them, but they bear little resemblance to the mathematics typically learned in school. People who make extensive use of mathematics in their work settings organize their ways of thinking mathematically around situations and problem contexts, not around the abstractions in school math textbooks. The research from situated cognition consistently has shown that virtually everyone engaged in solving problems in their own contexts is able to develop mathematical concepts and powerful conceptual tools for problem situations, even when they flunked math in school.

Using the Braid Model to Build Experiences and Understanding

The Braid Model emphasizes context and situations asking kids to imagine, visualize, and connect the mathematics to other math content and to the context. We encourage teachers to look for (or create) problems where the context facilitates access to the content and is not merely window-dressing. Figure 2.10 illustrates how a teacher can build experiences for students with multiple representations and multiple contexts. The figure may seem ridiculously complicated and, in fact, the interactions are complex. Life in the classroom is not all that simple, despite the pronouncements of policy makers who offer simplistic solutions to all our problems.

Start at the top of Figure 2.10 and work down. The teacher has a *concept* in mind when she plans her lesson (for example, "integers"— most especially negative integers). She decides to have the kids think about what happens in the winter in Chicago with temperatures frequently below zero on the Fahrenheit scale. We'll call that *context A*. The students work on several problems (three in Figure 2.10), and for each problem, they create representations (such as drawing a thermometer or number line) labeled REP A1, REP A2, and REP A3 in Figure 2.10. She debriefs the students on each problem and, through questions and explanations, she attempts to solidify their understanding of the *concept* in this *context* (negative integers as temperatures below zero). Note that the three REP As are surrounded by a dotted shape, which represents debriefing.

We'll call that Context A. The kids work on several problems (three in Figure 2.10), and, for each problem, they create representations (e.g., drawing a thermometer or number line) labeled REP A1, REP A2, and REP A3 in Figure 2.10. She debriefs the students on each problem and

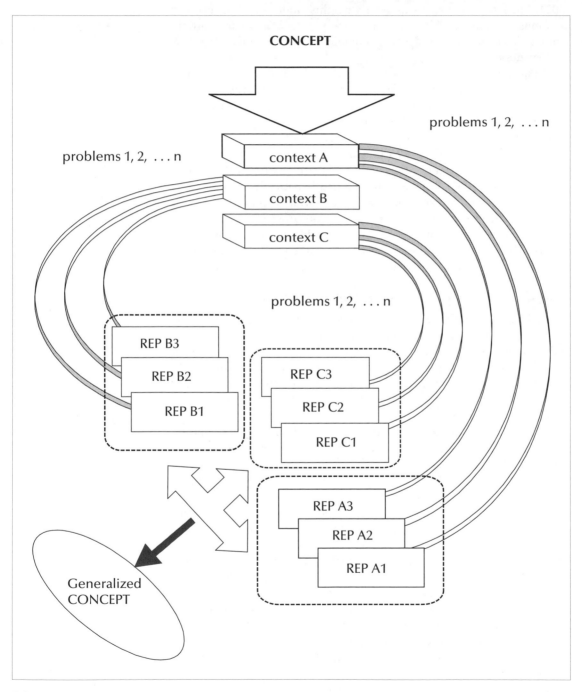

FIGURE 2.10

then, through questions and explanations, she attempts to solidify their understanding of the concept *in this context* (negative integers as temperatures below zero). Note that the three REP As are surrounded by a dotted shape, which represents debriefing.

Consider the following example of how a teacher planned to do this first context for the major concept of negative integers, based on the students' prior knowledge.

Context A: Temperature Prior work with context: Class and each individual examined a vertical thermometer. On graph paper they drew two vertical lines that would become a Fahrenheit scale and a Celsius scale. Students marked the freezing and boiling points at same heights on both lines and labeled them 32° and 212° versus 0° and 100°. Then they *interpolated* several times. Questions to prompt them were:

- What temperature is halfway between 0 and 100? (*50 degrees*)
- Then what temperature is halfway between 32 degrees and 212 degrees Fahrenheit? (*122 degrees*)
- What can you conclude from these facts? (*50 degrees C and 122 degrees F are the same temperature.*)
- Use interpolation to find other points of equivalence in the two scales.

The students found that they could go halfway between on both scales until they got to the Celsius values of 0, 25, 50, 75, 100. Then several noted that while Celsius went up by 25, Fahrenheit went up by 45. Both 25 and 45 have 5 as a factor. So one-fifth of the way between 0 and 25 is 5. At the same time the Fahrenheit scale goes from 32 to 77, up by 45. One-fifth of the way up would be 9, which must be added to the 32 degrees. The teacher asked what happens to Fahrenheit when you go up 5 on the Celsius scale? Will that always be true? What about if you go down 5 degrees in Celsius? The students then completed the table on the far right.

Problem 1: Record the high and low in Fahrenheit temperature for five straight days in January in Chicago. Draw five vertical thermometers including the scales at 10-degree intervals. Mark the high and the low for each day and write these temperatures onto the thermometers. Calculate: How many degrees change occurred? Which day had the greatest change? By how much?

Problem 2: Take the same days as problem 1 and record the high and low degrees in Celsius. Enter the data on a table. Repeat problem 1. Calculate: How many degrees Celsius change occurred? Which day had the greatest change? By how much?

Problem 3: We know that 0 degrees Celsius is the point water freezes, which is 32 degrees on the Fahrenheit scale. On each of the five days, how many degrees were below freezing? Represent it any way you prefer, but you must explain what you did and why.

Problem 4: Choose a city in Alaska and a city in Siberia. Record the actual low in Celsius for both cities over a ten-day period.

- Find the average low during that period for each city. Which city had the lower average? By how much?
- Find the difference between each city for each day and then take the average of those differences. What do you get?

FAHREN.	CELSIUS	FAHREN.	CELSIUS	FAHREN.	CELSIUS	FAHREN.	CELSIUS
212 =	100	212	100	212	100	212	100
						203	95
						194	90
						185	85
						176	80
		diff = 90	diff = 50	167 (122 = 45)	75	167	75
						158	70
						149	65
						140	60
						131	55
diff = 180	diff = 100	122	50	122	50	122	50
						113	45
						104	40
						95	35
						86	30
		diff = 90	diff = 50	77 (32 + 45)	25	77	25
						68	20
						59	15
						50	10
						41	5
32 =	0	32	0	32	0	32	0
						23	−5
						14	−10
						5	−15
						−4	−20
Go halfway		Go halfway		Go one-fifth of the way			

FIGURE 2.11

Problem 5 (Challenge): We know that Fahrenheit and Celsius are different and their "degrees" are not the same size. Freezing and boiling points are 32 and 212 versus 0 and 100. Is there ever a temperature when both scales would read the same number?

When sure that all the students have developed good *local conceptual development* of negative integers in the context of temperature, the teacher will introduce a different context for negative integers with multiple problems (for example, Context B— the planet Earth, with altitudes of mountains above sea level, depths of the oceans below sea level, and certain locations on the face of the earth as below sea level.) She repeats the process of debriefing of each problem and pulling together how these problems in this context conceive of the concept. If the students don't bring it up first, she asks them to compare and contrast the representations and the meanings of the concept in each context. The three-pronged arrows in Figure 2.10 are meant to signify this comparing and contrasting of the representation and meaning in different contexts (the figure shows three contexts interacting).

Then the teacher encourages the students to strip away all the differences among the three contexts and push for the commonalities. She guides them in building understanding, moving to more abstract representations that are less and less concerned with the particular features of each context. Through this guidance she is helping them build a generalized understanding of the concept that can be used in a variety of other contexts. (Note the solid arrow coming from the interactions among the three contexts to the generalization.) A reasonable assessment of how generalized the concept is within a student's knowledge would be for the teacher to introduce problems in new contexts in which the concept could possibly be used. Can the student make the connection (for example, debits and credits)?

Big Idea 5: Cognitively Based Planning for Language, Connections, Contexts, and Representations

How do you think about the mathematical concepts you teach and how do you talk about them to students? Motivating students by getting them to *buy into* the problem is extremely important. When planning lessons or units, write out a list of questions to ask yourself, such as:

- What is the main concept of this problem?
- Why am I choosing to use this problem?
- To what other concepts is this related?
- How will I initiate this problem, story problem, or activity? (How will I pitch it?)
- What questions will I ask?

- What representations will I encourage students to create?
- What patterns do I expect students to perceive? What questions may help them?
- What connections among concepts do I want students to see or understand?

For a more comprehensive list of "Planning Considerations," see the Appendix. The questions are not recipes or prescriptions that tell you precisely what to do. They are issues for teachers to consider and decide *how* they will attend to them. Collectively, they require teachers to integrate thinking and language into the students' problem solving and their own mathematics teaching.

Planning for teaching should include assessment, carrying out both informal, ongoing assessment of student progress and more formal, summative assessment of student achievement. Generally speaking, we want to monitor student thinking and understanding and help them become more metacognitively aware of what they are doing and thinking. We will illustrate these ideas in many of the problems. Some of these problems, though primarily used in the curriculum to teach specific concepts, can also be excellent assessment devices.

Big Idea 6: Integrating Reading Comprehension Strategies and Math Processes via Cognitive Principles

These two seemingly disparate areas are both based on cognition. Reading is the dynamic process of deriving meaning from written language and requires some special *thinking* about what one knows already (prior knowledge) and one's experiences (especially with language). Readers *interact* with what they read. They do not passively receive its meaning. They create it for themselves. They use what they know about the content of the text, how texts of this kind are structured, and the particular vocabulary.

Research has identified several highly effective cognitive strategies for students to use in reading comprehension, and specific teaching techniques for helping students use these strategies have been developed (Keene and Zimmermann 2007, Harvey and Goudvis 2007, Miller 2002). There are seven fairly broad reading comprehension strategies, each of which encompasses a number of more focused strategies, techniques, or activities.

1. *Making Connections:* activating relevant prior knowledge, linking what is in the text to their own experiences, discerning the context; relating what is in the text to other things they've read, to things in the real world, to phenomena around them;
2. *Asking Questions:* actively wondering, raising uncertainties, considering possibilities, searching for relationships, making up "what if" scenarios;

3. *Visualizing*: imagining the situation or people being described, making mental pictures or images;
4. *Inferring and Predicting*: interpreting, drawing conclusions, hypothesizing;
5. *Determining Importance*: analyzing essential elements;
6. *Synthesizing*: finding patterns, summarizing, retelling;
7. *Metacognitive Monitoring*: actively keeping track of their thinking, adjusting strategies to fit what they are reading.

Simply *applying* these strategies to math does not go far enough because meaning making and comprehension in mathematics requires deep conceptual understanding of abstract ideas. These strategies must be adapted to work in mathematics (Hyde 2006).

Students must engage in five mathematical processes if they are to understand mathematical concepts (NCTM 2000):

1. *Problem Solving*: building new mathematical knowledge, solving problems from many different contexts, using a variety of strategies;
2. *Reasoning and Proof*: making and investigating mathematical conjectures; selecting and using various types of reasoning and methods of proof; developing and evaluating mathematical arguments and proofs;
3. *Connections*: understanding how mathematical ideas interconnect and build on one another to produce a coherent whole; applying mathematics in contexts outside of school;
4. *Representations*: creating and using representations to organize, record, and communicate mathematical ideas; selecting, applying, and translating among mathematical representations to solve problems, using representations to model and interpret physical, social, and mathematical phenomena;
5. *Communication*: organizing and consolidating thinking; sharing one's thinking coherently and clearly with others; analyzing and evaluating the thinking and strategies of others; expressing mathematical ideas precisely via the language of mathematics.

Over the course of several years we investigated what can happen when we juxtaposed the five math processes with the seven reading comprehension strategies. Figure 2.12 is a matrix we used to organize our analysis. For each cell we systematically asked, "What principles from cognitive science can we use to modify this reading strategy to help students do this math process?" (Bransford, Brown, and Cocking 2000; Donovan and Bransford 2005).

For example, for many years we have had great success in our classrooms using an adaptation of Ogle's K-W-L, derived from the Asking Questions strategy (Blachowicz and Ogle 2001). K-W-L stands for the prereading questions "What do I *know*?", "What do I *want* to learn more about?", and, after reading, "What did I *learn*?" We asked ourselves,

"What kinds of metacognitive self-questioning can students use to enhance their problem solving?" This question is implicit in the cell in the second row, first column, asking questions/problem solving.

After experimentation and adaptation, we created our math **KWC**:

- What do I Know for sure?
- What do I Want to find out?
- Are there any special Conditions?

Math teachers may want to think of these as the *givens, goals,* and *constraints*, but we go far beyond the traditional use of those terms.

We found that our three KWC questions provided a good structure and focus for our students *during* the reading of a story problem. The teachers modeled these questions for the whole class. They became the key questions when students met in small groups to "Discuss the problem." These questions provided a structure for the students to work in their groups. They connected with their prior knowledge. After using this strategy in small groups, students used these questions when they worked on story problems individually.

READING COMPREHENSION STRATEGIES	MATHEMATICAL PROCESSES				
	Problem Solving	Reasoning & Proof	Connections	Communications	Representation
making connections					
asking questions					
visualizing					
inferring					
predicting					
determining importance					
synthesizing					

FIGURE 2.12

We filled in many cells in the matrix and tried out the adapted comprehension strategies with a variety of math problems (e.g., traditional story problems to open-ended or extended-response problems and mathematical tasks).

Next we took the classic four phases of problem solving used by George Pólya in the 1950s because they are simple to grasp, most teachers know them, and we wanted to organize the flow of the students' work, which becomes increasingly more complex.

1. Understand the problem
2. Plan what strategy to use
3. Use the strategy
4. Look back

Next we augmented Polya's phases with five aspects of problem solving that we have tried to build in to math activities for about ten years.

1. *Situations*: Teachers (or students) pose problems in real-world situations or contexts familiar to the students.
2. *Representations*: Students create one or more representations of the situation related to the problem or the question posed.
3. *Patterns*: Students look for patterns (or relationships) of any kind in the representations.
4. *Connections*: While debriefing the problem with the class (or with a small group), teachers ask questions to help students connect the patterns they see to their prior mathematical knowledge to crystallize their understanding.
5. *Extensions*: Teacher determines the appropriate extensions for each student as a form of differentiation.

The teacher decides what each child needs to work on next: something much more challenging, something much less challenging (perhaps some students did not fully understand concepts that were a prerequisite for the activity or problem), and finally, more practice problems (at the same level of difficulty as the one they just did) for the students for which the activity or problem was very appropriate. We did not include extension in the student model of the problem-solving process. However, many middle school students are quite able to assess what they need and could be included in this process.

We blended our way with Pólya's way of thinking about how kids could work on math problems and what the teacher should do and help them do. Then we blended them again with things that we were trying from the matrix of reading comprehension strategies and math processes. The result is the Braid Model, shown in Figure 2.13, from which you can see how our ideas fit together. When we begin a story problem, we spend a good deal of time making sure everyone understands the problem.

The Braid Model of Problem Solving

Understanding the Problem/Reading the Story

Visualization

- Do I see pictures in my mind? How do they help me understand the situation?
- Imagine the SITUATION. What is going on here?

Asking Questions (and discussing the problem in small groups)

K: What do I *know* for sure?
W: What do I *want* to figure out, find out, or do?
C: Are there any special *conditions*, rules, or tricks I have to watch out for?

Making Connections

Math to Self

- What does this situation remind me of?
- Have I ever been in any situation like this?

Math to World

- Is this related to anything I've seen in social studies or science, the arts? Or related to things I've seen anywhere?

Math to Math

- What is the main idea from mathematics that is happening here?
- Where have I seen that idea before?
- What are some other math ideas that are related to this one?
- Can I use them to help me with this problem?

Infer

- What inferences have I made? For each connection, what is its significance?
- Look back at my notes on K and C. Which are facts and which are inferences?
- Are my inferences accurate?

Planning How to Solve the Problem

- What REPRESENTATIONS can I use to help me solve the problem?
- Which problem-solving strategy will help me the most in this situation?

Make a model.	Draw a picture.	Make an organized list.
Act it out.	Make a table.	Write an equation.
Find a pattern.	Use logical reasoning.	Draw a diagram.
Work backward.	Solve a simpler problem.	Predict and test.

Carrying Out the Plan/Solving the Problem

- Work on the problem using a strategy.
- Does this strategy show me something I didn't see before now?
- Should I try another strategy?
- Am I able to *infer* any PATTERNS?
- Am I able to *predict* based on this inferred pattern?

Looking Back/Checking

- Does my answer make sense for the problem?
- Is there a pattern that makes the answer reasonable?
- What CONNECTIONS link this problem and answer to the big ideas of mathematics I am learning?
- Is there another way to do this? Have I made an assumption?

FIGURE 2.13

MAKING MEANINGFUL CONNECTIONS AMONG MATHEMATICAL CONCEPTS

When our students work on "cool" problems, we want them to actively look for connections of several different kinds. *Principles and Standards for School Mathematics* (NCTM 2000) reminds us to help kids see mathematics as a coherent whole. They ask us to help children see and make connections between concepts in mathematics, for example, fractions, decimals, percents, ratios. Few curricular programs aggressively promote connections for the kids. In rapid fire, textbooks blast out shotgun shells filled with unrelated "factlettes," chapter after chapter.

We have organized *Understanding Middle School Math* around several sets of connections that we have made. Consider all the aspects of probability that you would want students to know and be able to do. This list would contain some concepts that were fairly abstract (theoretical probability) but also many things that were more concrete, real, and hands-on (experimental probability). In fact, you might agree with us when we say that the teacher must lay a foundation of probability experiments to build up to the more abstract concepts of theoretical probability. Experimental probability is based on data and the analysis of that data with statistics. As we will describe later in detail, any time your students are doing a probability experiment you have the opportunity for them to learn or to practice significant number and computation work. You might imagine a Venn diagram such as Figure 2.14.

This shows us that there are three different source areas for concepts, problems, and activities. The part of PROBABILITY that is not in the intersection of the two sets would be Theoretical Probability. One might be tempted to assume that only theoretical data work (statistical theory) remains in the DATA part of the diagram. Not so. See Figure 2.15.

Figure 2.15 shows us that there are things to know and be able to do with measurement data, for example, keeping track of temperature for a certain interval for a period of time. You may think this is odd, but measuring all the heights of the kids in the class would not go into the same intersection. Why not? The heights are geometric measurements, a different category. And if the students were to collect all the height data and analyze it, the results would be yet another intersection of three sets—*geometric measurement data.* See Figure 2.16.

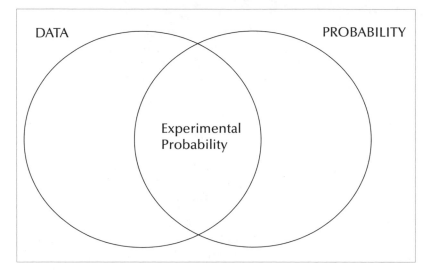

FIGURE 2.14

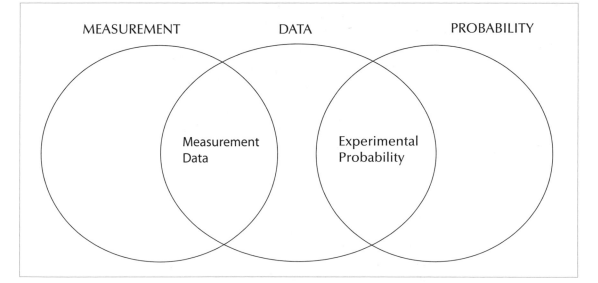

FIGURE 2.15

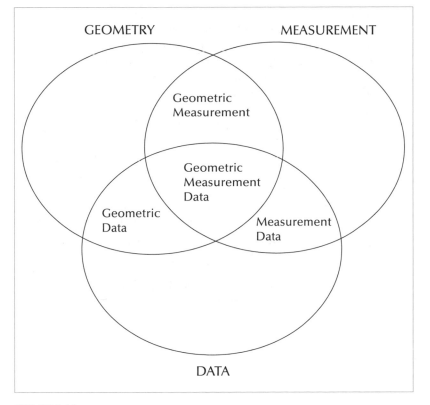

GEOMETRY　　　　MEASUREMENT

Geometric
Measurement

Geometric
Measurement
Data

Geometric
Data

Measurement
Data

DATA

FIGURE 2.16

We can see from Figure 2.16 that there are concepts—and therefore, problems and activities addressing those concepts—that come from different places in the complex interconnectedness of mathematics. For example, there are measurement concepts that do not involve geometry: temperature, money, time, mass/weight, capacity. Likewise, there are measurement concepts that are geometric in nature: length, area, volume, angular measure.

What would the intersecting geometric data include? Then what are the geometry concepts that do not involve data or measurement? Examples would be symmetry, similarity, tessellations. Why are we making such a big deal out of these distinctions? Several reasons are:

1. Intersections of these strands are places of "natural" connections in mathematics. If we are interested in helping students see mathematics as a coherent interconnected whole, these are great places to start.

2. We have less than 180 days each school year to teach about 100 concepts. (Granted some are review.) If we hit only one concept per lesson, kids would never have enough time to build

understanding of the concept. But if we purposely use activities, problems, or lessons with multiple interconnected concepts, the students stand a chance of working with a concept frequently.

3. If we deal only with strands as the curricular categories then we have a lot of ground to cover in order to connect things. By identifying these intersections we have explicitly made some important math connections.

4. In many textbooks, the geometry presented is almost entirely geometric measurement. Distinguishing between geometry and geometric measurement forces us to consider other geometric concepts that may have been neglected in the past. In some strands, identifying the concepts that are in the intersections draws attention to the concepts that still remain, and may reveal that more theoretical concepts remain while the concepts that went into the intersections are more experientially based.

THE CONNECTEDNESS OF STRANDS

Four Foundation Strands

geometry
measurement
data
probability

Four Intersection Strands

geometric measurement
measurement data
geometric measurement data
experimental probability

Note: We have left out some logically possible intersections because they are not especially potent in the middle school curriculum and we have incorporated any valuable ideas or concepts into a related strand (for example, geometric data is included in geometric measurement data).

Two Symbolic Strands

numbers
algebra

We use numbers and algebra to do mathematics. Both are symbolic representational systems, although algebra is more abstract. They pervade the other strands, continually used to represent and understand the relational concepts. They are so deeply connected that they flow, one into another, even more freely than an intersection.

Not easily. People have tried many times in many ways to conceptualize the math curriculum. What we can illustrate by example is the way we have arranged content for teaching math in the middle grades. Figure 2.17 shows the four foundation strands (geometry, measurement, probability, and data) and the four intersections, which we will also refer to as strands. When people talk about real-world uses of mathematics and real-life connections, these four intersections are where they reside. If you are looking for science and social studies connections to mathematics, here is where you'll find them.

The two other strands shown in Figure 2.17 are numbers and algebra. We believe that we need to seize every opportunity to build number work into activities and problems that come from the eight strands. Although there are some activities that reside solely in the realm of number, we are cautious to make sure they will really help students. Too often in their pasts, our students have been dramatically unsuccessful in working with "naked numbers"—computations that refer to nothing. We all have students who are not proficient in some, many, or all aspects of computation. We have found that the best ways to help them master computation is by first working in activities and problems that are sufficiently real that they can imagine the situation and are motivated to find a solution. They need problems to help them conceive of what these operations are really all about. Multiplication does not always make things bigger. Subtraction does not always take something away from a total. The textbook may be trying to get them to memorize the *order* of operations when what they need is to understand the *meaning* of operations. Therefore, you will find many activities in this book that you can use to "swing back" and have the kids work in an interesting motivating context, while learning the *arithmetic* they failed to learn when taught in a more traditional fashion.

What about algebra? Here is where it gets interesting. We think of algebra much in the same way we think of numbers. Both provide us ways to look at relationships and patterns and to symbolically represent real life situations. Granted, algebra is more abstract than numbers, but in many ways algebra is generalized arithmetic. Its abstractness comes in handy when we are trying to describe or represent the general case or to generalize across many cases. In every one of those eight strands, algebra is used in some way, for example, in tables, graphs, and equations to see how different representations of the same situation or phenomena reveal different features of its nature. In the same vein, you don't have to look hard to find algebraic formulas in geometry and probability. In this book we have explicitly built algebra into many places that traditional texts have not. Algebra should be as pervasive as numbers for students in grades 5–8.

Like number work, in algebra there is a place for working directly with the manipulation of symbols—the rules of the road—legitimate transformations of expressions, balancing equations, and the like. It is unfortunate that so many textbooks are dominated by symbol manipulation, leading people to believe that it *is* algebra. We must keep our eyes on the prize, not on the tools. The prize is being able to represent, model, generalize, and analytically describe the world. Learning to use the tools effectively is important but you don't win the game until you play it.

Figure 2.17 also shows that numbers and algebra are strongly connected to one another. In addition you should imagine both of these strands connected to the other eight. Numbers and algebra must be used

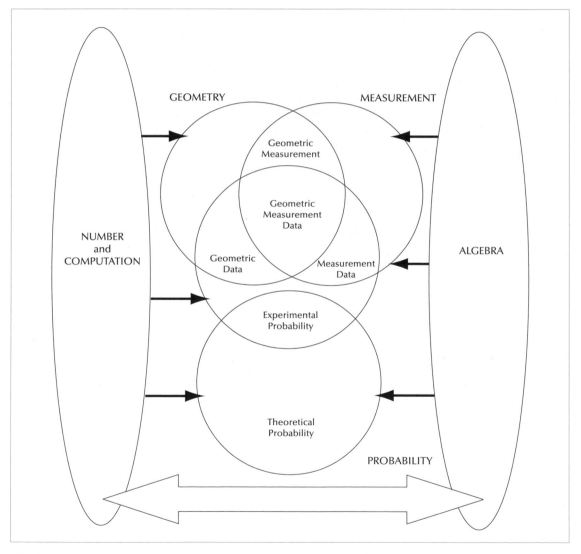

FIGURE 2.17

in all the others (this is what the abundance of arrows is supposed to show). Students learn to use these tools by using them in the rich real world contexts that the other eight provided.

We have purposely not included grade levels for the problems in *Understanding Middle School Math*. We believe that teachers are the *only* ones in a position to determine how a particular problem and its related concepts fit with their students and the curriculum to be taught.

3 | NUMBERS AND EARLY ALGEBRA

ALGEBRA IN THE CLASSROOM, THEN AND NOW

Students all across the United States now take formal algebra courses in middle school. Pushing the traditional Algebra I course down into eighth grade as the honors, gifted, or accelerated course for a handful of students may be justifiable, but wholesale herding all eighth graders into traditional Algebra I will not produce scholars. It will most likely produce failures.

I was in seventh grade in October 1957, when the Soviets sent Sputnik up and scared the marinara sauce out of U.S. politicians, educators, and mathematicians. Our first response was to sort students into tracks sooner and more diligently, accompanied by standardized testing of all sorts. Let's find the best and the brightest and funnel them into math and science. And by the way, we don't want our little Wernher von Brauns in any of the same classes with the pre–gas station track students.

Our second response was to slam-dunk the elementary schools with the *New Math*, rather abstract set theory–based arithmetic programs. *The Culture of the School and the Problem of Change* (Sarason 1971) includes a brilliant case study analyzing how the designers and implementers of the New Math completely misread the so-called behavioral regularities of schools that were far stronger than the ill-conceived implementation plans.

Morris Kline, mathematician and author of dozens of books that show the interconnectedness and coherence of mathematics, had his own critique of the New Math. In *Why Johnny Can't Add* (1964), Kline laid much of the blame of the failure of New Math on the mathematicians who insisted that math be taught in a highly deductive manner that they thought was "rigorous" but that inexorably led to students trying to memorize definitions, procedures, and formulas they didn't understand.

I am concerned that we are on the brink of making an analogous mistake with algebra, pressing its abstractness downward because with some students it appears that we can. For fifty years educators have used psychologist Jerome Bruner's (1977) ideas about teaching almost any concept in a developmentally appropriate way to any age student as the justification for introducing increasingly more geometry, measurement, data work, probability, and algebra into the elementary and middle schools. William Schmidt and his colleagues, when reporting on the TIMMS data, said that the U.S. math curriculum was a mile wide and an inch deep. They did not point fingers, but it's clear that this phenomenon did not happen overnight.

My junior high school in the late 1950s had grades 7, 8, and 9. All seventh and eighth graders took General Mathematics, which was dominated by arithmetic. At the end of eighth grade an amazing event occurred: The Algebra Fairy came to my junior high school and touched some of us eighth graders with her magic wand and allowed us to take algebra in ninth grade. And what of the others students, not so anointed? They got yet another year of General Math . . . and about one-third of the ninth-grade boys got their driver's licenses. They were sixteen years old and had been held back at least twice, usually because they failed math.

For the fortunate ones so blessed with access to algebra, our preparation was number work. There was no course called *Pre-Algebra*. Ten years later, I was teaching mathematics in a high school and we started seeing pre-algebra courses and books. When I looked at the books I discovered that pre-algebra was the same as the content of the first quarter of my ninth-grade algebra.

I am in no way suggesting that we return to those thrilling days of yesteryear. I don't want us to be hoodwinked into thinking that counting, sorting, and grouping objects is unimportant. A thousand times in my years of teaching algebra, a student's question was best answered by giving an example that was more concrete. That usually meant pulling the student back to his or her knowledge of *number* to concretize the algebraic abstraction.

Chapters 3, 4, and 5 in this book are about numbers and algebra. In them, we explore meaningful, exciting, and fun activities that help students' algebraic thinking become increasingly abstract by building on their concrete understandings.

PARTIAL PRODUCTS LIKE YOU'VE NEVER SEEN THEM

Starting Out with Base Ten Blocks and Graph Paper

Whenever anyone asks me what I think is the most important concept to learn in elementary school, I candidly tell them: *multiplication and division and their relationship to one another*. If students get to middle or junior high school without this knowledge, they'll be in trouble. (Refer to *Comprehending Math* [Hyde 2006] for a discussion about what elementary teachers can do to prepare their students.)

If students don't understand multiplication and division and their relationship, it is unlikely that teachers will get anywhere with the same approaches that failed the students—especially memorizing naked number procedures. Teachers will need *real* contexts and representations.

About twenty years ago, I was rummaging through some old math books, and I got a major shock. There were pictures of base ten blocks arranged to model the partial products of multiplication. My first reaction was, "Does this always work?" I thought for a second and said to myself, "Of course it does!" My second reaction was annoyance, "Why didn't someone show me this before now?" My third reaction was, "Wow! This is a great precursor to polynomial multiplication!"

I usually do the base ten blocks activity with sixth or seventh graders. I bring in zip-top bags that contain base ten blocks made up of cubic centimeters, so that when students lay the blocks flat on a table the surface of the blocks are in square centimeters. I make sure to have:

- 1 yellow hundreds square (10 centimeters on each side)
- 10 blue tens sticks (10 centimeters long, 1 centimeter wide)
- 15 yellow centimeter cubes (1 centimeter square)

I explain that base ten blocks are tools for measuring area or length. I give each pair of students a single sheet of centimeter square graph paper and tell them that each square centimeter represents a square foot, then I give them this problem to solve:

> I need to lay one-foot square tiles to cover the floor of my office, which is 13 feet by 14 feet. Draw the perimeter of my office on the graph paper, then fill the 13-by-14-foot rectangle with base ten blocks. What is the area of the rectangle?

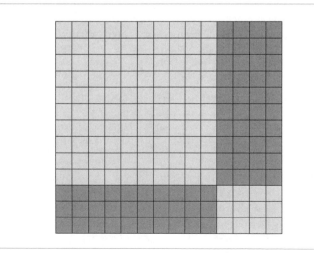

FIGURE 3.1

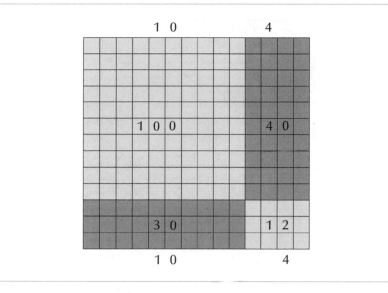

FIGURE 3.2

When everyone had filled their rectangles, I show them my way that groups all the ones blocks together in one corner, opposite the hundreds block, which makes it easier to see what is going on. See Figure 3.1.

Next I pass out blue and yellow pencils so students can shade in the two colors on their graph paper. I ask what shapes, and how many of them, they've created. They reply, "Four rectangles." I then ask them to write the dimensions of each rectangle on its outside and write the area of each rectangle on its inside. See Figure 3.2.

"How would you figure the area?" I ask. The students add up the areas of the four rectangles. "Do you have to add them in a particular order?" Some say no, some aren't sure. "The four rectangles would give us four partial products," I continue.

The tricky maneuver is the 10 times 4. It is much easier to ask students, "What color is it?" The 10-by-10 is, of course, the yellow hundreds square, which is easy for students to see. Armed with this information, students can now add the four partial products to find the overall product of 182:

$$
\begin{array}{r}
1\,4 \\
*\quad 1\,3 \\
\hline
1\,2 \\
3\,0 \\
4\,0 \\
1\,0\,0 \\
\hline
1\,8\,2
\end{array}
\qquad
\begin{array}{l}
3 * 4 = 12 \\
3 * 10 = 30 \\
10 * 4 = 40 \\
10 * 10 = 100
\end{array}
$$

We do a few more examples and then repeat the process without the base ten blocks, just using graph paper. See Figure 3.3.

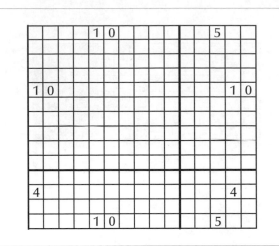

FIGURE 3.3

I ask students to draw the perimeter of a 14-by-15 rectangle on their graph paper and then draw two crossbars, one vertical and the other horizontal. The vertical bar cuts the side between the tens digits and the ones, reinforcing place value (just remind students to put the tens on the left). Then they can draw the horizontal line separating the tens digits from the ones digits.

I prefer they put the unit digit below the tens (see below) so that if anyone had trouble with partial products, I could easily show how the partial product of 14 * 15 works. I can also show the class how the distributive property works (4 * 15) = (4 * 5) + (4 * 10).

$$
\begin{array}{r}
1\,5 \\
*\quad 1\,4 \\
\hline
2\,0 \\
4\,0 \\
5\,0 \\
1\,0\,0 \\
\hline
2\,1\,0
\end{array}
$$

$4 * 5 = 20$
$4 * 10 = 40$
$10 * 5 = 50$
$10 * 10 = 100$

Moving on to More Abstract Representations and Mental Math

As students become more sophisticated in their thinking about partial products, they should move from the more *concrete* representations to the more *abstract* ones. I ask students to get a clean sheet of paper—no using base ten blocks or graph paper with this problem. See Fighure 3.4.

By this time some students are cranking out these products in their heads and if they think aloud they say, "20 * 30 = 600, plus 6 * 30 is another 180 or 780, plus 7 * 20 = 140, would give me 920, plus 6 * 7 = 42 added to the 920 would be 962." They invariably start with the biggest rectangle, which is an excellent place to start because it is essential to the product of front-end estimation—a great low estimate.

I'm thinking of a rectangle that is 26-by-37. Sketch the perimeter (no measuring!), put in the crossbars between the tens and units places, compute the area of the four smaller rectangles, and find the area of the big rectangle. See Figure 3.4.

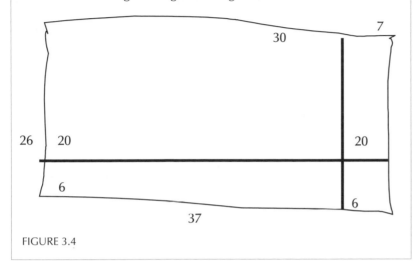

FIGURE 3.4

Some students become incredibly adept at doing math in their heads. I have yet to find a student who, if taught partial products using these multiple representations, fails to understand what is going on in multi-digit multiplication. Everyone gains immensely from this combination of representations.

Some teachers basically stop here and just use calculators hereafter for larger numbers because the students' understanding is so good. Others, including me, use the following base of conceptual understanding to help them see why the traditional algorithm works:

$$
\begin{array}{r}
{\scriptstyle 1} \\
1\,4 \\
*\ 1\,3 \\
\hline
4\,2 \\
1\,4 \\
\hline
1\,8\,2
\end{array}
$$

It takes about twenty minutes for students to make the connection: The four partial products that are made explicit by the rectangle model are folded into two partial products in the traditional algorithm. It is worth having students connect the procedure to the concept and not just use calculators. First, someone is going to show it to them anyway, and they may not try to make it as sensible as we can. Second, connections help students believe that math is understandable.

Red Dots

Slapping one or two zeroes on the end of a number is *not* a great way to help students understand what happens when a number is multiplied by ten or by one hundred. We have a better way. See Figure 3.5.

Figure 3.5 has five drawings that show a progression of drawing and thinking. Using a 100-foot roll of centimeter square graph paper, which is generally 75 centimeters wide, we give each pair of students a 75-by-60 centimeter sheet and a small 3-by-4 centimeter rectangle of oak tag or tag board. Then we give them the following instructions:

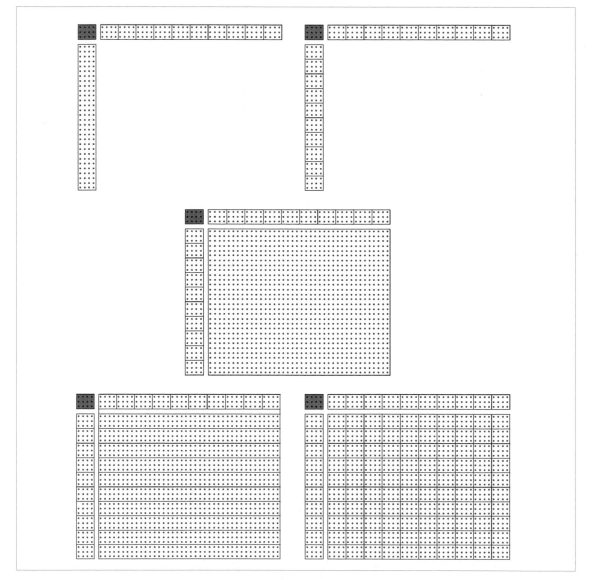

FIGURE 3.5

- Place the rectangle in the upper left corner of the centimeter square sheet and trace its perimeter.
- Use a red water soluble marker to put a single dot in each of the twelve squares. (Note: Some students like to use a red marker to color a 3-by-4 rectangle in the corner and then add in black dots.)

Next we give students a 3-by-40 centimeter rectangle of oak tag with these instructions:

- Place the rectangle just to the right of the 3-by-4 rectangle and line it up to run across the top of the sheet.
- Draw the rectangle's perimeter.
- Use a red water soluble marker to put a single dot in each of the one hundred twenty squares.

On a poster we have written this problem:

$3 * 4 = 12 \quad 3 * 40 = ?$

- How many of the 3-by-4 rectangles will fit in the 3-by-40 rectangle?
- Mark off the right side of the 3-by-4 rectangle each time you place it down on the 3-by-40 rectangle.
- So, the 3-by-40 rectangle is ___ times as big as the 3-by-4 rectangle.

$3 * 40 = 3 * 4 * (10) = 12 * 10 = 120$

Next we give them a 4-by-30 centimeter rectangle of oak tag with these instructions:

- Place the rectangle just below the 3-by-4 rectangle and line it up to run along the left side of the sheet.
- Draw its perimeter.
- Use a red water soluble marker to put a single dot in each of the one hundred twenty squares.

On another poster we have written this problem:

$3 * 4 = 12 \quad 4 * 30 = ?$

- How many of the 3-by-4 rectangles will fit in the 4-by-30 rectangle?
- Mark off the bottom of the 3-by-4 rectangle each time you place it down on the 4-by-30 rectangle.
- So, the 4-by-30 rectangle is ___ times as big as the 3-by-4 rectangle.

$4 * 30 = 4 * 3 * (10) = 12 * 10 = 120$

Okay, now the hard part. We ask students to draw the perimeter of a 30-by-40 rectangle, filling the left and lower part of the square centimeter sheets. Refer back to Figure 3.5.

- How many of the 3-by-40 rectangles will fit in the 30-by-40 rectangle? (Note: We are using the 3-by-40 rectangle now, not the 3-by-4 rectangle.)
- Lay the 3-by-40 rectangle across the 30-by-40 rectangle's dots and mark off the rows.
- How much bigger than the 3-by-40 rectangle is the 30-by-40 rectangle?

Last, we ask students to place their 4-by-30 rectangle vertically on the 30-by-40 rectangle and mark the columns to answer the following questions:

- How many of the 3-by-40 rectangles will fit in the 30-by-40 rectangle?

Consider:

- The 30-by-40 rectangle is 10 times as big as the 3-by-40 rectangle and the 4-by-30 rectangle.
- $30 * 40 = (3 * 10) * (4 * 10) = 3 * 4 * 10 * 10 = (3 * 4) * (10 * 10) = 12 * 100$
- How many of the 3-by-4 rectangles will fit in the 30-by-40 rectangle?
- How many times bigger than the 3-by-4 rectangle is the 30-by-40 rectangle?

We typically have students go through the red dots with the 3-by 4 rectangle and then two or three others to make sure that they fully understand what it means to multiply by powers of 10.

Algebra Tiles

To help students understand relationships expressed algebraically in formulas, equations, and expressions, it is valuable to take a step back from the symbolic abstractions and draw on geometric expressions, which are often better connected to students' experiences. Several geometric tools are available on the market today, but one in particular, Algebra Tiles, is directly related to partial products. Students who have had good experiences with the rectangle model of multiplication and partial products will be able to transfer that learning to Algebra Tiles because both are based on the distributive property of multiplication over addition.

There are three basic pieces to most Algebra Tile sets:

1. a small square
2. a large square
3. a rectangle with two of its sides equal to the length of the sides of the small square, and two equal to the sides of the large square

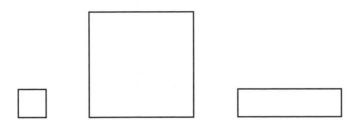

There are several different ways to use these pieces, but here I'll focus on polynomial multiplication. The small square may be considered to be 1-by-1(with an area of 1 square unit) and the large square x-by-x (with an area of x^2). The long rectangle would have side length of 1 and x and its area would be x square units.

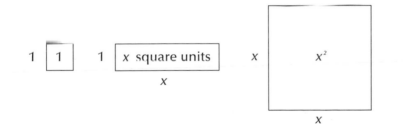

They fit together nicely. Can you figure out the area of the newly formed square?

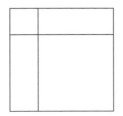

The area is $(x + 1)$ by $(x + 1)$, which equals $x^2 + 2x + 1$. Can you see the area of these pieces? There are two squares of area *1 square unit and* x^2 and two rectangles of area *x*. This point is often confusing to some students because *x* is a length and also an area in square units.

Figure 3.6 is a different example: If we had to multiply $(x + 3)(x + 4)$, we might FOIL:

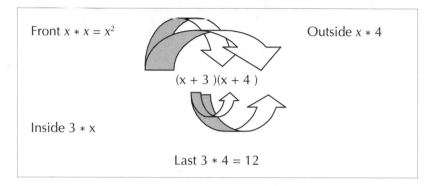

Front $x * x = x^2$ Outside $x * 4$

$(x + 3)(x + 4)$

Inside $3 * x$

Last $3 * 4 = 12$

FIGURE 3.6

Notice how FOILing creates four partial products as it makes sure that each of the terms in both binomials is multiplied by the two terms in the other binomial. We might have arranged the binomials vertically instead of FOILing horizontally. See Figure 3.7.

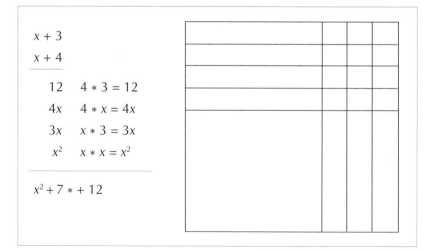

$x + 3$
$x + 4$
———
12      $4 * 3 = 12$
4x $4 * x = 4x$
3x $x * 3 = 3x$
x^2 $x * x = x^2$

$x^2 + 7 * + 12$

FIGURE 3.7

See how the rectangles (Algebra Tiles) on the right represent the four partial products.

Now let's try another example. Suppose this time that the small square is considered to be *y*-by-*y* (with an area of y^2) and the large square is *x*-by-*x* (with an area of x^2). In this case, the long rectangle would have side length of *y* and *x* and its area would be *xy* square units.

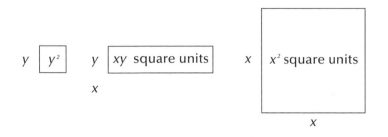

The area of the long rectangle, *xy* square units, is actually easier for students to understand than the long rectangle from the previous example that had 1-by-*x* as dimensions.

Again, the shapes fit together nicely. Can you determine the area of the newly formed square?

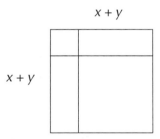

The area of the above square is (*x* + *y*) by (*x* + *y*), which equals x^2 + 2*xy* + y^2. Can you see the area of these pieces? There are two squares of area, one of which is x^2 and the other is y^2 and two rectangles of area *xy*.

There are many students who are visually inclined and need to see the geometric representations in order to understand *what* multiplication of polynomials entails and *how* it is connected to multiplication with whole numbers. It is extremely valuable to use tools such as Algebra Tiles, because they reinforce where the four partial products that result from FOILing originate.

PARTIAL QUOTIENTS

If students fully understand how *partial products* work, it is very useful to relate them to its inverse, *partial quotients*. When I meet with a group of teachers I often ask them, "What is the record for the most consecutive class periods of math devoted entirely to teaching the long division algorithm?" Answers vary but most are between eight and fifteen periods. *The envelope, please. . . . The award goes to Ms. Evelyn Hickenlooper of West Cupcake, Illinois. She kept her pupils practicing long division until 80 percent of them demonstrated 80 percent mastery in eight minutes—she drilled them for five weeks, twenty-five consecutive periods of math.* (Names have been changed to protect the excessive.)

Of course, Ms. Hickenlooper is not alone. Many teachers believe it is their civic duty, if not their moral obligation, to teach long division, but in reality they are just drilling the procedure—very little understanding is involved. When you think of drilling, don't you think of cavities and root canals? Practice and drilling are *not* the same.

Instead, if teachers were to teach for understanding, what would they do? First, they would help students develop number sense and understand the structure of our number system. Students need to understand addition and subtraction—not just as single digit facts, but as concept labels. There are different situations that we use addition and subtraction to *label* or *refer to*—for instance, the word *subtract* suggests removing something, taking it away, but is also used to determine the *difference* between two quantities, as in the altitudes of two mountains. By what verbal magic do we call these phenomena by the same name, *subtraction*?

Students attempting long division must understand what division is and how it is related to multiplication. There are three different models or situations of multiplication: *equal groups, arrays*, and *rectangular area*. It is the latter that makes partial products so simple to understand because the rectangular area model of multiplication treats place value explicitly. It is amazing how some textbook authors or textbook publishers include the partial products model but do not show *any* rectangles. Inconceivable!

When it comes to division, the key distinction is between *fair share* and *repeated subtraction*. Most elementary textbook math programs have about three times as many fair share problems as repeated subtraction problems. Consider this problem:

> Janie has 52 fun-sized candy bars that she is willing to share with her 3 friends Janice, Joanne, and Harriet. Each of the 4 friends will share equally. How many candy bars will each friend get?

In this situation, we know how much candy is to be divided, and we know how many people, but we don't know how many per person.

A different situation would be if Janice were making up packets from fifty-two fun-sized candy bars and each packet needed to have four candy bars. She could reach into the big box of candy bars, pull out four, and wrap them up. She'd continue to take out four *repeatedly* until she had no more. How many times can she do this before she runs out? In this situation, we know how much candy is to be divided, we know how much each packet gets, and we have to figure out how many packets.

Why am I going into this much detail? Students in elementary school don't get enough experience *thinking* about story problems, let alone working with repeated subtraction situations. What happens when students get hit with the long division algorithm that is based on repeated subtraction?

In an effort to help students cope with repeated subtraction, teachers invent concepts such as *guzinta* (as in, 4 *guzinta* 24 six times). To illustrate, let's use the problem 896 ÷ 8. The long division algorithm begins with estimating how many of the divisors can be subtracted from the dividend: 896 ÷ 8 is set up as 8⌐896. When we ask students to memorize *8 guzinta 8 one time,* we are really making the highest estimate possible in the hundreds column. Then we begin the subtraction process:

$$
\begin{array}{r}
112 \\
8\,\overline{)896} \\
\underline{8} \\
9 \\
\underline{8} \\
16 \\
16
\end{array}
$$

I have been told that in English schools, students do their sums and products on graph paper, one digit per square. It is very effective in keeping the columns straight. The inherent difficulty of the traditional algorithm is that, like many general algorithms, in order to accommodate all cases the procedure treats all numbers as if they were composed of individual digits. It is the Universal Blood Donor, O negative, everybody can get it. But it doesn't address place value—instead of learning it thoroughly in second grade, students are taught to ignore place value when working out algorithms. Talk about mixed messages—is it any wonder that many students go through elementary school and arrive at middle school not fully understanding place value of whole numbers, or decimals?

When we teach partial products, even when the situation concerns equal groups, our method is to have students use rectangles. Once students understand the situation, any multiplication can be abstracted as "naked numbers," and those numbers can be rethought as sides of a rectangle. With multiplication, we know the multiplier and the multiplicand and we are trying to determine the product. With division, we know the divisor and the dividend and we are trying to calculate the quotient. ("I'll take obscure arithmetic terms for 500, Alex!")

For example, refer to the problem and solution shown in Figure 3.8. The division is conceived in terms of a rectangle that has an area of 154 and one side of 7. Using this information, students must find out the length of the other side. First, students take out a sheet of graph paper and vertically draw one of the known sides, in this case, 7. Next, they draw two parallel lines extending out from the top and bottom of the known side. The problem is, we don't yet know how far to go. But we do know the area (154), so we can figure out the unknown side by repeatedly subtracting chunks that are multiples of 7. *WHY?* Because that way, we'll always have taken off (or accounted for or covered) one rectangle and still have one rectangle remaining.

Actually, our first move isn't to have students think about repeated subtraction because that's generally an unfamiliar topic. Instead, we have students place base ten blocks onto the graph paper and build a rectangle of the given area in order to determine what the unknown side is. (Later we will just use graph paper and no blocks.) Students draw the straight line of the known side and rays for the two unknown sides. Then they shade in the graph squares that correspond to how many squares they have covered up with the base ten blocks.

Andy's Inheritance

Andy's Inheritance is a problem from which students learn about regrouping in place value up through the millions. This is a great opportunity for students to incorporate KWC in the solving process.

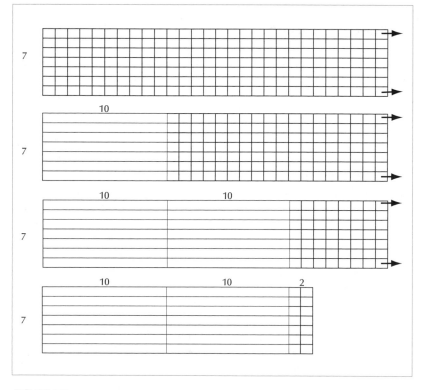

FIGURE 3.8

Andy has inherited one million dollars from his Great-Aunt Edna. He wants his money in cash but he doesn't want to carry around too many bills in a suitcase or briefcase. He wants a mixture of large and small bills. He decides that he wants some of each of the following *denominations* (the amount of the bill): $100,000, $10,000, $1,000, $100, $10, and $1.

Question 1: What are several ways Andy can accomplish his goal?

The first step is to imagine the situation. What's going on—What do I *know* for sure?

- Andy inherited $1,000,000.
- Andy wants his money in cash. Andy doesn't like to have a lot of bills.

Next, what do I *want* to figure out, find out, or do?

- How can Andy get his million dollars?
- What are some different ways Andy could get his million?

Last, are there any special *conditions*, rules, or tricks I have to watch out for?

- Andy's money can only be in $100,000 bills, $10,000 bills, $1000 bills, $100 bills, $10 bills, and $1 bills.
- Andy must have some of each denomination.

Try creating a table like the one shown below. Then, starting with the $1 denomination, explain the regrouping you would do to prove this is a million dollars:

$100,000	$10,000	$1,000	$100	$10	$1
9	9	9	9	9	10

Question 2: Andy wants some of each of the 6 denominations, but he only wants to carry 100 bills. Can you figure out several ways he can do this?

Question 3: In the table below, there are several examples of ways to make $1,000,000 with these bills. However, some of these examples violate the special conditions that Andy required in question 2. Which examples will not work? Note the new constraint: only use 100 bills.

$100,000	$10,000	$1,000	$100	$10	$1
9	9	9	9	9	10
9	8	18	20	0	0
9	6	38	18	19	10
8	15	49	9	9	10
8	19	8	19	9	10
8	18	18	18	18	20

Do you see any patterns in the table above? In the ones column, the number of $1 bills must be a multiple of ten to get a zero in that place for the million. That multiple of ten then would be added to the tens column (the $10 bills). Most of the numbers in the table end in either 8 or 9 because when the column to the right of them groups by tens in order to become a zero, regrouping will occur in that cell to make it a multiple of ten, and so on through the table.

The Andy's Inheritance problem helps reinforce the concept of place value in our base ten system. Students must group and regroup each of these denominations. There are other denominations of bills that are in circulation (for example, $2, $5, and $20); we ask students to talk about why those bills aren't included in the problem.

Square the Digits and Sum the Squares

Square the Digits and Sum the Squares is a rather inductive activity I have done with students and teachers alike. I have a collection of pink index cards, at least enough for each student. The cards are blank on one side and have a number that may be one, two, or three digits long on the other. I fan the cards out in my hand face down and ask each student to take one card at random, then I tell them to put the cards away for a moment.

On the board I write four digits, for example, 1245, and I tell students that these numbers are the last four digits of my phone number (or my social security number or my dog's birthday).

Next I demonstrate a simple recursive procedure, which I call Square the Digits and Sum the Squares:

1. Take each individual digit and square it (raise it to the second power), then add the four numbers together. For example:
   $1^2 + 2^2 + 4^2 + 5^2 = 1 + 4 + 16 + 25 = 46$
2. Now do it again with 46: $4^2 + 6^2 + = 16 + 36 = 52$
   and again: $5^2 + 2^2 = 25 + 4 = 29$
3. How long can I keep doing this procedure?

"What happens if I start with 8600? $8^2 + 6^2 = 64 + 36 = 100$. Then what?" Some students reply that 100 just goes to one and then they're stuck forever. "Why?" I ask. Because 100 squared is 1, they say. This iterative procedure is simple but unusual. It treats 86 and 68 the same. Squaring and summing works on digits, not on place value and thus ignores the order of the numbers.

Now it is the students' turn. They pick a four-digit number of their own (such as the last four digits of their phone number or social security number) and may use calculators, but I also require they write down what they do (as in the numbered example above). As I circulate around the room I spot-check each paper. I say, "Each of you selected an index card with a number on it. I predict that if you do not have to stop at one, you will continue to square and sum the digits until you get to the number on your card."

In a class of twenty-five students, usually two or three make mistakes performing the procedure. A dead giveaway that they've made a mistake is when a student yells from the other side of the room, "I did it twenty times and I didn't get my number or one!" I ask the troubled soul to go back to the beginning and try it again or to check what they did.

If students go to one very quickly, I ask them to choose a different four-digit number and start again. The balance of the class, about fifteen or so students, have performed ten or fewer iterations and gotten the number on the card. I ask them to go the board and write down their sequences, for example:

$7265 \Rightarrow 114 \Rightarrow 18 \Rightarrow 65 \Rightarrow 61 \Rightarrow 37 \Rightarrow 58$

$6788 \Rightarrow 213 \Rightarrow 14 \Rightarrow 17 \Rightarrow 50 \Rightarrow 25 \Rightarrow 29 \Rightarrow 85 \Rightarrow 89 \Rightarrow 145$

$1123 \Rightarrow 15 \Rightarrow 26 \Rightarrow 40 \Rightarrow 16 \Rightarrow 37 \Rightarrow 58 \Rightarrow 89$

$3333 \Rightarrow 36 \Rightarrow 71 \Rightarrow 50 \Rightarrow 25 \Rightarrow 29 \Rightarrow 85 \Rightarrow 145 \Rightarrow 42$

Note that the operator $\Rightarrow$ that signifies squaring and summing digits is not an equal sign $(=)$, which would not be appropriate.

When I ask students if they see any patterns, their usual response is, "Mine stopped at the number you gave me. Would it go on forever?"

I tell them to take theirs further. "What do you see?" Several blurt out, "It starts to repeat." I ask for volunteers to put their sequences up on the board:

$7265 \Rightarrow 114 \Rightarrow 18 \Rightarrow 65 \Rightarrow 61 \Rightarrow 37 \Rightarrow 58 \Rightarrow 89 \Rightarrow 145 \Rightarrow 42 \Rightarrow 20 \Rightarrow 4 \Rightarrow 16 \Rightarrow 37$

$6788 \Rightarrow 213 \Rightarrow 14 \Rightarrow 17 \Rightarrow 50 \Rightarrow 25 \Rightarrow 29 \Rightarrow 85 \Rightarrow 89 \Rightarrow 145 \Rightarrow 42 \Rightarrow 20 \Rightarrow 4 \Rightarrow 16 \Rightarrow 37 \Rightarrow 58 \Rightarrow 89$

$1123 \Rightarrow 15 \Rightarrow 26 \Rightarrow 40 \Rightarrow 16 \Rightarrow 37 \rightarrow 58 \Rightarrow 89 \Rightarrow 145 \Rightarrow 42 \Rightarrow 20 \Rightarrow 4 \Rightarrow 16$

$3333 \Rightarrow 36 \Rightarrow 71 \Rightarrow 50 \Rightarrow 25 \Rightarrow 29 \Rightarrow 85 \Rightarrow 145 \Rightarrow 42 \Rightarrow 20 \Rightarrow 4 \Rightarrow 16 \Rightarrow 37 \Rightarrow 58 \Rightarrow 89$

Some of the students have difficulty grasping the pattern. I explain that there are eight numbers that repeat, so we call it an eight-cycle. Some students have figured out that these were the numbers I put on their pink cards:

$$145 \Rightarrow 42 \Rightarrow 20 \Rightarrow 4$$
$$\Uparrow \dots\dots\dots\dots \Downarrow$$
$$89 \Leftarrow 58 \Leftarrow 37 \Leftarrow 16$$

Students often argue about which numbers are part of the cycle. For example, some are certain the 85 is part of the cycle. They say that 85 always makes 89. I just tell them that if they go through the cycle twice, they won't see 85 again; it allows them to enter the cycle at 89, but 85 is not part of the eight-cycle. Along the way they find a few numbers that get stuck at 1:

$$7 \Rightarrow 49 \Rightarrow 97 \Rightarrow 130 \Rightarrow 10 \Rightarrow 1$$
$$13 \Rightarrow 10 \Rightarrow 1$$
$$19 \Rightarrow 82 \Rightarrow 68 \Rightarrow 100 \Rightarrow 1$$
$$23 \Rightarrow 13 \Rightarrow 10 \Rightarrow 1$$
$$28 \Rightarrow 68 \Rightarrow 100 \Rightarrow 1$$

I ask students to describe the patterns they see in the example above. Their responses are all very similar: "When you square and sum the digits of a number repeatedly, you will eventually stop at one or go into the eight-cycle."

My response is that this pattern is true for the examples we looked at, but is it always true? That gets them thinking. "What if we find a number that does not fit that pattern?" I continue. "Examples are great for helping us develop hypotheses, but all it takes is one counterexample to negate our hypothesis. How would a mathematician prove that this pattern holds for every whole number?"

"There must be some formula," they say.

I tell them, "No. There is no formula. You have to check every number; mathematicians call it *proof by exhaustion*. But you really don't have to check them all." And I give these examples:

- What is the largest four-digit number? 9999. It will go immediately to 4 * 81 or 324, a three-digit number.
- How about 99999? It would go to 5 * 81 or 405 on its first iteration.
- Even 9,999,999,999 goes to 10 * 81 or 810 on the first shot.

The procedure of summing the squared digits will go to a three-digit number immediately unless you start with:

- 9,999,999,999,999 or 13 * 81 = 1053, which becomes a three-digit number on the next iteration.

So you only have to test three-digit numbers, and mathematicians have cut it down even smaller than that. I ask then to go to 243 (3 * 81) or (3 * 9²).

I assign each student about twenty numbers to check (for example, 1 to 20, 21 to 40, and so on). If they are sharp, they'll realize they actually don't have to check 71 if they have already checked 17. (See www.braidedmath.com for Summing Squared Digits and a table of this work.)

Square the Digits and Sum the Squares has been around for decades; however, most math educators are more interested in the sequences that end at 1, or "happy numbers." Personally, I am fascinated by the cycles, and I am struck by the fact that we cannot predict whether it will stop at one or go into the eight-cycle. *What* will happen is already strictly determined—it is going to happen in a preordained fashion. And yet we cannot predict *which* will happen—unless, of course, we have done it before or consult a chart. But in one of many wonderful twists and turns in mathematics, when you raise the digits to the third power and sum them repeatedly, you *can predict,* to a great extent, what will happen.

Extension

Ask students if all eight numbers are points of entry into the cycles. If so, are they equally likely? The front cover of this book gives an answer. All eight have entry points to the eight cycle, but they are not equally likely. For a full treatment, see our website, www.braidedmath.com.

Summing the Cubes

After working with Square the Digits and Sum the Squares, very often one or two students ask, "What happens if you cube them?" I ask them to predict: Students frequently say that if they get one thousand or one hundred or ten, they only cube the one and that will stay at one.

Once again, students need to investigate to see the patterns. It is possible for students to cube each digit and sum them on a scientific calculator, but the error rate really goes up. Therefore, a number of years ago I started the Summing the Cubes activity in the classroom.

After the initial explanation of the activity, we discussed together how we could incorporate an Excel spreadsheet into the activity. The students came up with a list of criteria; in general, students said that the spreadsheet should:

1. take the number and break it up into its individual digits;
2. take each digit and cube it (raise it to the third power); and
3. add up all the cubed digits.

These are pretty much the actions I had already built into the spreadsheet for this activity. (I did not use the spreadsheet to break up the number into its individual digits, however, because I did not want to explain functions such as *mod* and *div*, which I believed would sidetrack students.) See Figure 3.9.

I had students pair up at the computer lab and they jumped right in with both feet, trying random starting numbers. After a few minutes, I could hear a variety of comments:

- I found one that stops at a three-digit number.
- I haven't found any cycles. It just keeps stopping at different numbers.
- I don't see any pattern. You said there was a pattern.

To which I simply replied, "You need more data."

I circulated around the room, waiting for them to find a two-cycle, which classes like to call a "bouncer" because it bounces back and forth between two numbers, or a three-cycle, which some call a "tricycle." I saw that they had found several "stoppers," which they think of as the *1* they hit when they're stuck.

A	B	C	D	E	A^3	$...B^3$	$...C^3$	$...D^3$	$...E^3$	SUM
1	2	3	4	5	1	8	27	64	125	225
		2	2	5	0	0	8	8	125	141
		1	4	1	0	0	1	64	1	66
			6	6	0	0	0	216	216	432
		4	3	2	0	0	64	27	8	99
			9	9	0	0	0	729	729	1458
	1	4	5	8	0	1	64	125	512	702
		7	0	2	0	0	343	0	8	351
		3	5	1	0	0	27	125	1	153
		1	5	3	0	0	1	125	27	153

FIGURE 3.9

After about ten minutes, I asked them to stop so we could debrief. I wanted to broaden and deepen their appreciation of these numbers, so I asked, "Did you find a number that returned to its original number when you raised each digit to the third power and summed them?"

Most students looked puzzled and several asked me to repeat what I'd said. I did, and they chimed in with, "Oh! You mean the 'stoppers.' Yes, 153 came up a lot. We also found 370 and 371." (Rarely does anyone find the other stopper, 407. Occasionally one or two students will say, "135," and I simply ask, "What does that go to?" Then they see that 153 is the stopper.

Mathematicians call stoppers *pluperfect digital invariants* (PPDIs). There are not many of them—they must be the same number of digits as the exponent. There are no PPDIs for two-digit numbers raised to the second power; however, three-digit PPDIs are 153, 370, 371, and 407.

Cycles are not PPDIs, but cubing and summing do yield a few. For two-cycles, students may stumble upon 136 ↔ 244 and may need some suggestions to find 919 ↔ 1459 (for example, "Try some big three-digit numbers, like in the 900s.") For three-cycles, they'll find 55 ↔ 250 ↔ 133 (and 133 goes back to 55). A little less frequent is 160 ↔ 217 ↔ 352.

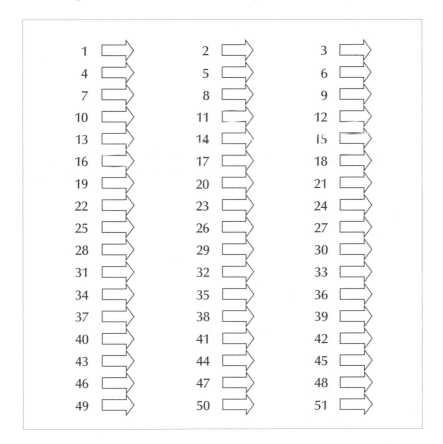

FIGURE 3.10

#		#		#	
1	1	2	371	3	153
4	55>250>133	5	371	6	153
7	370	8	371	9	153
10	1	11	371	12	153
13	55>250>133	14	371	15	153
16	160>217>352	17	371	18	153
19	370	20	371	21	153
22	160>217>352	23	371	24	153
25	55>250>133	26	371	27	153
28	55>250>133	29	371	30	153
31	55>250>133	32	371	33	153
34	370	35	371	36	153
37	370	38	371	39	153
40	55>250>133	41	371	42	153
43	370	44	371	45	153
46	55>250>133	47	407	48	153
49	919<>1459	50	371	51	153

FIGURE 3.11

At some point in the Summing the Cubes activity, a few of the students will start asking about patterns and predicting, especially if I have stated or implied that the cubing will differ from the squaring. As before with squaring, I assign a chunk of numbers in an organized fashion for students to check. However, this time they have the spreadsheet to help them and I give them a special recording sheet. See Figure 3.10. (See www.braidedmath.com for Summing Cubed Digits recording sheets.)

Students must enter only the ultimate result for the given starting number in the spreadsheet. Even single- or double-digit numbers can give students quite a run. They can easily check if they have correctly entered numbers into their spreadsheet because *I know the pattern*—and as soon as they get enough data down in the tree-column formats, *they will, too.*

Even with only fifty-one data points, all of the possible end results except one pops up. If, during the investigation, someone discovers 136 ↔ 244, I would ask what column it would go into. See Figure 3.11.

The pattern in the table above is really quite amazing—any number that is a multiple of three when its digits are cubed and summed is *still* a multiple of three. Of the numbers that are possible end results, only one, 153, is a multiple of three. In number theory, we refer to them as "$3k$" numbers. If we numbered the rows in this table, then we would call the second column $3k - 1$ and that column is almost entirely filled with 371, except for the sixteenth row, where $k = 16$ and $3k - 1$ is 47, where we see the very unlikely 407. All other ending numbers—stoppers 1, 370 (both two-cycle bouncers, and both three-cycles)—appear only in the first column ($3k - 2$). Beautiful!

The Irrational Tangram

The seven-piece tangram is thought to be an ancient Chinese puzzle and a voluminous mythology has been created around it in story books, particularly propagated by the great American puzzlist, Sam Lloyd. The first published reference in Chinese about the seven-piece puzzle was in 1803 (AD, not BC). The term *tangram* originated in the 1850s and in 1903 Lloyd published a preposterous legend about the origin of the tangram, which many people took as fact (Gardner 1988, p. 29). Actually, the tangram was created in the 1890s by the great America puzzlist Sam Lloyd. See Figure 3.12.

The tangram is a versatile tool that teachers can use with students to explore the concept of similarity because so many geometric shapes can be made from the seven pieces, including:

- sixteen right isosceles triangles; each right isosceles triangle can be called *half squares*.
- thirteen convex polygons; each polygon can be made in multiple ways, by all of the tangrams, except the square

And another important thing to know:

- The two small tangram triangles have one 90-degree angle and two short legs—the length—which we call one *unit*. The *unit square* is the standard for area. If all seven tangram pieces are used to create a polygon, for example, its area must be eight square units.

(See www.braidedmath.com for Tangram masters and solutions.)

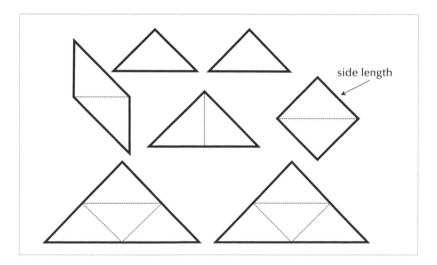

side length

FIGURE 3.12

In this activity, I explore with students an introduction to irrational numbers using tangram pieces. After the students become thoroughly familiar with the tangram through a variety of activities, such as making thirteen convex polygons, creating the square, and investigating each tangram's fractional part to the whole, I have pairs of students pool their tangram pieces. Each pair of students takes a unit square, arranges all four of the small triangles and fit them together—which I have learned is wicked hard for some students—then makes a third square from two big triangles. See Figure 3.13.

Their task is to compare the three squares and try to estimate the side length of the middle square. A little verbal scaffolding sometimes is necessary:

You can tell that the small square is 1 by 1, so its area is 1 square unit. The biggest square has 2 units on a side, so its area is 4 square units because it is 2 by 2. But the middle square is made from 4 half-squares, so it must have an area of 2 square units. What is its side length?

$$1 * 1 = 1 \text{ and } 2 * 2 = 4. \text{ But } \_\_\_\_ * \_\_\_\_ = 2?$$

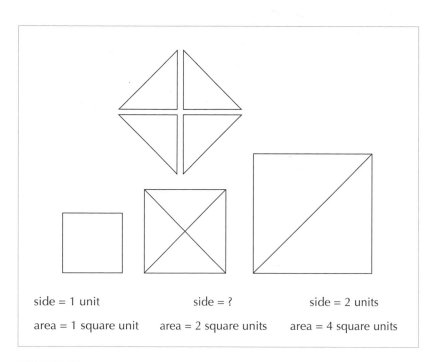

side = 1 unit   side = ?   side = 2 units

area = 1 square unit   area = 2 square units   area = 4 square units

FIGURE 3.13

By matching the sides to each other, students can see that the unknown side is between 1 and 2, perhaps 1 and half. So I suggest that they get out calculators and try 1.5 * 1.5 and I make a table on the board with a large gap between 1 and 2. We start to fill it in.

side length	area	side length	area	side length	Area
1	1	1	1	1	1
				1.4	1.96
		1.5	2.25	1.5	2.25
2	4	2	4	2	4

Students found 1.5 to be too large (2.25) and 1.4 to be too small (1.96). What number "squared" will make 2? They realize that it must be between 1.4 and 1.5. Some want to try 1.45, but others say that it must be closer to 1.4 because 1.96 was so close. Some try 1.41 and others try 1.42.

side length	Area	side length	area	side length	area
1	1	1	1	1	1
1.4	1.96	1.4	1.96	1.4	1.96
1.41	1.9881	1.41	1.9881	1.41	1.9881
				1.415	2.002225
		1.42	2.0164	1.42	2.0164
1.5	2.25	1.5	2.25	1.5	2.25

This is an excellent form of interpolation that teachers can build upon to clarify place value in the decimals. I let students go for as long as they want within reason, getting ever closer but never reaching exactly 2, until the calculator rounds the number to 2. We take a quick digression to examine some repeating decimals that begin as fractions, such as $\frac{1}{3}$, $\frac{2}{3}$, and $\frac{1}{6}$. And then we do some fractions that repeat cyclically, such as $\frac{1}{7}$, which is .142857 repeated.

By now students are ready to hear that there are some special numbers that will never repeat as *decimals*, basically ratios that go on to infinity with no repeating pattern. And what we have been looking for is one of them: 1.414213562373 . . . it doesn't repeat and it doesn't cycle. In fact, these twelve decimal places will only round to 2 when squared—raised to the second power. Instead of remembering this twelve-decimal place number and saying it is "2 when squared," we have a better, faster way to deal with this: The side length, that when squared is 2, we call the *square root of* 2 and write it $\sqrt{2}$. It can never be expressed as a repeating decimal because it is not the ratio of two numbers, like $\frac{1}{6}$ or $\frac{3}{8}$. Therefore it is called *irrational*. There is nothing wrong with irrational numbers, you just have to be careful when working with them.

I suggest that students try the square root key on their calculator to see how many decimal places they get. After some discussion, we write on the board: $\sqrt{2} * \sqrt{2} = 2$, and to wrap up the Irrational Tangram activity, there are several directions we can go. We can:

- stay with the tangram and examine each piece as either a multiple of the unit length or a multiple of $\sqrt{2}$;
- investigate other irrational numbers and use a spreadsheet to organize our data; or
- facilitate a discussion that introduces geoboards or dot paper that uses squares, some of which have rational side lengths and some of which have irrational side lengths.

4 | PROPORTIONAL REASONING

Ever since the time I was asked to teach a lesson on proportional reasoning, I have been amazed at the number of connections it has to related concepts. Recently I found a great resource, *Teaching Fractions and Ratios for Understanding* by Susan J. Lamon (2005). Lamon defines proportional reasoning as the "ability to scale up and down in appropriate situations and to supply justifications for assertions made about relationships in situations involving simple direct proportions and inverse proportions" (p. 3). True understanding of proportions and the ability to reason with them requires far more than merely working with procedures based on $a/b = c/d$.

WHAT PROPORTIONAL REASONING LOOKS AND SOUNDS LIKE IN THE CLASSROOM

We can create rich contexts for students to analyze situations where a *natural* relationship exists between two quantities, where as one changes, so too does the other in a specific, constant manner. Unfortunately, many textbook problems are *contrived* relationships, for example, comparing eyeballs to gummy worms. In this section, we present several natural relationship proportional reasoning problems: Shampoo Bottle, Cats and Rats, and Making Seismometers.

Shampoo Bottle

Consider the following simple direct proportion problem:

> If one large bottle of shampoo contains 40 fluid ounces and the salon recommends that you use 1¼ fluid ounces per application, how many shampoo washes can you do with one large bottle?
>
> Think:
>
> | | |
> |---|---|
> | 1¼ fluid ounces | 1 wash |
> | 2½ fluid ounces | 2 washes |
> | 5 fluid ounces | 4 washes |
> | 40 fluid ounces | 32 washes |

After analyzing this problem, we can agree that the ratio of fluid ounces to washes is 1¼:1. We first begin by doubling the amount of shampoo being used, which causes the number of washes to double as well. Using a pattern to determine the number of washes in forty fluid ounces of shampoo enabled us to arrive at the answer, thirty-two washes, fairly quickly, but it is *not* clear exactly *how* we can use proportional reasoning to arrive at the same answer.

Instead of working through several cases as in the problem above, especially in situations where the answer does *not* come as quickly, we could instead analyze the ratio of one quantity to another in its simplest form—called the *constant of proportionality*, or the *unit rate*—and use it to calculate the desired amount.

For instance, in the Shampoo Bottle problem, the ratio of fluid ounces to washes is 1¼:1, 5:4—which means that each time the number of fluid ounces is precisely 1.25 times the number of washes available. In order to use the constant of proportionality or the unit rate, students will need to remember the related mathematical sentences that can be formed using simple multiplication and division. For this problem, if the number of fluid ounces is 1.25 times the number of washes, then the following related division statement is also true:

> The number of fluid ounces divided by 1.25 is equal to the number of washes.

This means that the Shampoo Bottle problem boils down to taking $^{40}/_{1.25}$ washes per bottle, which is equal to 32.

This direct solution is not what middle school students would immediately "see," which would require strong understanding of division, particularly repeated subtraction, to reason, "How many times can I pour out 1.25 ounces from 40?" Keeping that in mind, using a table makes working on the problem more accessible to students. Notice how the table emphasizes *both* horizontal and vertical patterns:

times 2	1¼ to 1	times 2
times 2	2½ to 2	times 2
times 8	5 to 4	times 8
	40 to 32	

Cats and Rats

Another way to foster proportional reasoning skills is to present problems where it is not *as* easy for students to see how they could skip the proportional reasoning process and jump to using $a/b = c/d$. I based the Cats and Rats problem on Lewis Carroll's *Alice in Wonderland* (1936).

Carroll's real name was Charles Dodgson and he was a professor of mathematics at Oxford. In his book *The Mock Turtle's Story*, Carroll named the different branches of arithmetic—ambition, distraction, uglification, and derision.

If 6 cats can catch and kill 6 rats in 6 minutes, how many cats will it take to catch and kill 100 rats in 50 minutes? Try solving this problem in more than one way.

The most common interpretation by middle school students—and their teachers—to this problem is, "Okay, then one cat can kill one rat in one minute." This is not accurate. We need to help students imagine this situation and *represent* the key elements in this complex relationship by encouraging them to use objects, draw pictures, or act it out. See Figure 4.1.

Let's think about the problem. It states, "6 cats can catch and kill 6 rats in 6 minutes." If each cat goes after the rat nearest to him, how long does it take the cat to catch and kill that rat? One minute? No—6 minutes. Once students understand that basic relationship, they need to realize or reason proportionately. If they multiply the number of rats, to keep the "balance"—the correct proportional relationship—then they must either increase the number of cats by the same factor or increase the number of minutes by the same factor—that is, *multiply*, not add.

I ask students to consider: "If you have more rats, you'll need more cats to exterminate them at the same rate as before: Each killer feline gets 1 rat in 6 minutes. Similarly, if you increase the cats by a factor, you must either increase the rats or decrease the time. *Why?* If you have more cats, they can do the job faster or they can get more rats." The chart on the next page illustrates these proportionalities while working toward a solution.

FIGURE 4.1

Cats	Rats	Minutes
6	6	6
1	1	6
100	100	6
4	100	150
12	100	50

Notice for the third row, if we multiply minutes by 25, then we would have to divide the number of cats by 25. Alternatively, for the fifth row, if we divide minutes by 3, then we would have to multiply the number of cats by 3.

From the table we can generalize the following:

Actor	Task	Time
Number of people	Number of objects	Number of hours (or days)

Which implies the following:

actor $*$ time = person hours
(to do or to make a certain number of objects)

person hours per object $\quad \dfrac{\text{PERSON HOURS}}{\text{OBJECT}}$

Actor	Task	Time
Number of people	Number of objects	Number of hours (or days)
x	y	z
a	b	c

$$\frac{x * z}{y} = \frac{a * c}{b}$$

Actor	Task	Time
Number of people	Number of objects	Number of hours (or days)
6	6	6
?	100	50

$$\frac{6 * 6}{6} = \frac{50 * z}{100} \qquad z = \frac{3600}{300} = 12 \text{ cats}$$

Ultimately, when our understanding of proportionality is used to reason both mathematically and logically, we must recall what it means for one to reason. Typically, we "do not associate reasoning with rule-driven or mechanized procedures, but rather, with mental, free-flowing processes that require conscious analysis of the relationships among quantities" (Lamon 2005), The very idea of moving beyond pattern analysis to proportional analysis by using reasoning in a variety of representations, such as tables, graphs, pictures, and so on, is necessary to build a solid foundation of proportional reasoning. In that vein, here is another problem for your students to try:

If 3 people can make 5 electrical seismometers in 8 hours, how many people are needed to make 100 seismometers in 24 hours?

TABLE			PROPORTION
people	product	time	
3	5	8	$3 * 8/5 = x * 24/100$
3	15	24	$100 * 24/5 = 24x$
1	5	24	$100/5 = x$
20	100	24	$20 = x$

DEVELOPING STUDENTS' PROPORTIONAL REASONING SKILLS

Understanding Differences Between Additive and Multiplicative Transformations

All of the story problems in the previous section, and others of similar mathematical structure, require some form of multiplication of quantities. However, students deserve the chance to understand specifically *why* multiplication, as opposed to addition, is the appropriate operation. It certainly takes, as Lamon states, some "degree of mathematical maturity to understand the difference between adding and multiplying and contexts in which each operation is appropriate" (2005). In fact, one of the most difficult concepts for students to understand is the multiplicative, not additive, nature of proportionality. As a result, before using the Shampoo Bottle, Cats and Rats, and Making Seismographs problems, it's necessary for teachers to get an idea of their students' understanding of the difference between additive and multiplicative transformations.

I knew that helping students to understand transformations in objects would be far more complex than just teaching a simple lesson on interpreting change. In fact, after I did more research to guide my future lesson planning, I discovered that there are a number of core ideas that need to be strongly considered when teaching students to build proportional reasoning ability, such as contexts, representations, operations, and ways of thinking.

As a result, before I implemented my proportional reasoning activity, I spent time analyzing my students' understanding of enlarging objects. I gave them a mini-problem in which they had to analyze the relationship between two objects that had undergone a transformation. See Figure 4.2.

Obviously, the officer on the right is larger than the officer on the left, but in what way? I asked students to consider the following questions:

- Over time, how would you expect their sizes to change?
- Over time, which officer will experience the most overall growth?

Students who have difficulty determining the difference between an additive or multiplicative transformation might initially think that the officer on the right just grew taller. Lamon states, "These children simply do not know that shrinking or enlarging affects more than just the heights" (2005, 7). Understanding the difference and the value of each different type of transformation is key to building proportional reasoning skills.

Understanding Ratios

Once my students had a solid understanding of the differences between additive and multiplicative transformations, I moved back a step further and asked, "*How* do students initially conceive of ratios?" Lamon's research suggests that:

When children prefer the ratio interpretation and classroom instruction builds on their intuitive knowledge of comparisons, they develop a richer understanding of rational numbers and employ pro-

FIGURE 4.2

portional reasoning sooner than children whose curriculum used the part-whole comparison as the primary interpretation of rational numbers. (2005, 9)

So I posed a prompt in class:

> Draw a picture of what 2 to 3 looks like to you.

Among the variety of students' drawings, two distinctly different images were often repeated. See Figure 4.3.

Students who created images such as that on the left show that they have a very narrow understanding of ratios, an understanding strictly limited to part-to-whole relationships (two parts out of three, to be exact). Those who created images such as that on the right, where 2:3 is clearly illustrated, were better able to answer questions about what enlarged images of this same ratio would look like. They were beginning to use pictures to develop their proportional reasoning skills. As a result, I gradually implemented the following activity to help students begin to understand, using ratio concepts, what being in a proportional relationship means.

The Party Problem

At the school social, there were 4 boys for every 3 girls. If there were 133 people at the social, how many of them were girls? How many were boys?

After beginning with a KWC, the students got to work quickly. I watched for a few minutes while they worked. Most students wrote something like ⅔ = 133. A few added an *x* to one of the sides (as one students said, "when in doubt, stick in an *x*"). Those who did "stick in an *x*" solved the equation and got something like *x* = 399.4, or 99.8. When I asked if there were 99.8 boys or girls, they were rather stumped. Clearly, students did not understand the problem.

As a class, we decided to go back to our KWC and talk about the problem as a large group. What did we *know* for sure? We knew the number of total people at the social was 133. One boy said that the girls were

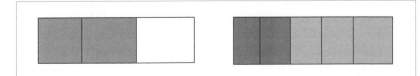

FIGURE 4.3

luckier; although we laughed at his response, it did cause the students to reveal that the ratio of 4:3 told them that there had to be more boys than girls. What were we trying to find out—what did we *want to know*? Students quickly told me that they had to find out how many of the 133 people were girls and how many were boys. Students felt that there were no special constraints or concerns.

I asked them to get into groups of three and determine a strategy for working on the problem. After a few minutes of brainstorming, we shared the different strategies. Most groups said they would draw a picture. I asked what would be in the picture and they said *B* for boys and *G* for girls. Several other students said they would make a chart with the number of boys and girls on it. As I walked around, I saw several papers with *B*s and *G*s all over, but with no discernable pattern. The chart makers had a lot of guesses, but no definitive pattern.

I suggested that we take a moment to fully understand what was happening by modeling the problem as a class. Four boys and three girls leapt to their feet, eager to attend the party. I asked the class to keep in mind that there were only seven people standing and the original problem stated that there were 133 total people at the social. When the next group of four boys and three girls stood up to join the party, I asked if we met the party conditions. All of the students acknowledged that there were eight boys and six girls present, bringing the total only to fourteen.

I knew we would soon run out of students, so I suggested they go back to their small groups and work on the problem. As I walked around, I noticed the picture drawers frantically getting clusters of four *B*s and three *G*s on their papers; it was apparent to me that the students understood that their clusters needed to be composed of the correct ratio of boys to girls. When I asked how they knew when to stop, my students' answers convinced me they were keeping a running total, hoping to reach 133. Those who worked on tables added more columns to the table. They had a column for the number of girls, the number of boys and, most importantly, a total column. See Figure 4.4.

Most groups could explain that they had increased the total students by fours for the boys and increased by threes for the girls. Their observations were not only an incredible attempt at proportional reasoning, but also an amazing foreshadow to what they were to learn with linear Diophantine equations in the coming quarter!

Within several minutes, students were able to ascertain that fifty-seven girls and seventy-six boys were at the party. I asked one group of picture makers to explain their process, then I asked the chart makers to explain their process of incrementing by four and three. Students seemed comfortable with the processes. I asked for any advantages or disadvantages of each process if the whole school attended and not just 133 students (assuming still that the ratio of boys to girls was 4:3). The picture makers said that they would not want to do all of that drawing; the chart makers said that they would want to use some patterns, namely increasing *B*s by four and *G*s by three, to shorten the process.

At the school dance there were 4 boys for every 3 girls. If there were 133 people at the party, how many were girls and how many were boys?

Boys	Girls	Total
4	3	7
8	6	14
12	9	21
16	12	28
20	15	35
24	18	42
28	21	49
32	24	56
36	27	63
40	30	70
44	33	77
48	36	84
52	39	91
56	42	98
60	45	105
64	48	112
68	51	119
72	53	126
76	56	133

76 boys and 56 girls

FIGURE 4.4

Next, I asked the original group of party goers to stand up again. Then I asked for the second set. I asked what each group had in common besides being in a four-to-three ratio. Students easily saw that there were seven people in each cluster. "So," I said, "we will always have to deal with seven total people at a time. Where does this seven come from?"

Immediately students responded that 7 people = 4 boys + 3 girls. I replied, "How can we use the fact that we are always dealing with clusters of seven people at a time to shorten the process?"

At this point, a student innocently asked if seven always had to "go into" the total number. I rephrased this a bit and asked students if seven was a factor of 133. They agreed that 7 * 19 = 133. This meant that there were nineteen clusters of seven-person groups.

"What do nineteen groups look like?" I asked. They responded that each of the nineteen groups had four boys and three girls. This meant that there were nineteen groups of three-girl clusters and nineteen groups of four-boy clusters, or fifty-seven girls and seventy-six boys—exactly what the students had originally discovered with their tables and pictures.

I let this digest a bit and then called on one student who was ready to burst. "You mean we could have added those ratio numbers to get the number in a group, then divide to get the number of groups? And then we multiply that number by the ratio numbers?" See Figure 4.5.

Was this student's final comment even more evidence that my students were using proportional reasoning skills to figure out the number of girls and boys at the social? Yes, most definitely. My students finally understood, after a variety of representations in their problem-solving process, how to use their proportional reasoning to figure out that the total number at the party comprised partitions of its component parts, all in the required ratio. Certainly a jump into $a/b = c/d$ would not have done any justice!

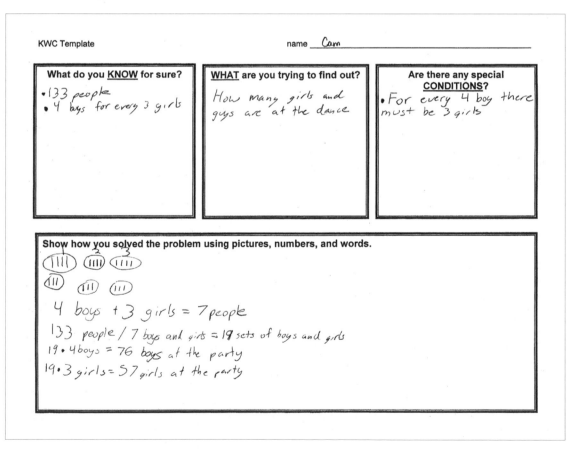

FIGURE 4.5

To get students to move even deeper into proportional reasoning, it is natural to transition from ratios that compare measures of the *same* type to ratios that compare measures of *different* types, commonly known as *rates*. The following problem is one that I use to introduce students to *rate of change (slope)*, *unit rate*, and *cost analysis*.

Two Brands of Clementines

Sunnyside Clementines (SC) cost $3 for 2 pounds, where as Juicy Gem Clementines (JG) cost $4 for 3 pounds. What does each brand cost for 4, 6, and 12 pounds? What are the changes you observe for each brand? What does each brand cost per pound? Using your table and a graph, decide which is the better buy, assuming the quality of the two is equally good.

Pounds	Cost *rounded to nearest cent*	Cost/pound *in simplest form*	Pounds	Cost *rounded to nearest cent*	Cost/pound *in simplest form*
2	$3	$3/2	3	$4	$4/3
4	$6	$3/2	4	$5.33	$4/3
6	$9	$3/2	6	$8	$4/3
12	$18	$3/2	12	$16	$4/3
1	$1.50	$3/2	1	$1.33	$4/3
1	$1.50	$3/2	1	$1.33	$4/3

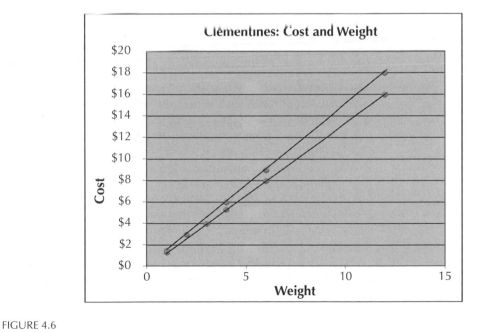

FIGURE 4.6

First, notice in the table that, in both cases, $a/b = c/d$ can be replaced with mental math to calculate the cost for four, six, twelve, and one pounds of clementines. Looking closely at the cost per pound column for each brand, we can easily see that while both the number of pounds and cost are increasing, they are indeed increasing at a constant fixed rate of change. That is, SC will always change such that the cost and the number of pounds are in a ratio of 3:2 and JG will always change such that the cost and pounds are in a ratio of 4:3.

Second, notice in the graph that the top line, which represents SC, is always steeper—or has y-values that are always greater—than the JG line. The positioning of the SC line in comparison to the JG line implies that the cost of SC will always be greater than the cost of JG, which means JG is always going to be a better buy. We can validate this conclusion by using both the tabular and graphical representations of the data. Solving this problem just using $a/b = c/d$ would rob students out of the chance to see the rate's *extendibility* and the connection between *rate of change (slope)* and *unit rate* in the graph and the table. (See www.braidedmath.com for further extensions and applications of the Two Brands of Clementines problem involving percents and price value.)

Rate of change is often developed through contexts in which certain quantities change with respect to a specific time frame. I always enjoy story problems related to rate of change—The Rendezvous of the Two Spies is a very cool problem that had my students thoroughly engaged and understanding math without having to learn a set of procedures and that made a huge impact on their proportional reasoning skills. (Note that although the original problem provided the average speed, I did not provide this information to the students.)

The Rendezvous of the Two Spies

One December day, two spies decide that they must meet to exchange documents. One is in New York City and the other is in Indianapolis, 700 miles away by train. The spies want to be together for only a brief moment. They consult train schedules and find that there is a stop that will meet their needs. The Midwest Flyer leaves Indy at midnight and arrives in NYC at 2 P.M., 14 hours later. The Silver Streak leaves NYC at 2 A.M. and arrives at Indy at noon, 10 hours later. How far from each city do the spies plan to rendezvous and at what time?

I provided each student with a copy of the problem to read on his or her own, and then as a class we read the problem aloud. I led the KWC discussion:

What do we know about the problem?

The students responded with appropriate facts about each train.

What are we supposed to find out?

We need to find out when the spies meet.

We also need to find out where they meet.

We will need to know how fast they are going.

Are there any constraints?

The spies have to stay on the train they started on. No transfers.

I returned to the suggestion that we need to know how fast the trains are going. My students were familiar with the $d = rt$ formula, but they had not yet made the connection between the formula and speed being a ratio that compares distance to time. How could they innately understand that speed is the ratio of distance to time?

Prior to this activity, I spent a great deal of time discussing the two quantities of which speed is composed of—distance and time. In my classroom, I conduct *brain-a-canes*, which are far more powerful than a brainstorm. Students in my classes know that during a brain-a-cane, desks are pushed back, they sit in a circle by the front of the room, and their minds are wide open. There are no foolish replies during a brain-a-cane; there are only the foolhardy who refuse to participate . . . though I always find a way to break the seal!

For the Rendezvous of the Two Spies brain-a-cane, I wrote two words on opposite sides of the board, *distance* and *time*. Within ten minutes we had generated two separate lists of distance measures and time measures. This brain-a-cane not only gave me an idea of their understanding of how to measure distances and time, but it also revealed a lot about their hobbies and after-school lives. For distance, several students offered *parsec, fathom, furlong, pixel, cubit*. For time, they suggested several strange ones like *cock-crow watch, tropic year, fortnight, Olympiad*. When each list seemed to be done, in the middle of the two lists I wrote, *speed is a ratio that compares distance* TO *time*.

Next, students generated several somewhat-crazy measures of speed using one word from the distance list and comparing it *to* another word from the time list. For example: *parsecs per tropic year, furlong per Olympiad*, and *cubit per cock-crow watch*. While most of the measures of speed were familiar, like *miles per hour*, the creative ones really helped the students to solidify the idea that speed is a ratio comparing distance to time. As a class, we then progressed through various symbolic representations until we reached the familiar generalized form, $\frac{d}{t} = r$, and used the relationship between multiplication and division to generate the following related statements: $\frac{d}{r} = t$ and $d = rt$.

At this stage, I felt it was appropriate to ask my students whether $d = rt$, $\frac{d}{r} = t$, or $\frac{d}{t} = r$ would be most helpful to us right away. They decided that since we knew time and distance and we needed the rate of each train, that the last form would be good to use.

Students then broke into groups of three and discussed the problem. Most of the groups began by listing important information, such as the distance and rate. Many groups drew a rough map with NYC on the east and Indy on the west, connected them, and wrote *700 miles*. Several groups started making different representations, such as setting up horizontal lines on the floor, using masking tape to mark increments of one hundred miles. I then led a group discussion by prompting my students with a variety of questions:

What do you know now? From the equation $\frac{d}{t} = r$, we found that the Indy train traveled at a rate of 50 miles per hour and the NYC train went 70 miles per hour.

What did you do next? I drew a map with NYC and Indiana; we started to write down times; we worked with distances.

Could we use people to model the situation? Of course, there were many volunteers. We selected our human train, one for NYC and one Indy, and then I had the rest of the class tell them where to stand (one on each side of the room).

How far apart are they? 700 miles.

What time shall we say it is? Midnight.

So what is happening then? The Indy train starts to move.

We will tell Indy to travel for one hour and then stop. The Indy train started, but the students decided he went too far for one hour.

Why do you think he went too far? He was only supposed to go $1/14$ of the distance (fifty miles) and he went too far across the room for only one hour. The students helped position the train correctly; I reassured them all that the actors do not have be exact, we just have to visualize what is going on—the relationships between the two trains.

How far did he travel? How many miles were covered? He went fifty miles and there are 650 miles left.

Now it is 2 A.M. What happens? Indy traveled one hundred miles (fifty miles each hour). There are six hundred miles left. (We agreed that the person moved correctly.) Now NYC has to get ready to leave.

Now it is 3 A.M. What is going on? Indy is now at one hundred fifty miles and NYC is at seventy miles.

How far between them? 700 − (150 + 70) = 480 miles left. They covered 120 miles.

How will we know when to stop? They will be at the same place and the total miles covered will be seven hundred miles.

At this point we returned to our groups for students to complete the problem. I noticed all groups used some form of table or chart that indicated time and miles covered. As I walked around, I asked groups what they were looking to do. Students answered that the miles covered by each train would add up to seven hundred. Most continued using a model similar to the one established by the role-playing model, translating it into a chart with time and distance traveled. Each group very quickly determined that the trains met at 7 A.M. and had both traveled three hundred fifty miles, although the train from Indy traveled longer. See Figure 4.7.

Extensions

1. Both trains travel 50 mph. When and where will they meet?
2. Both trains travel 70 mph. When and where will they meet?
3. The faster train leaves 2 hours earlier than the slower train. When and where will they meet?
4. Both trains leave at the same time. When and where will they meet?

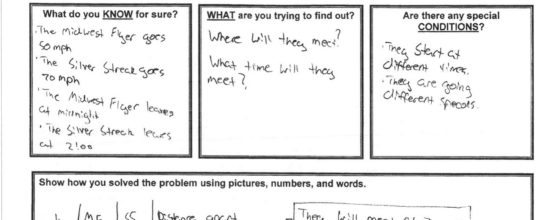

FIGURE 4.7

It was clear from my own personal observations and the students' enthusiasm that they thought acting the problem out helped them understand what to do. When they saw the picture of what was going on, it was easy for them to continue the pattern they observed on the chart. The richness of the patterns should not be lost: Most students noticed in their tables "up by 50 miles for Indy, up by 70 miles for NYC" for each hour. Some noticed that the mileage between the trains decreased at 120 miles per hour. When I asked how they knew a table was the best representation for identifying this pattern, students said it was a way for them to see the big picture, to stand above the action, have an aerial view. By recognizing the value of using a table in this problem, students essentially told me that they had made a *math-to-math connection*.

Interesting Applications of Rate

Math curricula tend to leave out or not connect several proportional reasoning concepts. More often than not, for example, students get to middle school with a very narrow and procedural conception of the mean. Technically, they may know how to calculate the arithmetic mean, but they don't necessarily understand it.

There are several good ways to use cool problems to help build conceptual understanding in elementary school. For instance, the mean is a lot like fair share division. If you had a big bowl of gum balls and you let each child take one hand and pick up as many as he or she could, different amounts of gumballs will be pulled out. But what if everyone pulled out the exact same amount? How many would that be? If you put the chosen gum balls into a pile, counted them, then divided that total by the number of people, the quotient would be the *arithmetic mean*. It's the answer to, "What if everyone had gotten the same amount?"

My students used this conception of the mean to determine the average rates of the two trains in The Rendezvous of the Two Spies problem. The average rate of 50 miles per hour is the answer to "What If?"—what if the train had gone at the same rate for every one of those 700 miles and every one of those 14 hours? With the train making stops at towns along the way, it was frequently accelerating and decelerating; perhaps between cities it ran at a constant rate for 100 miles, but it was definitely not 50, and was more like 70, because to average 50 with all the stops it would have to spent some time running considerably faster than 50, more like 70, to average out at 50.

However, the arithmetic mean is not the only measure of central tendency; it is not even the *only* mean. There are other means. What follows are two different rate problems that Susan did with her students. The problems not only require students to tap into their proportional reasoning skills, but they also allow a different mean to appear.

The Two Painters: Laverne and Shirley

I began my opening activity for the day with a sixty-second video clip of Laverne and Shirley attempting to paint a house. Older audiences might assume that in the video clip, the paint ended up pretty much everywhere except where it needed to be—the walls. While my students were watching, they were also responding to the question I distributed on slips of paper as I welcomed them at the door: "What's going on in this video clip?"

When the video ended, I gave students an additional two minutes to respond to the question. As I walked around the room, I noticed that only one or two of the students had actually recognized the actresses as Laverne and Shirley—interesting given their age group, but it still did not give them any advantage.

When time was up, I initiated a large-group discussion by asking, "So what's going on here?" Hands shot up immediately; I called on a girl who said, "These two ladies are trying to get a job done, but they're being too silly about it."

"A job?" I said. "What kind of job do you guess they are trying to accomplish?"

Several boys harmonized a response, "They're paintin'."

"Painting what?"

"Well, Mrs. F.," said a usually shy boy in a "duh" tone, "Can't you tell that they are trying to paint the inside of that house, but they can't get along because it looks like each one does it at different speeds?"

Aha!

Another girl added, "It looked like my sister and I trying to clean the bathroom—we don't really want to do it, but we usually end up making such a mess trying to beat the other one to finish."

And so a realistic context, even a silly context, was built around one of the biggest ideas in the middle school mathematics curriculum—rate! I distributed one copy of the following problem to each of my six groups and gave them instructions to begin a KWC. (Note: Including the hint depends on how much scaffolding teachers predict their students need.)

Laverne and Shirley are partners who paint houses (exteriors and interiors). They have estimated how long it will take to paint the kitchen and dining room of Mr. Ragusa's house. Laverne estimated that she could do it in 10 hours by herself; Shirley estimated that she could do it in 15 hours by herself.

How long would it take them to do the job if they worked together?

Hint: How much of the job (what part of the whole job) could be done if they worked 1 hour together? If they worked 5 hours together?

After about five minutes, I pulled the groups together to generate a large KWC on chart paper using ideas from each of my six groups. See Figure 4.8.

Based on their previous practice with multiple representations, several students jumped right into creating a table, because "It helps us to see what's going on hour by hour." One team in particular proudly announced that they were completely finished with the problem. I asked the class to halt all current work and asked the team, "How did you do it?" They described summing the two rates, ten and fifteen, and dividing the result by two—which gave them a value of 12.5 hours. Most of the students were quiet—probably because of the very different results they were beginning to see in their own tables.

I took time to praise the team for their efforts and willingness to share, and reminded the class that they only really "lose" when they give up. Then I asked the class to examine more closely the team's strategy for solving the problem—averaging the two rates, or the *arithmetic mean calculation* strategy. As a group, we determined that this particular strategy could not be correct, because according to the problem Laverne could do the whole job by herself in ten hours, so with Shirley helping, the answer had to be fewer than ten hours.

Once we'd determined the arithmetic mean calculation strategy to be an inaccurate method, I proceeded to dramatize utter confusion (as I often do to let students have opportunities to teach *me* what *they* know—and not always the other way around). I then told students to look again at the hint and asked how they were using tables to find their answers. Several groups chimed in to help me establish the column headings for my own table and as a whole group we completed the first row of the table. See Figure 4.9.

The key question that starts the first row is: "What part of the job did each person do in the first hour?" Laverne could do the whole job in ten hours, so she could do one-tenth of the job in one hour. Shirley needed

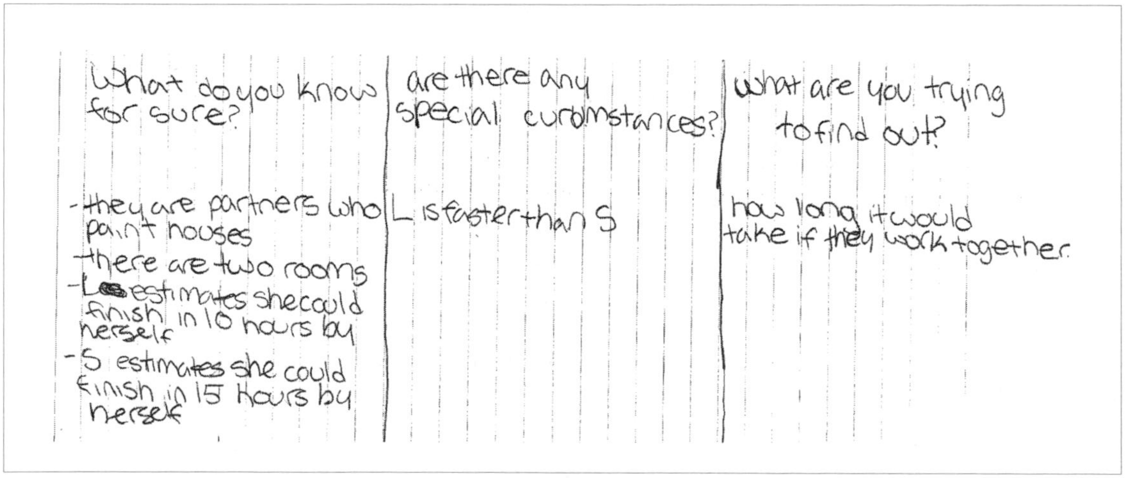

FIGURE 4.8

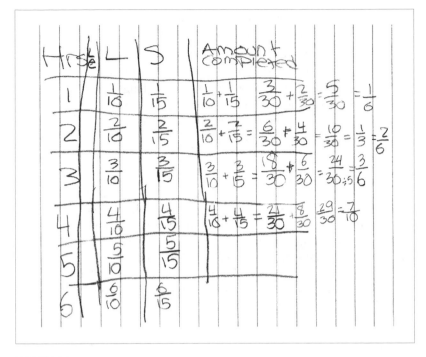

FIGURE 4.9

fifteen hours, so would do one-fifteenth of the job in one hour. The table shows the amount completed by the pair in that first hour would be $^1/_{10}$ + $^1/_{15}$ = $^1/_6$.

It was clear for several students, just after the first entry in the table, exactly how long it would take Laverne and Shirley collectively to complete the job. If they can do one-sixth of the job in one hour, they'd need six hours to do the job. But because I knew just how dangerous drawing conclusions could be by looking at just one case, I encouraged them to complete the table to prove to me that the pattern they'd begun to recognize was indeed true for the entire table. I also prompted students with the following questions:

- Suppose you figured out the pattern after two hours of work. What would your train of thought have been?
- Suppose you figured out the pattern after three hours of work. What would your train of thought have been?

The groups enthusiastically worked with their new level of understanding the rate problem. After a few minutes, I noticed that there was just enough time left in the class period for debriefing. We again discussed the value of using a table to uncover the data.

Extensions   For homework, I instructed my students to complete the following two extensions to The Two Painters: Laverne and Shirley problem:

1. Laverne and Shirley are thinking about adding a new partner, Lenny, who is a very fast painter. He estimates that he could paint Mr. Ragusa's rooms by himself in 6 hours. How long would it take the 3 of them to do the job if they worked together? See Figure 4.10.
2. Suppose Laverne and Shirley have been working for x hours. Using a table, write and simplify a variable expression that represents the part of the job completed in x hours. Explain your reasoning. See Figure 4.11.

We reviewed the tables like the one in Figure 4.10 on the next day. Because students understood the basic relationships in the tables we'd previously created, they could see why in x hours the painters could do $x/10 + x/15$ parts of the job. If we want to determine the time for the entire job, then they could work with $x/10 + x/15 = 1$ and $x = 6$.

Some of the students asked if there was a quick calculation that would allow them to solve this problem faster, so I helped them work through the most abstract formula:

If one painter takes a hours and the other takes b hours, then:

$$\frac{x}{a} + \frac{x}{b} = 1 \qquad \frac{bx + ax}{ab} = 1 \qquad x(a + b) = ab \qquad x = \frac{ab}{a + b}.$$

The expression $x = \frac{ab}{a + b}$ is quite amazing: the product of two numbers divided by their sum. The harmonic mean is $\frac{2ab}{a + b}$. Therefore, $\frac{ab}{a + b}$ is one-half of the harmonic mean.

I told the class we'd revisit these special relationships in subsequent problems.

The College Visit

I typically give students The College Visit problem after the two painters problem. In the past, I have seen that once students begin to recognize similarities in mathematical structure, it is important to create a new context for which they can develop the same concepts.

Will and Grace recently visited their old college buddy, Faith. Driving to the college (120 miles away), they averaged 60 miles per hour (mph). Coming home, there was more traffic and they only averaged 40 mph. What was the average rate in miles per hour of the round trip?

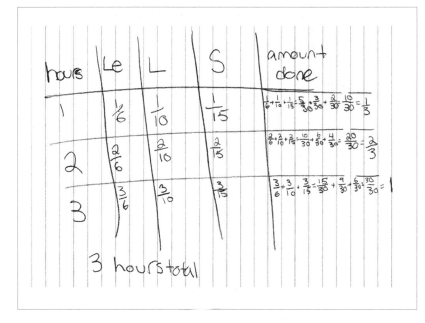

FIGURE 4.10

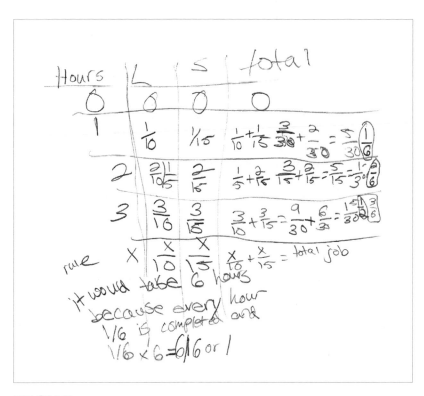

FIGURE 4.11

Initially, after students work through a KWC for this problem, I notice most are reluctant to use the arithmetic mean due to their previous experience with the problem of the two painters.

	R	*	T	=	D	
to	60 mph		( )		120 mi	using $D/R = T$, we have:
from	40 mph		( )		120 mi	120 mi/60 mph = 2 hrs
						120 mi/40 mph = 3 hrs

	R	*	T	=	D	
to	60 mph		2 hrs		120 mi	
from	40 mph		3 hrs		120 mi	using $D/T = R$, we have:
total			**5 hrs**		**240 mi**	**240 mi/5 hrs = 48 mph**

While the students were interested to discover that the average speed was 48 miles per hour, they were even more excited to find out the symbolic representation below, which uncovered the harmonic mean:

Let a = speed driving to the college and b = speed driving back home from the college.

Then as a class we generated the following:

	R	*	T	=	D
to	a		D/a		D
from	b		D/b		D
total			(D/a) + (D/b)		2D

$$R = \text{total distance} = \text{total time} = \frac{2D}{(D/a) + (D/b)} = \frac{2D}{D\,(a+b)/ab} = \frac{2ab}{a+b} \quad \text{known as the harmonic mean}$$

Two Ladders

Imagine two buildings separated by a narrow alley. One building is 10 feet high, the other is 15 feet high. The alley between them is 8 feet across. A ladder is placed from the base of one building up to the roof of the other building. A second ladder is placed on the opposite building in the same manner (from the base of one to the roof of the other).

Larry goes up one ladder and Mo goes up the other. Curley stands on the ground at the place where the two ladders cross each other so that he can hand materials to Larry and Mo. How high off the ground is the place where the two ladders cross?

First, the class thought through the basic facts using KWC:

What Are the Known Facts?

- There are two buildings, with heights of ten and fifteen feet.
- There are three guys.

- The buildings are eight feet apart.
- Two ladders are there at the same time.
- The ladders go from the ground of one building up to the roof of the opposite building.
- Two guys go up the ladder (one guy per ladder).
- The other guy is on the ground underneath where the ladders cross so he can hand things to the other guys.

I explicitly ask them to try to imagine the situation. To ensure students could visualize the Two Ladders problem, I asked them to work in groups and draw the problem as they saw it. The students' prior experience is always important to consider—for example, not all middle school children have knowledge of different types of ladders and an urban student might picture a scaffold rather than a ladder. In addition, some rural students may not visualize an alley between buildings and some students may not realize why ladders are put at a slant. In fact, most students think all ladders are adjustable; about 98 percent of students' drawings have ladders ending exactly at the top of the building.

After walking around and observing, I selected one student to put her drawing on the board, and suggested that everyone make a copy so they could start with the same diagram. See Figure 4.12.

As a teacher, you might consider the following questions:

- What mathematical concepts did *you* use to help solve the problem?
- What would your students do?

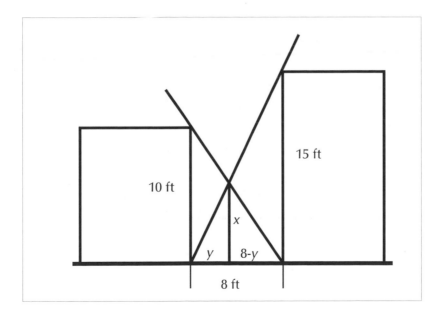

FIGURE 4.12

- Did you think of the Pythagorean Theorem? That may generate some very messy mathematics that no one wants to deal with!
- How about setting up several proportionalities using similar triangles? Notice that you don't need to know how long the ladders are . . . so forget Pythagoras.

In the Two Ladders problem, students have to see that the distance they are trying to figure out, x (the distance from the ground to where the ladders cross), is the height of two right triangles, back to back, with base lengths of y and $8 - y$. It is easy for our adult minds to see that the distance of eight feet between the two buildings can be partitioned into y and $8 - y$, but for many students, it's a magic trick. As a result, it is very important to give students as many experiences with examples of partitioning as possible.

It is also important for students to have prior experience with the concept of similarity and similar triangles; the Two Ladders problem helps to extend their conception of similarity. How do students know that the triangles are similar? They need to understand that the big right triangles formed by the ladder and the buildings have heights and bases of 10 and 8 and 15 and 8. The two smaller right triangles are made by "cutting off the tips" of the big triangles.

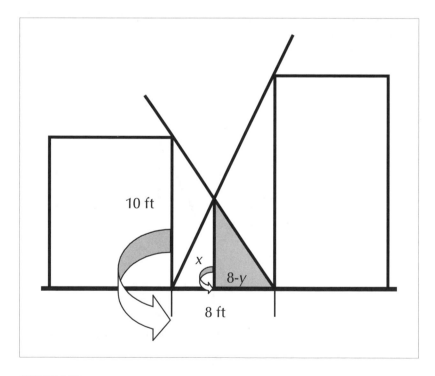

FIGURE 4.13

The small shaded right triangle in Figure 4.13 shares the same angle as the large right triangle on the left with sides of 10 and 8. Since they are both right triangles, their third angles must also be equal. Three equal angles makes them *similar* and their respective sides *in proportion to* one another.

Of the several proportions possible in the Two Ladders problem, our class chose to use HEIGHT:BASE = height:base. I encouraged the students to work in small groups to work through the remainder of the problem and to use their knowledge of similar triangles and proportional reasoning. As I walked around the room observing, I noticed that one group in particular had a few interesting ratios on their papers, $\frac{10}{15}$ and $\frac{8}{5}$. I also noticed that they had labeled the bottom partitions with actual lengths of 4.8 and 3.2.

After several minutes, I asked the groups to share their findings. The first group to raise their hands explained the initial ratios, $\frac{10}{15}$ and $\frac{8}{5}$, and the partition lengths, 4.8 and 3.2. They explained to the class that the two large vertical heights, 10 and 15, are in a 2:3 ratio. This told them that the 8-foot section was split into two partitions, but in a 3:2 manner. As a result, they used the 8:5 ratio, with a total length of 8 feet, split into 5 (3 + 2) portions, with each portion 1.6 feet long. From there, the group multiplied 1.6 by 2, finding a partition length of 3.2. Similarly, they multiplied 1.6 by 3, finding that that segment was 4.8. I decided to prove their answer in a more step-wise fashion:

A. $\quad \dfrac{15}{8} = \dfrac{x}{y}$ (larger triangles)

B. $\quad \dfrac{10}{8} = \dfrac{x}{8-y}$ (smaller triangles)

C. $\quad 15y = 8x$

D. $\quad 8x = 10(8-y)$

E. $\quad 15y = 10(8-y)$

F. $\quad \dfrac{15}{10} = \dfrac{8-y}{y}$

G. $\quad \dfrac{3}{2} = \dfrac{8-y}{y}$

The step approach above confirmed the students' analysis of partitioning. Since they now knew the base lengths, they could set up the base-to-height ratios easily and solve for the missing height. See Figure 4.14.

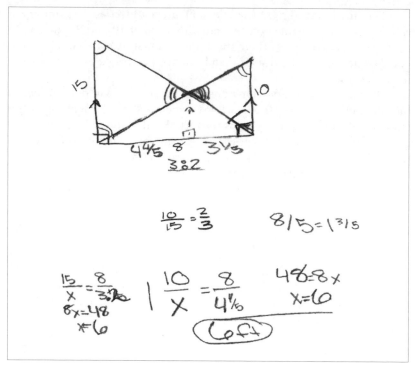

FIGURE 4.14

Alternatively, other groups used a similar proportional reasoning method by choosing to solve directly for height:

A. $\dfrac{10}{8} = \dfrac{x}{8-y}$

B. $\dfrac{15}{8} = \dfrac{x}{y}$

C. $8x = 80 - 10y$

D. $4x = 40 - 5y$

E. $8x = 15y$

F. $5y = 40 - 4x$

G. $8x = 3(5y)$

H. $8x = 3(40 - 4x)$

I. $20x = 120 \quad x = 6$

Any time our students have to do symbol manipulation, we as teachers have to make a point of thinking about what they are doing, why, and what we see at each step. We may find the sequence of steps used in the Two Ladders problem to be a bit different from those commonly shown in textbooks. When faced with a system of equations—what used to be called *simultaneous linear equations*—we solve by elimination or substitution.

The solution shown above was done by substitution, but consider the following. Some students might notice that equations C and E both have an equation with $8x$ and are prone to substitute $80 - 10y$ from equation C for $8x$ in equation E. Although that is a legitimate substitution, it will give values for y only and they are trying to solve for x, not y. Of course, students can plug in the solution of y back into one of the original equations and solve for x if they want to do so and still understand what they are doing.

Instead, notice that in equation D, the coefficient of y is 5 and in equation E the coefficient of y is 15. These facts allow us to rewrite E as equation G: $8x = 3(5y)$. Then we can substitute $40 - 4x$ for $5y$ and get equation H. Will this confuse some students? If they have always substituted for a variable with a coefficient of 1 and never realized that they can legitimately substitute any equivalent quantity, they might be confused. If so, they do not have a very deep understanding of substitution. If they try to express y with coefficient of 1 in terms of x they'd get $\frac{40 - 4x}{5}$ or $(8 - \frac{4x}{5})$ for y and then they'd have an annoying little equation to work with. It can be done—the solution of a height of six feet off the ground for the ladders crossing sounds reasonable.

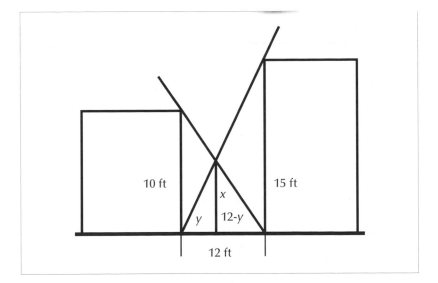

FIGURE 4.15

Extension

What would happen to the height if the buildings were 12 feet apart? Think for a minute. Would the crossing height be less than 6 or more than 6 feet off the ground? See Figure 4.15.

See Figure 4.16 for two students' solutions to the extension. Or, we could solve the extension as before, and get:

A. $\dfrac{10}{12} = \dfrac{x}{12-y}$

B. $\dfrac{15}{12} = \dfrac{x}{y}$

C. $12x = 120 - 10y$

D. $6x = 60 - 5y$

E. $12x = 15y$

F. $5y = 60 - 6x$

G. $12x = 3(5y)$

H. $12x = 3(60 - 6x)$

I. $30x = 180$

J. $x = 6$

How could the answer be six feet again? Is this a mistake? What is going on?

The power of algebra is in its ability to represent complex situations and to show us what is going on in a more general case. This is a very counterintuitive problem. The two buildings are different heights. One would assume that changing the distance between them (like changing the heights) would change the height at which they cross. Surprise! Of course, that means that this is not just one problem. At least two are needed to see what is going on. Then proof comes from the generalization of algebraic representations of proportions. See Figure 4.17

Note that two different manipulations of the symbols in Figure 4.17 both have the variable d drop out. It is not related to the x variable, which is only dependent upon a and b. This means the distance (d) between buildings has no effect on the crossing height of the two ladders (x). That height is only effected by the heights of the two buildings (a and b). The crossing height (x) is one-half the harmonic mean of a and b. *Wow!*

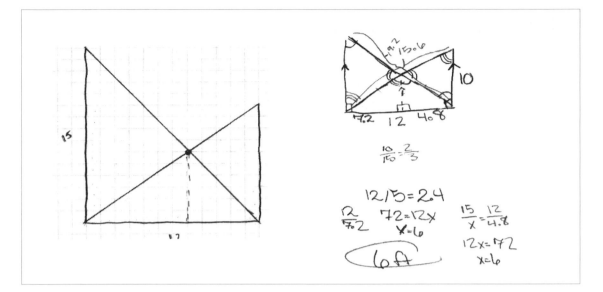

FIGURES 4.16a and 4.16b

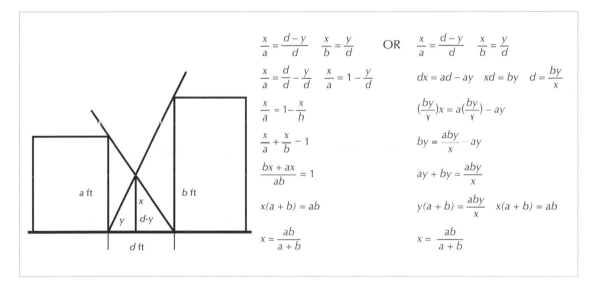

FIGURES 4.17a and 4.17b

Of Renegades and Rockets

Whenever I have given students the Of Renegades and Rockets problem, it is typically after the Two Ladders problem. Once the students begin to recognize the similarity in the mathematical structure, using proportional reasoning in conjunction with similar triangles, it is important to create a new context for which they can develop the same concepts.

123

Of Renegades and Rockets

1. The Trandeskian army has a surplus of tents that they now use to hide their Hummus 47 rockets. The tents are the same color as the burning sand of the Great Abysmal Wasteland of Upper Trandeskia (GAWUT). The rockets are packed in wooden crates that are squares on the left and right side and by some amazing coincidence fit snugly and perfectly into the tents. (See Figure 4.18.) If the altitude of the tent is 36 decimeters and the base of the tent is 45 decimeters, what is the length of the side of the square of the crate?

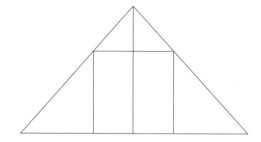

FIGURE 4.18

2. Meanwhile, Ichabod Dobachi, brilliant but demented physicist, has created his own rockets to be smaller, yet even more powerful than the Hummus 47. They are also packed in crates with square ends. By yet another amazing coincidence, they fit snugly in tents with altitude 28 decimeters and base of 21 decimeters. This information was obtained at a great personal risk by CIA operative (code name Butts) who penetrated Dobachi's network in Brazil. However, Butts was never very good at math and he can't figure out the size of the square. He has broken radio silence to ask his CIA handler (code name Artist) to figure it out for him. What is the side length of the square?

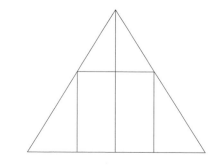

FIGURE 4.19

3. Generalize these problems by expressing side length *s* in terms of altitude *a* and base *b*.

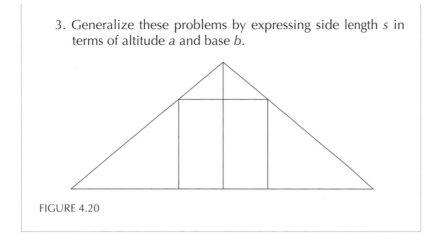

FIGURE 4.20

Before students even begin the first problem, ask them to look at the relationship between the altitudes and bases for each tent in questions 1 and 2. Do they notice anything familiar about the numbers 36 and 45 and 21 and 28? Why, they're consecutive triangular numbers! Remind students that the product of any two consecutive triangular numbers (in this case, 36 and 45 and 21 and 28) is always divisible by their sum—the quotient of which is always one-half the harmonic mean. Of course we want our students to develop their proportional reasoning skills using similar triangle properties, so discuss solving questions 1 and 2 in the following manner:

By using similar triangles we can set up the following proportions:

Question 1

$$\frac{36}{35} = \frac{36 - s}{s}$$

$$36s = 45(36 - s)$$

$$36s = 1620 - 45s$$

$$81s = 1620$$

$s = 20$ decimeters $\rightarrow$ check . . . is 20 the ½ harmonic mean of 36 and 45? (Yes!)

Question 2

$$\frac{28}{21} = \frac{28 - s}{s}$$

$$28s = 21(28 - s)$$

$$28s = 588 - 28s$$

$49s = 588$

$s = 12$ decimeters → check . . . is 12 the ½ harmonic mean of 21 and 28? (Yes!)

Now solve question 3 using the same proportional reasoning strategy and see just what pops up . . . Remember in question 3, we are supposed to let a = altitude, b = base, and s =side length of square.

Question 3

$$\frac{a}{b} = \frac{a - s}{s}$$

$$as = b(a - s)$$

$$as = ab - bs$$

$$as + bs = ab$$

$$s(a + b) = ab$$

$$s = \frac{ab}{a + b} \qquad \textit{½ the harmonic mean!}$$

Clearly, the quest for one-half the harmonic mean was victorious, not only in the initial sense when students recognized that 21 and 28 and 36 and 45 were pairs of consecutive triangular numbers, but also because after using similar triangle proportionality, they could easily progress in to a general form where a = altitude, b = base, and s = side length of square, where after using cross products the harmonic mean jumped out!

That harmonic mean is a tricky concept; students could easily believe that using the harmonic mean to average rates is *not* always obvious. The way in which students collaboratively revealed the harmonic mean (or one-half the harmonic mean) in The Two Painters: Laverne and Shirley, The College Visit, Two Ladders, and the Of Renegades and Rockets problems was amazing!

5 | ALGEBRAIC THINKING AND MODELING

As traditional approaches to algebra are pushed down to middle school, procedures for symbol manipulation dominate the algebra curriculum and the purpose of algebra has become obscured. The virtue of algebra for all of our students, regardless of grade level, is that through algebra they are able to represent, model, generalize, and analytically describe the world. Rules, tools, and procedures are important for our students to know and be able to do, yet students must do more than just practice skills. I would love to see the day when all the symbol manipulation rules are taught with and through problem solving.

If we truly value students representing, modeling, and generalizing in algebra, then we cannot continue to teaching the traditional steps (given an equation, make a table, make a graph, now go home, you're done). Our students should have myriad opportunities to reflect on their development of algebraic thinking and modeling on a regular basis in the classroom. They must have opportunities to:

1. collect real data;
2. organize the data into a table;
3. graph their data;
4. discern pattern(s) in the table and the graph;
5. and then generate a rule that can be represented as an equation.

In this chapter, we present three different methods for our students to create algebraic equations: line of best fit, linear combinations (also known as linear Diophantine equations), and finite differences—all of which cycle through multiple representations of tables, graphs, and equations. Our students naturally come to use and adopt these tools through doing and debriefing in authentic experiences that inspire them to use their insight and curiosity and, ultimately, reorganize their knowledge and understanding of algebra. First, Susan explores problems that convey line of best fit and then linear combinations; Art follows with problems centered around finite differences.

Susan's activities are in the order she presented them to her sixth graders, who already had some prior knowledge of linear relationships. She begins with some messy, real-world data that provokes students to form predictions from linear data, then supplements the curriculum with opportunities to investigate negative slope situations because the math curriculum had none.

LINE OF BEST FIT AND LINEAR COMBINATIONS

Positive Slope Situations

The Vitruvian Man

Vitruvius was a Roman engineer of the first century B.C. who greatly influenced Leonardo da Vinci's architecture and human drawings. The Vitruvian Man, created by Leonardo, is largely based upon the ideal human body proportions that Vitruvius himself created. See Figure 5.1.

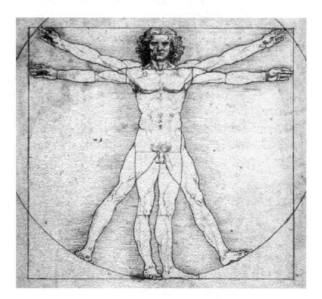

FIGURE 5.1

The drawing shows a man with outstretched arms and legs, in fact two pairs of each, which touch both the circumference of a circle and the sides of a square. From the drawing the conclusion can be made that the length of a man's arm span is equal to the height of the man. The ratio of the Vitruvian Man's arm span to his height equals 1. But how can we be sure? Do students measure up to these proportions?

My inspiration for this investigation came from an activity created by Suzanne Alejandre of the Math Forum. I modified the activity in a variety of ways to suit the needs of my highly motivated and academically talented sixth graders. Instead of asking my students to just collect data, graph their points, and describe the data trend, they investigated, analyzed, interpolated, and extrapolated their data in a manner that enabled them to draw on their prior knowledge of linear data and establish a solid framework for a unit on linear modeling.

I chose Vitruvian Man to be the anchor activity in a unit on linear modeling in multiple representations: tables, graphs, and rules. Prior to our investigation, my students had an understanding of ratios and rates only in the numerical (fraction computation and problem solving) and geometric (similar polygons) sense. I wanted my students to understand—and eventually synthesize at the end of the unit—the strong connections among the various mathematics concepts we'd discussed earlier in the year: the mathematical relationships, namely those that are linear, found in the human body and the usefulness this data has for archeologists and forensic scientists. I knew archeology and forensic science were especially interesting to my students because of a survey I'd taken at the beginning of the year asking them to name their favorite "cool math jobs."

Our Vitruvian Man investigation took place in the second half of the school year over a four-day period, at a time when my students were well accustomed to working cooperatively. I knew they understood the academic and behavioral expectations of group work without requiring a lot of redirection from me.

Vitruvian Man, Day 1

On the first day of this activity, I began as I would any other math period, with a "sponge" question, named in honor of my students' favorite cartoon character, SpongeBob SquarePants. A sponge is also a common device used to soak up maximum amounts of liquid whenever the two are in direct contact—a metaphor for the way I want my students to enter class and begin to be productive.

I asked the sponge question to get things rolling:

What do you know about the relationship between your arm span and your height?

Students pulled out their math reflective logs and began to jot down their thoughts for five minutes. My students are very good at using their math logs to communicate a variety of messages to me—their understandings, confusions, predictions, questions, and analyses—all of which they communicate in a variety of representations—pictures, drawings, graphs, tables, equations, words, and lists. During those five minutes, I saw a number of students hone in on the length of their arm span and their heights almost immediately. Students also worked in small groups to estimate one another's arm span and height in order to form educated conjectures about the relationship of the two. These sixth graders were used to my open-ended questions that required thoughtful investigation, even in the hypothesis stage.

Over the next five minutes, students showed me they were ready to discuss their responses by closing their logs. Despite some middle school "knuckle dragging" chuckles, I noticed that the students found a relationship between arm span and height. As one student said (using some prior, albeit misplaced, geometry vocabulary), "I think arm span and height are similar measurements, but not congruent."

I responded, "What do you mean?"

Another student from the same group jumped in and said, "She means the arm span [he showed me with his arms] is similar and not always equal to the height [he showed me by standing tall]."

"Yeah," another group piped in, "and the bigger your arm span, the taller you are, unless you're a chimp or something." I had to laugh and clarify that we would focus on humans in our investigation.

As students continued to openly discuss their conjectures, I recorded snippets of the comments on large chart paper in hopes of using them in a debriefing session at any point in this multiclass period activity. After about three more minutes in our whole-class discussion, I proceeded to hand out the Vitruvian Man activity sheet.

In this activity, students investigated the lengths of, rounded to the nearest inch, and the relationship between the arm span and height of a human being in their classroom. They needed to collect at least twenty different data entries to compare to the results of Leonardo da Vinci, archeologists, and forensic scientists. My goal was for students to see that despite how messy their data might be, they could still see a linear trend. This activity would prepare them for investigating linear functions.

The moment I said "linear functions," puzzled looks appeared on more than half the students' faces, so I asked, "Anybody have an idea what a linear function is?" Several students said in unison, "Something to do with lines and data." I was pretty impressed that they had taken an abstract phrase like "linear functions" and extracted what they knew: linear—line and function—relationship with data. I made sure to record bits of information from this informal questioning on the large chart paper I had set up. Acknowledging and emphasizing the importance of students' prior knowledge builds connections among new information and previous understandings.

After I finished describing the purpose, process, and data analysis, the students immediately plunged into the activity by delegating tasks, materials, and due dates. Because this activity was taking place during the second half of the school year, I did not assign specific tasks to each group member, nor did I designate individual due dates for parts of the entire assessment. I am not opposed to assigning specific tasks (for example, material manager, data collector), but it depends on the maturity and familiarity your students have with working cooperatively; mine had developed their cooperative learning skills all year long through a variety of formative and summative assessments. I have always allowed my students to safely explore mathematical phenomena in a nonthreatening environment.

I visited each group during class and listened to their thoughts and responses. By the end of day 1, I noticed that most of the students had completely finished collecting at least twenty data entries. See Figure 5.2.

Name _____
Date _____

⚲ Investigate/ Gather Data 📝

In your group, measure the arm span, radius(for information on the location of the radius, see the teacher and height in inches of everyone in the group. Also be sure to record the gender of each person. Share your data with other groups. Be sure to gather at least 20 people.

ARM SPAN	RADIUS	HEIGHT	GENDER (M OR F)	
* 56 in	* 8.5 in	* 56 in	* F Megan	
* 59 in	* 8 in	* 61 in	F Jessie	
* 60	* 9 in	* 60 in	M matt	
* 67.5 in	* 12.5 in	* 65.5 in	* F Amanda	
* 52.5 in	* 16.5 in	* 59.4	* F Lea	
* 58 in	* 8.5 in	60.5	* F Shana	
* 50 in	* 7.5 in	* 53 in	* F Allie	
* 56 in	* 9.5	* 52.5 in	* M Tommy	
* 60 in	* 9	* 58 in	* F Thalia	
* 54 in	* 9 in	* 56 in	* F Stacy	
* 63 in	* 15.5 in	* 63 in	* F M & F.	
* 62	* 11	* 65	* F	
* 61	* 10	* 63	* F	
* 58½	* 8½	* 57	* F	
* 42½	* 16	* 62	* F	
* 59½	* 9	* 59½	* M	
* * 63	* 9	* 63	* M	
* 58	* 14	* 62	M	
* 60	* 10	* 67	* M	
56.5	8.5	58	F	

use INCHES

- Most of the Males hight is higher than 60 in
- Sometimes when the radius is longer, the person is taller. vice versa.
- not many people are in porportion

FIGURE 5.2

Day 2

On the second day of the activity, I asked another sponge question:

> When you are ready to move from the tabular representation of your data to the graphical representation of your data, what do you predict you will see? Why?

One student said, while demonstrating with his hands, "It'll be a line, 'cuz as one thing increases, then so does the height."

"What kind of a line?" I asked. I showed them with my arm different types of slanted, vertical, and horizontal lines. I could tell immediately that while students could follow directions on the activity sheet about which variable to put where on the coordinate plane, they did not understand *why* they were placed that way. My question lead into an incredibly valuable discussion on independent and dependent variables and how we figure out conceptually where to place each variable. The discussion came in handy during later linear function activities.

I walked my students through the meaning of the statement "the dependent variable depends upon the independent variable" by referring to a variety of activities we had done earlier in the year. One of the activities was a campsite problem that involved two variables, the number of campsites rented and the amount of money made. In that context, my students understood that the amount of money made clearly depended upon the number of campsites rented—which is why when we graphed our data, we plotted the amount of money made (the dependent variable) on the y-axis and the number of campsites rented (the independent variable) on the x-axis.

One persistent student then asked, "So, what's this got to do with our arm span and height topic? Couldn't it technically be that either one depends on the other?"

"Yes," I replied, "mathematically and graphically you'll see a similar picture."

Most of the class responded with, "Huh?", which prompted me to go to the board and sketch the pictures using what I call "nice numbers." See Figure 5.3.

Students agreed that both tables graphed a similar picture—a straight line that rose to the right. One student suggested that it would be more reasonable to use option 1 because, she said, "our spinal cord is developed before our arms" before we are born—which implied that *the length of our arm span should depend upon our height*. I was impressed with her math-to-world connection! I heard a lot of "Oh yeah!" and "That's what we just learned in human development class!" from other students. I couldn't help but remind them just how *connected* mathematics is to the real world, especially *their* school world. As a result of our conversations,

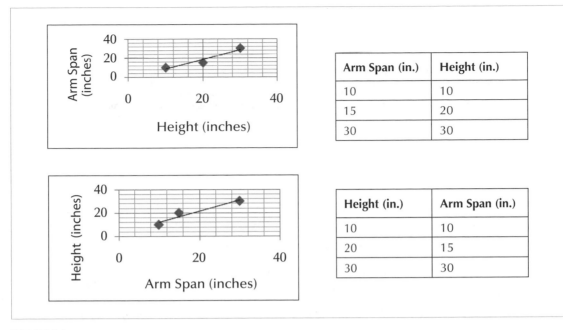

Arm Span (in.)	Height (in.)
10	10
15	20
30	30

Height (in.)	Arm Span (in.)
10	10
20	15
30	30

FIGURE 5.3

we decided to keep the height as the independent variable and the arm span the dependent variable, while maintaining an understanding that in *this* context, the assignment of the independent and dependent variables did not largely affect the graphical representation of their data.

As the students progressed in day 2 of their investigation, most of them were far on their way to working through the data analysis question portion of the activity. See Figure 5.4.

Day 3

As the third day of our Vitruvian Man activity began, some students voiced surprise that their data from the previous day did not form a perfectly straight line and asked if creating a *line of best fit*—a term they had either heard or learned the previous year, and something we would return to at the end of our unit—would help them understand that the data had a linear progression. See Figure 5.5.

I jumped in immediately and said, "Yes, it would, and later we'll talk about how to figure out the exact rule for the line of best fit and we'll even ask the folks at Texas Instruments what they think." I got the idea from Art to have my kids use angel hair pasta *instead* of rulers, because the rulers— yes, even the clear ones—are often too thick and wide to see through, often resulting in much inaccuracy. I made the decision to come back to the messy data at the end of our unit so that students could better understand how to use their newly acquired algebra language (*slope, intercepts, slope-intercept form*). In the meantime, I proposed a variation of our activity:

Purpose (What you will learn):

Leonardo Da Vinci's famous drawing The Proportions of the Human Figure(1492) is accompanied by calculations for measurements of the human body. Archeologists and forensic scientists are also concerned with the measurements of the body. They use measurements of bones and body parts (namely the radius bone) to predict height and body type of a person. In this activity you will explore the relationship between body measurements. You will compare your results to those of Leonardo da Vinci, archeologists and forensic scientists. The most significant purpose of this activity is to lay the foundations for our study of linear functions.

Process (What you will do):

In your groups, you will measure each other's arm span, radius (distance between wrist and beginning of inner elbow) and the height in INCHES of everyone in the group. Also, be sure to record the gender of each person. You are then to share your data with other groups. Be sure to gather data for at least 20 people. After you have collected data for at least 20 total people (you may include yourself in this data), please create two different scatter plots on graph paper (yes, one per piece of paper) that represents the following:

HW
1. Graph height on the x-axis and arm span on the y-axis. (height, arm span)
2. Graph height on the x-axis and radius on the y-axis. (height, radius)

label axis

HW Analysis (What did you observe and how can you apply and extend this new knowledge):

Using your two different graphs, please answer the following questions:

1. In words, explain what each of your graphs showed. That is, tell the "story" of each graph by describing any particular trends in the data.
2. Suppose a person has an arm span of 65 inches, what do you predict their height to be? How do you know this a reasonable estimate?
3. Suppose a person has a radius that is 7.5 inches long, what do you predict their height to be? How do you know this is a reasonable estimate?
4. Da Vinci concluded that arm span is equal to height. Do your results verify his conclusions? Support your answer with evidence.
5. How do you suppose an archeologist or a forensic scientist would use the information displayed on the second graph?
6. Scientists use the following formulas to approximate an adult's height H, in inches, when they know the length of their radius r. Does your data support either of these formulas? Be sure to separate male and females. Why might your data NOT reflect the same information as these formulas?

| Male | $H = 3.7r + 31.7$ |
| Female | $H = 3.9r + 28.9$ |

7. Complete the following statement *"Today I learned that…"* (Be as specific as possible)

FIGURE 5.4

Extension

Determine the line of best fit by considering every point in the data set, instead of the minimum requirement, which is 2.

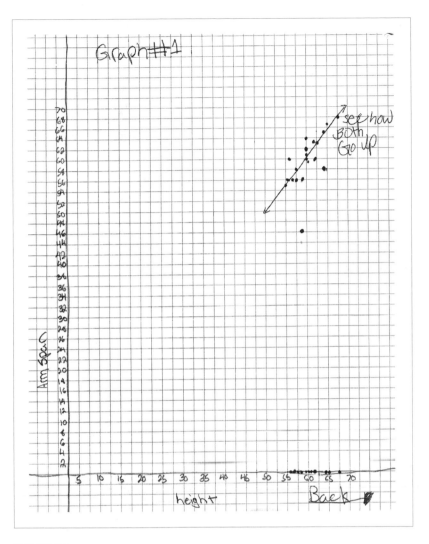

FIGURE 5.5

In the past I have had students calculate average ranges for a fixed domain. Because these points have the same domain, they lie right on top of one another, with the line of best fit in between them. In essence, students predict that for a given value of our *x*-variable, what is a likely value for the *y*-variable? Depending on your students' mathematical ability, you might have them examine the correlation coefficient to see just how closely fitting their line of best fit is to their data. This conceptual approach can be accomplished by having the students analyze their graphs, their tables, and the position of the points they plotted in relation to their line of best fit.

By the end of the third day, in our debriefing session, we discussed the results of students' Vitruvian Man data analysis. It was really interesting to hear how students used their tables and graphs to interpolate and extrapolate. See Figure 5.6.

Many students understood the positive relationship between arm span and height, although they seemed disgruntled by the fact that the relationship was *not* proven to be a 1-to-1 ratio, as most had predicted at the beginning of the activity. This sparked a heated discussion that was nicely corralled by one student who suggested, "Well, we're just students and we're not done growing! Let's check out Mrs. F., because she's already full grown."

To my amazement, I was measured on the spot and students could see that the ratio of my arm span to my height was indeed 1-to-1. I asked, "What if I went around your town and school measuring adults' arm span and heights and then did the same for students? Who do you think would be more likely to have this 1-to-1 ratio, the adults or the students?" They proceeded to discuss the answer to this question in their small groups.

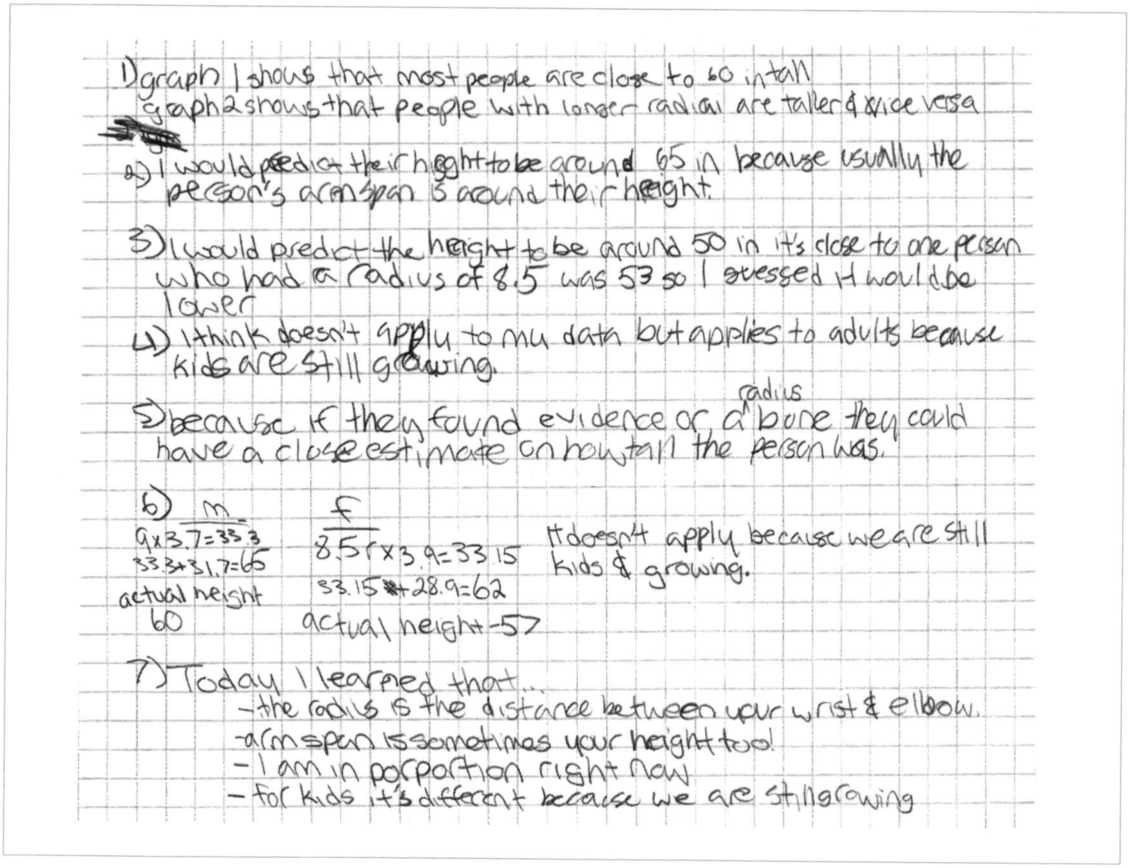
1) graph 1 shows that most people are close to 60 in tall
graph 2 shows that people with longer radiai are taller & vice versa
2) I would predict their height to be around 65 in because usually the person's arm span is around their height.
3) I would predict the height to be around 50 in it's close to one person who had a radius of 8.5 was 53 so I guessed it would be lower
4) I think doesn't apply to my data but applies to adults because kids are still growing.
5) because if they found evidence or a radius bone they could have a close estimate on how tall the person was.
6) m
9x3.7=33.3
33.3+31.7=65
actual height 60
f
8.5 r x 3.9 = 33.15
33.15 + 28.9 = 62
actual height - 57
It doesn't apply because we are still kids & growing.
7) Today I learned that...
- the radius is the distance between your wrist & elbow.
- arm span is sometimes your height too!
- I am in porportion right now
- for kids it's different because we are still growing

FIGURE 5.6

As I walked around the room, I overheard one girl make an interesting connection and conclusion that caused me to exclaim *"Eureka!"* (to boost her confidence), stop the discussion, and have her repeat it loudly. She stated simply, "1 think one-to-one doesn't apply to my data because we are students and we are still growing. But most adults are finished. Like Mrs. F. *But* this idea is not totally garbage. What if a forensic scientist or an FBI agent finds an arm bone of a dead body? You know they can closely predict the height—even if it is a student like me."

Just a simple mathematical model for predicting, that's all folks. In fact, precisely the next thing students looked at was some rules generated by scientists that represented the relationship between arm span and height. I required students to determine if either of the presented formulas, which related height to radius, represented their data and to use mathematical evidence to support why or why not. I then asked them to use the data they collected on the spot (my height, radius, and arm span) and compare how those values were different from their values. Students come within *25 thousandths* of an inch over my height of 63 inches. Pretty darn close! See Figure 5.7.

Day 4

On the final day of our Vitruvian Man activity, students gathered their tables, graphs, and data analysis to complete, partially in groups and as individuals, a final discussion. See Figure 5.8.

I required students to use an inductive reasoning approach to form generalizations about the human body's actual proportions. As I mentioned earlier, my goal was for students to understand and be able to synthesize the connections among various mathematics concepts, the mathematical relationships in the human body, and the usefulness of this data for archeologists and forensic scientists.

Students achieved success not only in their highly reflective student work but also in their clear display of how much prior knowledge they had on linearity—far more than any pretest would ever have shown. The Vitruvian Man activity also provided a springboard from which students could bounce new ideas and concepts off a variety of contexts that

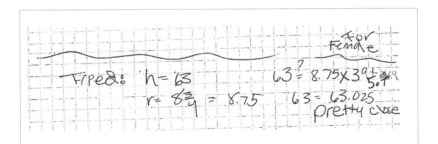

FIGURE 5.7

interested them and also connected to ideas within mathematics and out-side of mathematics to other content areas.

Inverse Linear Relations

Chocolate Algebra

Chocolate. Smooth, velvety, rich luscious chocolate. Algebra. Structured, patterned, intensely functional algebra. Both can be equally dangerous if certain precautions are not taken while consuming them. How could *anyone* ever think to fuse together such a bittersweet relationship in such a way to derive a deep synthesis in middle school mathematics? Art Hyde (2006) cooked up this investigation, which consists of several problems, "in order to fully integrate (synthesize) the different representations, data

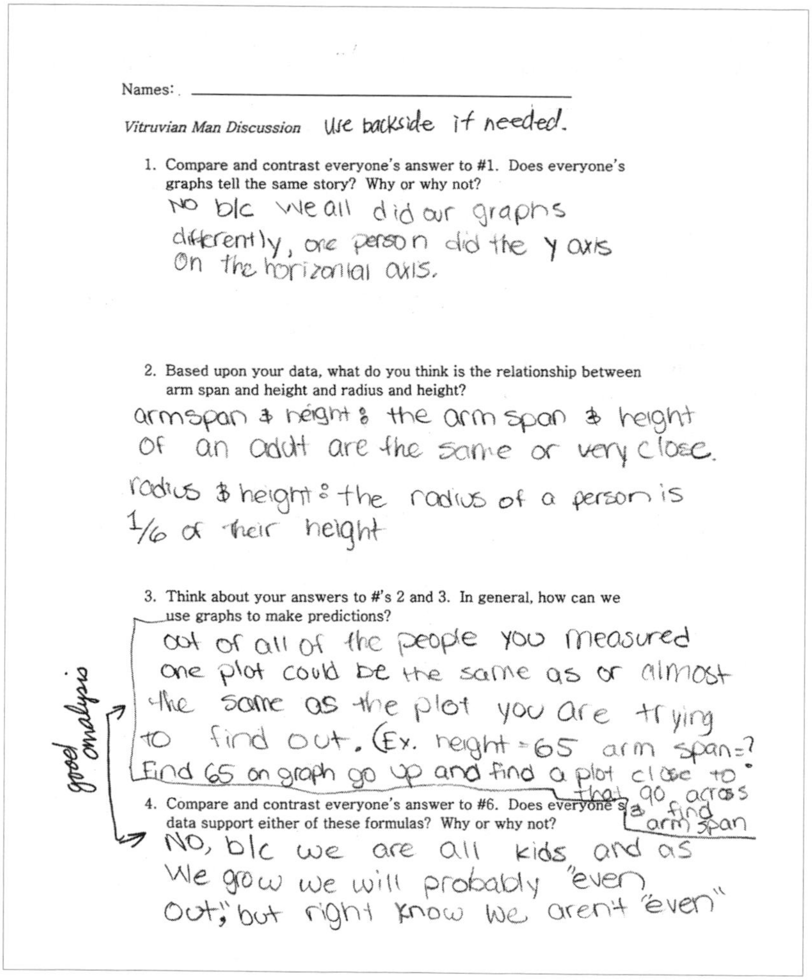

Names: _____

Vitruvian Man Discussion Use backside if needed.

1. Compare and contrast everyone's answer to #1. Does everyone's graphs tell the same story? Why or why not?

No b/c we all did our graphs differently, one person did the y axis on the horizontal axis.

2. Based upon your data, what do you think is the relationship between arm span and height and radius and height?

armspan & height: the arm span & height of an adult are the same or very close.

radius & height: the radius of a person is 1/6 of their height

3. Think about your answers to #'s 2 and 3. In general, how can we use graphs to make predictions?

out of all of the people you measured one plot could be the same as or almost the same as the plot you are trying to find out. (Ex. height = 65 arm span = ? Find 65 on graph go up and find a plot close to that. go across find arm span

good analysis

4. Compare and contrast everyone's answer to #6. Does everyone's data support either of these formulas? Why or why not?

No, b/c we are all kids and as we grow we will probably "even out," but right know we aren't "even"

FIGURE 5.8

tables, graphs (and equations for the older students) within a real-life situation. It is done in the context of *chocolate* and *money*, two of the seven deadly sins." I had no idea how my students' excitement would continue to grow throughout every stage in this investigation.

Just Like a Kid in a Candy Shop   My sixth graders know to be ready for anything the moment they hear we will be doing one of Art's investigations. At the end of class the previous day, I simply told them to bring their minds and sweet tooth to our next class meeting, because those were two of the most necessary supplies needed for our next mission.

What they weren't ready for was a large canister of Tootsie Rolls with a $1 price tag attached and a 2-pound Hershey's bar with a $2 price tag attached. As the students settled into class, somewhat unnerved by my audacity to place so much chocolate within their reach, I handed each student their very first Chocolate Algebra problem with a KWC prompt:

Chocolate Algebra #1

Suppose I have $10 to spend, and I want to buy $1 Tootsie Rolls (TRs) and $2 Hershey's bars (HBs). I have to use all of my money. What combinations of chocolate goodies can I buy? Begin with a KWC.

I had placed, next to the chocolate, a large blank sheet of chart paper and a collection of play money in denominations of $1, $2, and $5. "We get to use that chocolate *and* that money today!" I exclaimed as I circulated around the room handing out the problem.

My sixth graders immediately began working in small groups on the KWC. Within moments, many students were furiously raising their hands to write parts of their KWC on the board. See Figure 5.9.

Show Me the Money   Once I'd established the context, constraints, and question of the Chocolate Algebra problem, I distributed a bag of play money to each group. For this first problem, each group received a bundle of $1 bills and $2 bills. I made sure that each group had more than enough bills to be able to visualize as many different combinations as possible. Also, I knew that because my students had successfully completed the KWC that they knew each $1 bill represented a TR and each $2 bill represented an HB. I said to my students, "Show me the money! Hold up an example of a possible purchase that I could make." After about thirty seconds, each group held up a possible purchase.

I stopped at each group, announced what I saw they held for money, and asked the rest of the class to verify if it was a valid purchase. I noticed that not one group held up an amount that was either less than or greater than $10—all groups had paid close attention to the special condition

What do I **KNOW**?	What do I need to **FIND OUT**?	Are there any special rules or conditions?
Hershey Bars → 2$ Tootsie Rolls → 1$ I have → 10$	What are the different combos of HBs & TRs.	Must use all 10$ - NO CHANGE ↓ No partial candy ↓ Possible to buy only 1 candy type

FIGURE 5.9

listed in their KWC. I also noticed that one group held up ten dollars, but only in $1 bills.

As I approached this group, I asked the class to verify if it were possible to not purchase any HBs. One boy said, "Just look at the KWC. It just says that we have to spend *all* of our money—it doesn't say how!"

"So is it okay to assume that I'm allowed to purchase zero HBs?" I responded.

A student from the ten $1 bills group said, "Of course. Well, we don't know *for sure* if it's *not* okay to do that, so let's add this comment to our 'C' and then we can all agree that it's okay." I nodded in approval and then sent her immediately up to the board to add her insightful comment to the KWC.

Once the girl returned to her seat, I asked the class, "Are the examples you're holding up *all* of the possibilities?"

"*No way!*" students replied in unison. "How do you know?" I asked, with a curious look on my face. One boy replied, "If it's possible to have zero HBs and stick to the problem's rules, then it's possible to have zero TRs too! So there's at least one more for ya!" I nodded in approval.

Tabular Representations I then asked "How can we keep track of all this information in such a way that helps us be sure that we have found all possible cases?" I suddenly heard a groan from a boy who rarely speaks up in class, "Oh gosh, it's one of your favorites again—isn't it?" he said, rolling his eyes.

"One of my favorite whats?"

Another child from his group joined in and said, "*A table!*" I eagerly praised their predictions and approved the table strategy. Before I set them off in their small groups to work on the table, I wanted to make sure that they all knew how to construct the table around the data they were

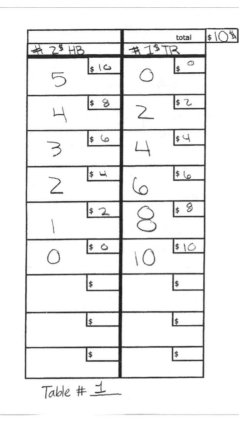

total	$10

# 2$ HB		# 1$ TR	
5	$10	0	$0
4	$8	2	$2
3	$6	4	$4
2	$4	6	$6
1	$2	8	$8
0	$0	10	$10
	$		$
	$		$
	$		$

Table # 1

FIGURE 5.10

collecting. Because this group had been accustomed to working with organizing information for a table, they knew from looking back at their K and W from the KWC that each candy bar type and cost, as well as the total amount of money to spend, had to be represented in their tables. As a large group, we sketched on chart paper the outline for their first table in Chocolate Algebra. See Figure 5.10.

When Art first created this activity, he was working with an intellectually heterogeneous group of third graders. He wanted to help them focus on the relationship between the two variables in the cells of the T-table while still keeping track of the cost. Rather than have these third graders remember or recalculate the costs of buying that many of each item at its stated price, Art started using a box in the upper right hand corner of each cell for the students to enter the cost of those items. (This is like adding two more columns, but students have difficulties dealing with the over load of four columns.) (See Figure 5.10.) The box in the corner can be easily made with a computer. Some teachers favor a circle, half or quarter circle and refer to these as total bubbles. This simple idea has proven to be disproportionately profitable because:

1. It saves short-term memory (as described above) and offers a simple check on possible solutions because the numbers in the two corner boxes must sum to the total.
2. When the number of items or the costs becomes too large for mental math to compute, students are glad to be able to compute the product of items times price per item and record it once.
3. Items and their costs is a good place to start because they are different entities and cost is signified by a dollar sign. Once comfortable with this format, the students can use the total boxes or bubbles to record their portioning of anything. For example, how many ways could we put twenty-nine students into groups of either three or four?

Groups of Four	Groups of Three	Total to Cover 29
20	9	
5	3	

4. The contents of the total bubbles or boxes can be used as expressions that are instrumental to the creation of the standard form of the relevant equation ($4x + 3y = 29$).

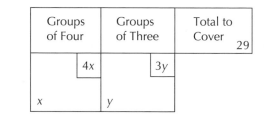

Groups of Four	Groups of Three	Total to Cover 29
$4x$	$3y$	
x	y	

"One more question before you work," I said to the class. "How can you be sure that you satisfy the special conditions in your table?" Several students piped up, "Because the rows in your tables should always sum to *exactly* ten!" I nodded in approval and sent the students off on their way to construct the table for Chocolate Algebra #1.

After several minutes of the groups working, I pulled the class back together to record their data on chart paper. Again, before I recorded each possibility, I asked the class to verify the accuracy by holding up the dollar amounts to make sure that we did indeed satisfy our special condition. Also, I recorded their data in no apparent order, because I planned on discussing the importance of order in the next several moments—and, to my surprise, it was the students who brought it up!

Once I felt that I had exhausted the class for possible solutions, I asked, "How can we be sure that we've got all the possible combinations of TRs and HBs?" Several students commented, "Because we have zero to ten possible TRs up there."

"So what does that mean?" I asked. A girl from that group said, "Well, if you start with no TRs, then move slowly up by one, the price for each TR, then you keep going until you reach the maximum number of TRs, which is obviously ten because we only have ten dollars to spend. *And* Mrs. F., it would help if you ordered your table like that so that we could all keep track while we move from least to most number of TRs."

I then posed the following question: "Using the technique of starting with the least number of TRs and moving through to the greatest number of TRs, what's happening to my HBs?" All of the students agreed that when the TRs went up, the HBs had gone down to ensure that we were only spending exactly $10. This marked one of the first real-world examples that my students had with inverse linear relationships. In the beginning of their unit on linear modeling, the students had primarily dealt with positive, or direct, linear relationships—that is, as one quantity increases, so does the other. I made a point of connecting our previous investigation of positive linear relationships to our new investigation of negative linear relationships. After I told them what a negative linear relationship was—when one quantity increases, the other decreases—I asked them to describe how Chocolate Algebra Problem #1 exemplified the qualities of a negative relationship. Most students easily referred back to the large table we recently created together to point out that as the TRs went up, the HBs went down.

Once I was confident that the students had a solid understanding of how we created the table and had a strategy to ensure that they found all possible combinations, I told the class to work in their groups to generate a list of any patterns they observed in Chocolate Algebra #1. See Figure 5.11. I compiled their observations in a class list using the chart paper for later use in a debriefing session.

Chocolate Algebra #2

At the end of class, I decided to take the time to distribute and discuss with students their evening's homework assignment, which was to complete Chocolate Algebra #2, including a KWC and a detailed list of observations made from their tables.

Chocolate Algebra #2

Suppose I have $20 to spend and I want to buy $1 Tootsie Rolls (TRs) and $2 Hershey's bars (HBs). I have to use all of my money. What combinations of chocolate goodies can I buy? Begin with a KWC and be sure to include any patterns you observe from your tables.

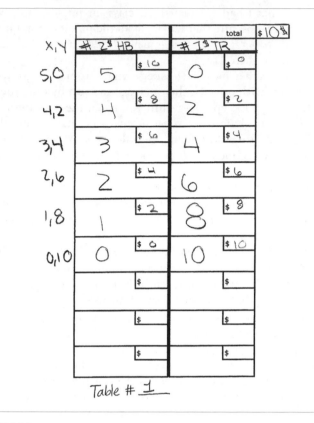

x,y	#2$ HB		#1$ TR		total	10
5,0	5	$10	0	$0		
4,2	4	$8	2	$2		
3,4	3	$6	4	$4		
2,6	2	$4	6	$6		
1,8	1	$2	8	$8		
0,10	0	$0	10	$10		
		$		$		
		$		$		
		$		$		

Table # __1__

FIGURE 5.11

At the beginning of the next class, as my students entered the class, I greeted them with a small slip of paper that contained their questions for the daily opener, or "sponge":

1. In what ways are Chocolate Algebra #1 and #2 similar?
2. In what ways are Chocolate Algebra #1 and #2 different?
3. Look up at my display on the board. What do you suppose the next Chocolate Algebra problem will be about?

After five minutes, I noticed most of the class had completed their sponge and had already begun to debrief last night's homework in their small groups, so I opened up the floor for a whole-class discussion to share their answers to the sponge. For the first question, most students agreed that the KWCs were very similar and the way in which they constructed their tables for both problems had striking resemblances. See Figure 5.12.

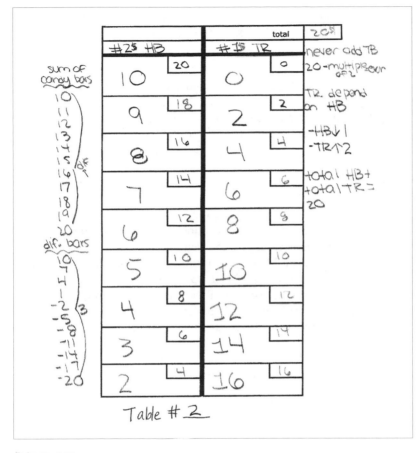

FIGURE 5.12

For the second question, I received a variety of responses that appeared to reach the same conclusions: more money and more possibilities—twice as many, to be exact. For the third question, most students noticed the new chocolate candies and their corresponding price values, which led them to assume that we'd be doing another Chocolate Algebra investigation.

From Tables to Graphs   Prior to the next Chocolate Algebra investigation, I wanted my students to change their Chocolate Algebra #1 and #2 data from a tabular representation to a graphical representation. So I posed the following two questions to my class:

1. How could you graph this data?
2. Why would you graph this data?

Before the students were permitted to discuss their answers in groups, I required them to write down their answers anonymously on a small slip of paper. Once they were confident with their answers, they placed them into a hat. I then planned to distribute the slips of paper randomly to students around the room so they could get a chance to look at one another's ideas. I use this strategy frequently for three main reasons:

1. It gives students a chance to ponder their own answers before any eager beavers shout out their answers.
2. It requires students to think about their responses before they blurt them out.
3. It enables students to be more willing to share because they are reporting someone else's anonymous answer.

As the students shared their answers, I heard the following:

- We could graph the data from tables #1 and #2 on two different coordinate things.
- We could make two graphs, one for each problem.
- TRs are independent because *we* chose those values and HBs are dependent 'cuz their values always *depended* on what we had for TRs . . . so, TRs = *x*s and HBs = *y*s. You're gonna need another column on your table to write (*x*, *y*)s (the ordered pairs).
- We would graph because Mrs. F. says graphing is one of the three representations and we just did tables.
- We would graph to make predictions and to have another way to analyze data.
- Graph to see if data is straight line, even though I already know it is by looking at those constant changes.

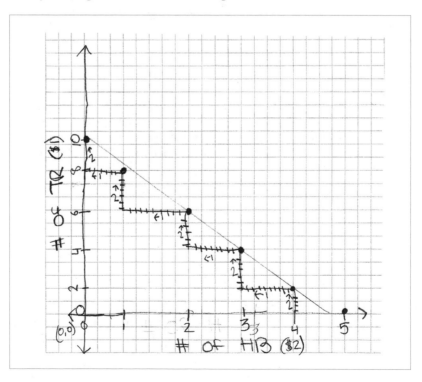

FIGURE 5.13a

The point here was to get students thinking about how and why we would graph the data, not just to claim ownership over the ideas generated. Once a clear purpose and procedure had been established for the graphical representation, the students took out their graph paper and began to construct a graph for Chocolate Algebra #1 and #2. See Figures 5.13a and b.

Then several small-group discussions took place over the differences and similarities that they had observed among the two graphs and the graphs and tables. One of the most important similarities I overheard was in reference to the stair steps being the same for each graph and table. The moment I heard this, I stopped class to allow this student to openly share his insight. First I asked him to clarify what he meant by *stair steps*. His response was, "You know, how the chocolate changes in the table. Down by 1, up by 2. See how that's the same in my graphs?"

At that moment all the students shifted back into their groups to verify if what he had said was indeed true for their tables and graphs. This connection and verification of this connection are key to understanding the bridge between these two representations of the same data: tables and graphs. I wasn't so concerned that their name for slope or constant rate of change was *stair step*, because the connection they made proved to be more powerful than I predicted. I planned to introduce the formal name for *stair step* after the next set of Chocolate Algebra investigations.

In addition to working with students on moving data from a tabular to a graphical representation, I also wanted to discuss with them before

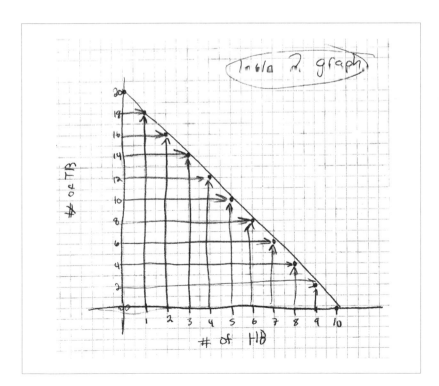

FIGURE 5.13b

our next Chocolate Algebra investigation the way in which they connected the data points on their graphs. My students had already looked at a variety of real-world situations in which they had to decide whether to connect data points with a solid line or a dashed line. From my students' perspective, they understood a solid line to *include* data between points and a dashed line to *exclude* data between points.

To prompt a discussion, I asked, "Which way should we connect the dots on your graphs? A solid or dashed line?" A dozen hands shot up; one girl stated, "In other problems we did before it was okay to use solid because it was possible to have data in between, but here it is not."

I nodded in approval, but then asked why this was true. Another dozen hands shot up, and a boy said, "Because you only have whole-number candies, like there isn't any possible way to go the store and buy one-and-a-half Hershey's bars, they just won't let you do that."

I certainly agreed with that statement and added, "Yes, in this situation you are correct. A dashed line would be best."

Just about every student in the class took the next moment or two to adjust their lines. Once they finished adjusting their graphs, I had the students place their work into a Chocolate Algebra folder that they were building in their small groups. The folder assured that their work wouldn't get lost, and they could freely refer back to the earlier stages of this investigation as they continued to build their synthesis of linear modeling.

Chocolate Algebra #4, #5, and #6

I then presented the students with another set of Chocolate Algebra problems:

Suppose I have $40 to spend and I want to buy $5 Russell Stover bars (RSs) and $2 Hershey's bars (HBs). I have to use all of my money. What combinations of chocolate goodies can I buy? Begin with a KWC.

Suppose I have $45 to spend and I want to buy $5 Russell Stover bars (RSs) and $2 Hershey's bars (HBs). I have to use all of my money. What combinations of chocolate goodies can I buy? Begin with a KWC.

Suppose I have $50 to spend and I want to buy $5 Russell Stover bars (RSs) and $2 Hershey's bars (HBs). I have to use all of my money. What combinations of chocolate goodies can I buy? Begin with a KWC.

I added separately that students should make sure to include all their table observations and to graph all three data sets on different coordinate planes, and then I added this last question: "What do you notice about the stair steps?"

Immediately, students recognized the mathematical structure and the similar context of the three Chocolate Algebra problems. Some students made a math-to-math connection that I had not even thought of—they recognized that the total bubbles will always fluctuate by the least common multiple (lcm) of the candy bar prices, regardless of whether the candy bar prices were relatively prime or not. When I asked them how they came to this idea, most students admitted that they were initially looking for shortcuts or ways to complete the table in an efficient manner and made the assumption that if there was a pattern in the fluctuation of number of candy bars based on their individual costs, then there must be a pattern also in the fluctuation of the cost of candy bars (as observed in the total bubbles).

I asked how students saw this pattern. One said, "Well we've certainly done a lot with greatest common factor (gcf) and lcm this year, it was

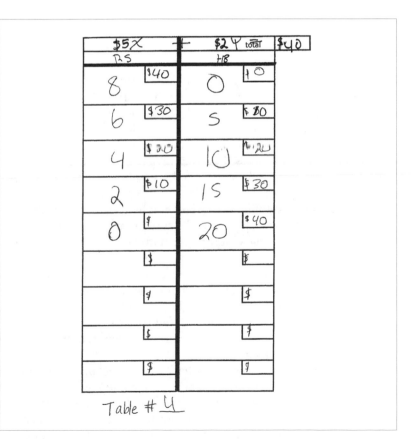

FIGURE 5.14a

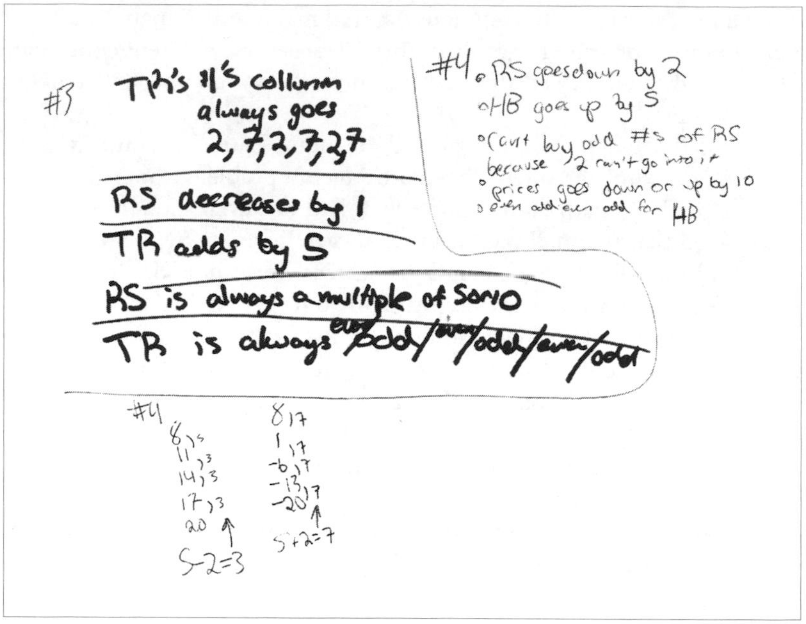

FIGURE 5.14b

bound to pop up here somewhere." To *me*, that meant they were using a critical mathematical eye to connect prior knowledge to new understandings. To *them*, that meant they were clever and working in a time-effective manner. Either way, I was impressed! In groups, the students used the remainder of the class period to find all possible combinations for each problem in this third round of Chocolate Algebra. See Figures 5.14a–d.

On the next day of class, I greeted my students at the door with a slip of paper for their daily sponge and a graphing calculator. They've been using graphing calculators in class since January and can use its basic functions (computing, listing, and graphing equations using the *y* = function *with* a known equation and stat plots and using the data from lists students input *without* a known equation). The sponge for this class period was for students to enter their data from yesterday's investigation into a *list* on their calculators. I asked students to place each data set in a specific order so that we would all be on the same page as I checked for their comprehension. Once I concluded that everyone was ready, I plugged in my overhead calculator and walked the students through the steps for creating a graph using the stat plot function from the data they input into their lists (L1 through L6).

The students quickly seemed to pick up on the fact that all three lines not only had the same stair steps but also did not intersect. I said, "When the slope or rate of change (a fancy name for stair steps) are the same among different data sets, the lines they form in their graphs will always either *fall directly on top* of one another if they are the same line, or, like

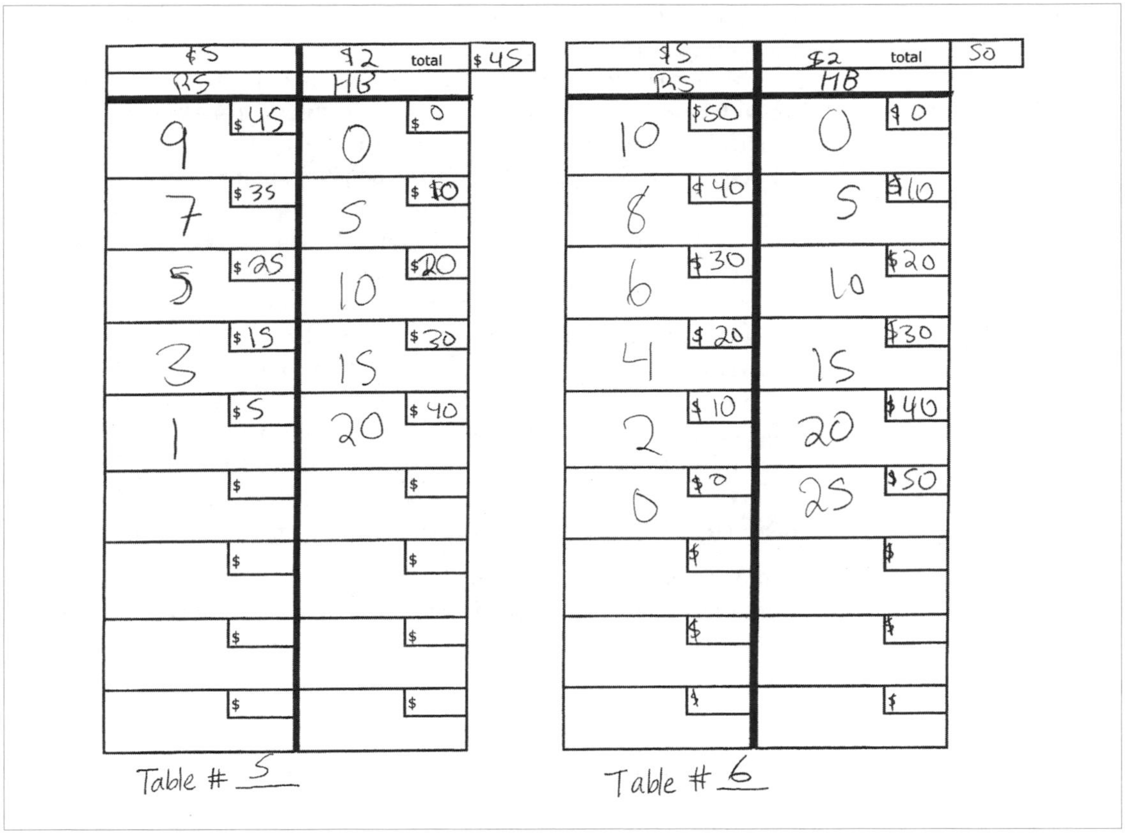

$5		$2	total	$45
RS		HB		
9	$45	0	$0	
7	$35	5	$10	
5	$25	10	$20	
3	$15	15	$30	
1	$5	20	$40	
	$		$	
	$		$	
	$		$	
	$		$	

Table # __5__

$5		$2	total	50
RS		HB		
10	$50	0	$0	
8	$40	5	$10	
6	$30	10	$20	
4	$20	15	$30	
2	$10	20	$40	
0	$0	25	$50	
	$		$	
	$		$	
	$		$	

Table # __6__

FIGURE 5.14c

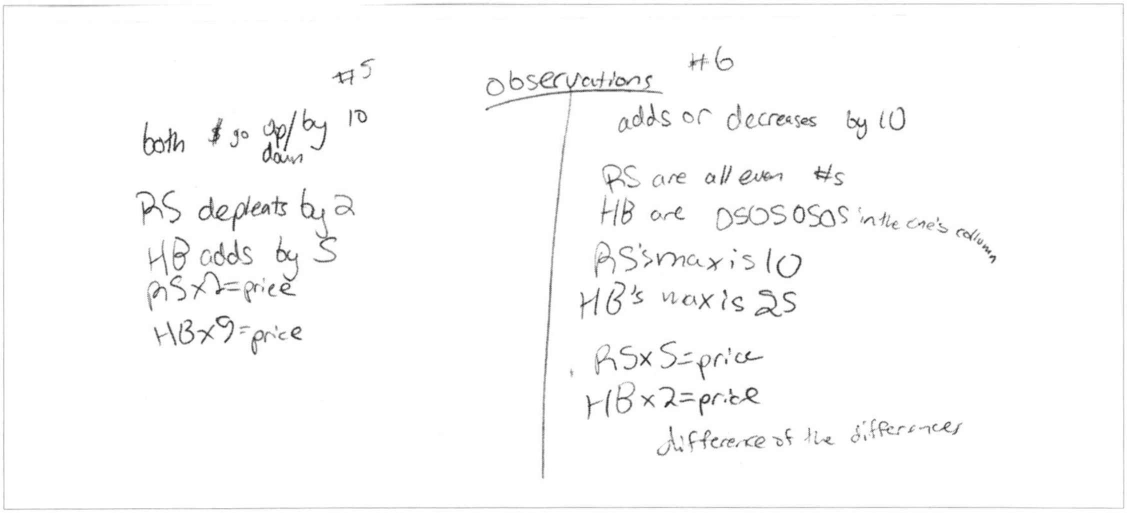

#5

both $ go up/by 10
down

RS depleats by 2
HB adds by 5
RS×2=price
HB×9=price

observations   #6

adds or decreases by 10

RS are all even #s
HB are OSOSOSOS in the one's column
RS's max is 10
HB's max is 25

RS×5=price
HB×2=price
    difference of the differences

FIGURE 5.14d

in our case, *they will never intersect.* Does anyone remember what we call lines that don't ever intersect?"

About thirteen hands (and feet!—yes, they do get *that* excited) shot up and in unison the class replied, "Parallel lines!" The students acknowledged this statement and understood that each of the three problems in Chocolate Algebra #3 had the same constant rate of change, or slope, because their chocolate prices were kept constant. This provoked me to ask, "If the candy bar prices were constant, why weren't the lines all on top of one another—what *was* different?"

One boy quickly said, "The amount of money you gave us to spend in each case." I nodded in approval and replied, "That is precisely what causes the lines not to fall right on top of one another."

Prior to moving to the next representation of the Chocolate Algebra data—equations—I wanted my students to take a step back to look at all five of their Chocolate Algebra problems and to reflect on the patterns they observed as a whole. The students began their work in small groups and I instructed them to complete the remainder for homework that night.

From Tables to Equations At our next class meeting, the students were once again greeted by me at the door, not with a slip of paper but instructions to read the sponge on the board:

> Debrief last night's homework with your group members. Don't worry about adding or subtracting any ideas, just share.

While the students were debriefing in their small groups, this gave me the perfect opportunity to rotate around the room to see what they came up with last night. I was impressed not only by their insights and observations but also by their ability to connect past math language to newly acquired math language. To me, it sounded as though a group of distinguished mathematicians were having a deep discussion about linear Diophantine equations! See Figure 5.15.

Before moving on, I did compile their responses on large chart paper in an effort to generalize the patterns they were seeing in Chocolate Algebra. The generalizations that my students were able to make were not made overnight. In fact, they were not made after just one or two class periods. For this entire activity, I spent a total of two and a half weeks on eight Chocolate Algebra investigations. Only after the first five, which took a little less than two weeks of having my students naturally go through cycles of reconceptualization (for example, going back to any of the previous investigations to establish and prove accuracy of their patterning), was I confident that every student fully understood that *how* the candy bar numbers and prices fluctuated could help them fill in any Chocolate Algebra table and how to build expressions using the total bubbles in their tables—which would eventually assist with equation building.

Name _____

All Chocolate, No Change!

Use your data to draw conclusions.

1. On the back of each of your six data tables, please record what you observe. Please feel free to draw conclusions—but use your data to support these ideas.

2. If the prices of chocolate bars are **relatively prime**, then what patterns do you observe in your tables?

   - Fluctuate by eachothers prices

   - The # of bars goes up or down by the price of the opposite bar

3. If the price of chocolate bars are **not** relatively prime, then what patterns do you observe in your tables?

   - Fluctuate by simplified ratio

4. Look at all six of your tables. Notice the "total bubbles". What do you suppose is the relationship between the numbers in the total bubbles and the prices of each chocolate bar?

   $N \times p = total$
   $N = number\ of\ bars$
   $P = price\ of\ bars$

FIGURE 5.15

Next, I wanted my students to take their data from Chocolate Algebra #1, #2, #3, #4, and #5 from a tabular representation into an equation representation. So I posed the following two questions to my class:

1. How could you create an equation for each Chocolate Algebra data set?
2. Why would you create an equation for each data set?

Before I permitted students to discuss their answers in groups, I required them to write down their answers anonymously on a small slip of paper, place them into a hat, and later pull one out randomly. As the students read the slips, I heard the following:

- Two things are always changing and because algebra has variables each problem has to have two different variables.
- The sum of both amounts, whatever they are, has got to add to be the total $ you gave us.
- (In reference to Chocolate Algebra #4): If x = #RSs, then $5x$ = amount $ spent on RSs (Teacher note: This is because for every RS purchased, this contributes to five times as much toward the total cost, a pattern

easily established by analyzing the tabular representation.) and then if y = #HBs, then $2y$ = amount $ spent on HBs—which has got to add to be the total cash. (Teacher note: This is because for every HB purchased, this contributes to twice as much toward the total cost, a pattern also easily established by analyzing the tabular representation.)

- Well, the equation gives us a general way to represent the data. We could plug and chug to check answers too.

Using the suggestions directly taken from my students, I modeled the method for creating the equation for Chocolate Algebra #1 and #2 by letting x represent the number of TRs, and y represent the number of HBs, using the total bubbles in the table to establish the total cost for each individual candy (x, one times the number of RS, = cost of RS and $2y$, two times the number of HB, = cost of HB). Then I took the sum of the candy costs, $x + 2y$ and set that equal to the total amount of money that they were supposed to spend (all chocolate, no change), which in Chocolate Algebra #1 was $x + 2y = 10$ because I had given them ten dollars to spend and in Chocolate Algebra #2 was $x + 2y = 20$ because I had given them twenty dollars to spend. I then instructed the students to generate equations for the remainder of the Chocolate Algebra problems on their own. As the class period came to a close, I pulled the large group back together and as a class we debriefed and shared the following four equations:

- Chocolate Algebra #3: $5a + b = 27$, where a = # $5 RSs and b = # $1 TRs
- Chocolate Algebra #4: $5x + 2y = 40$, where x = # $5 RSs and y = # $2 HBs
- Chocolate Algebra #5: $5x + 2y = 45$, where x = # $5 RSs and y = # $2 HBs
- Chocolate Algebra #6: $5x + 2y = 50$, where x = # $5 RSs and y = # $2 HBs

Before we parted for the day, I assigned homework that required the students to investigate and practice changing between two different forms of equations: standard form and function form.

At the beginning of the next class, I greeted the students at my door with their sponge for the day:

Put Chocolate Algebra #4, #5, and #6 equations into function form. What's similar about all three of these equations in function form? What's different?

As I circulated through the class, I noticed that most of my students had a good understanding of what function form was and the procedure to follow to convert an equation from standard form into function form. Most students also quickly saw that the numbers next to their x variables were all the same, but the numbers without an x variable were the only ones to differ for each equation. I was impressed, but still hoped that another connection would have been made.

Incorporating the "Fancy" Algebra Language   When a connection wasn't made, I prompted the class with the following question, "How can you 'see' the stair steps, or as we now call it, the slope, in each of your equations?" A dozen hands went up. One boy said, "The steps are the numbers right before the *x* variable! And this is true for all six Chocolate Algebras! I just checked."

"Well, we better check to verify this interesting conclusion," I said. Sure enough, he was right! I instructed the students to take Chocolate Algebra problems #4, #5, and #6 and let *x* = 0 and solve for *y* in each of those cases. The fancy name I gave this term was the *y*-intercept. Without too much detail, I told students that this is the point where our line crosses the *x*-axis. Of course, because I always demand verification, they too were suspicious and checked their graphs to make sure I was right. When students search for evidence themselves, they construct their own knowledge and not just receive whatever I decide to teach them.

After they verified the *y*-intercept on their graphs, one girl asked, "Well, if there's such a thing as a *y*-intercept, is there such a thing as an *x*-intercept where line crosses the *y*-axis?"

I responded, "Well, let's investigate in a similar manner, except this time, let *y* = 0 and solve for *x* in each of those cases. What do does everyone observe?" I gave them several minutes to perform their calculations and sure enough, not only did they agree upon the existence of an *x*-intercept, but they also verified it on their graphs.

Next, I threw my students another question for them to ponder over the evening: "What do the *x*- and *y*-intercepts mean in terms of the data in the Chocolate Algebra problems?" Students were eager to share answers, such as, "In number four, when RS = 0 and HB = 20, you know that's the *y*-intercept not only from the table, but just look at that point on the graph—it's on the *y*-axis, where the *x*-coordinate is always zero."

Another student chimed in, "Yeah and same problem, when RS = 8 and HB = 0, it's the *x*-intercept because the *y* value, the number of HBs, is zero in the ordered pair and on the graph." As another milestone had been reached in the Chocolate Algebra investigation, one girl asked an insightful question: "If two points determine a line, like from geometry, then can we just find the *x*- and *y*-intercepts in our tables to make the graphs even faster?"

I responded, "Yes, most definitely; however, I would caution you to not get in the habit of only using *x*- and *y*-intercepts to graph because not all lines have *x*- and *y*-intercepts." I then proceeded to show students several examples involving horizontal and vertical lines and Chocolate Algebra #3, which did not have a whole-number *x*-intercept, $5a + b = 27$.

Chocolate Algebra #7 and #8

Later in the day, I presented my students with their final two Chocolate Algebra problems, #7 and #8.

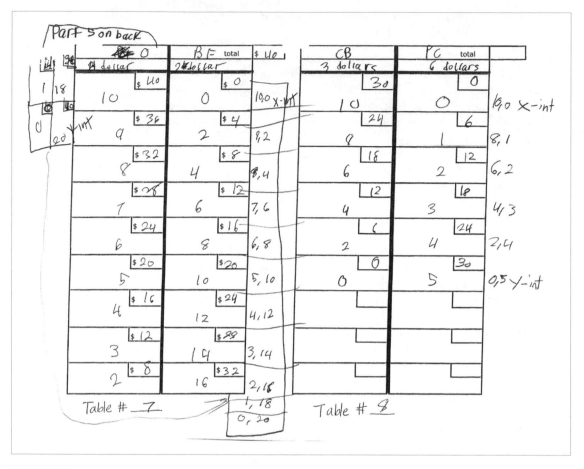

FIGURE 5.16

Chocolate Algebra #7 $4x + 2y = 40$
Chocolate Algebra #8 $3x + 6y = 30$

What was different about #7 and #8 was not only the type of chocolate used—Butterfingers (Bs) and Oreos (Os) for #7 and Crunch Bars (CBs) and Peanut Butter Cups (PBs) for #8—but this time I prompted them with specific questions about the equations and intercepts. See Figure 5.16.

The students used the remainder of the class period to work on the new Chocolate Algebra problems and I instructed them to finish any leftovers for homework that night.

During our next class, after we debriefed Chocolate Algebra #7 and #8, the last task for the students to complete was to neatly organize all of their compiled Chocolate Algebra data that had accumulated inside their group folders. In addition to giving students specific organization instructions to demonstrate their newly pulled-together, or synthesized, understanding of linear modeling, I had each of them respond to the following prompt:

After completing eight Chocolate Algebra investigations, I learned
THAT . . .

I reminded them that it was very important that they not leave out
the word *THAT* in their responses because doing so would not enable
them to fully express their new found understandings and appreciations
of linear modeling. As a result, I did receive rather detailed and insightful
responses. See Figure 5.17.

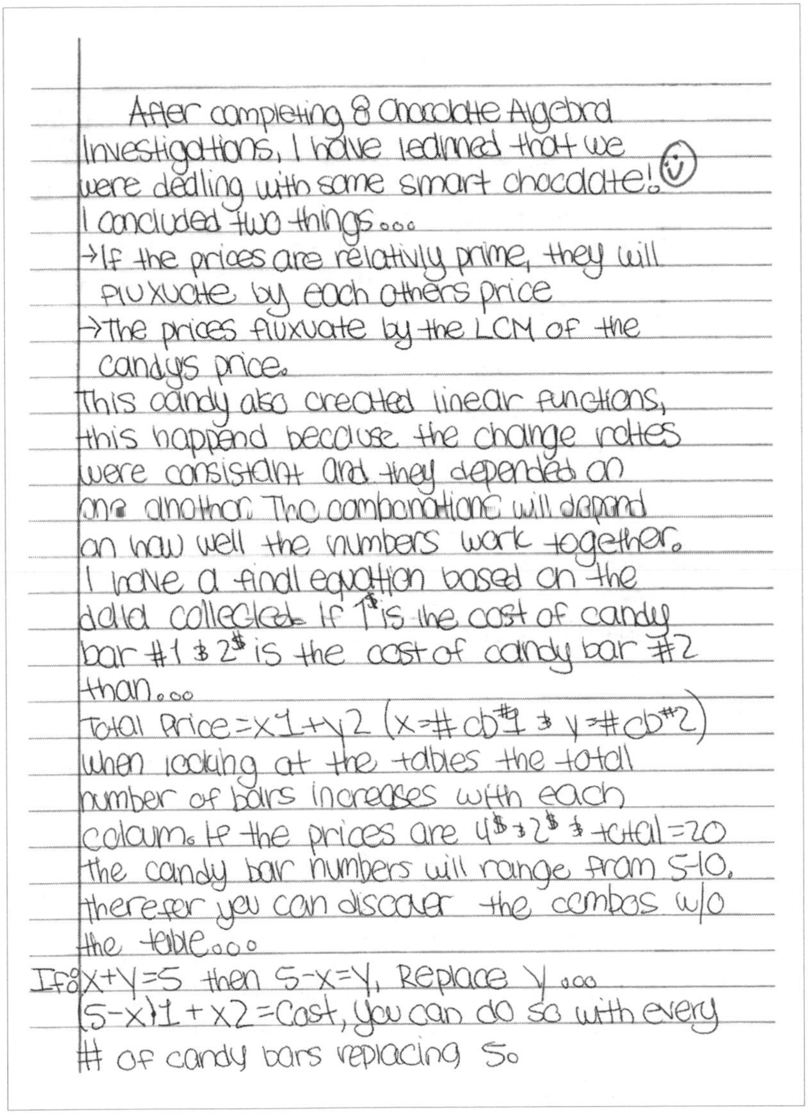

After completing 8 Chocolate Algebra
Investigations, I have learned that we
were dealing with some smart chocolate! ☺
I concluded two things...
→ If the prices are relatively prime, they will
   fluxuate by each others price
→ The prices fluxuate by the LCM of the
   candys price.
This candy also created linear functions,
this happend because the change rates
were consistant and they depended on
one another. The combonations will depend
on how well the numbers work together.
I have a final equation based on the
data collected. If 1$ is the cost of candy
bar #1 & 2$ is the cost of candy bar #2
than...
Total Price = x1 + y2 (x = # ob#1 & y = # cb#2)
When looking at the tables the total
number of bars increases with each
coloum. If the prices are 4$ & 2$ & total = 20
the candy bar numbers will range from 5-10.
therefor you can discover the combos w/o
the table...
If x + y = 5 then 5 - x = y, Replace y...
(5 - x)1 + x2 = Cost, you can do so with every
# of candy bars replacing 5.

FIGURE 5.17

Chocolate and Algebra: A Mathematically Rich Relationship

Anyone who tries the Chocolate Algebra investigation will agree that the "depth of understanding of the concepts and their interconnectedness is astonishing" (Hyde 2006). My discussion of how this activity played out in my classroom only scratched the surface. The fluency with the new and old mathematical language and the confidence that my students spoke with can be largely attributed to the consistency within the multiple representations and the highly attractive context of chocolate and money. Each representation was clear and "directly linked to the real-life situation from which it sprang" (Hyde 2006). Also, because each representation was deeply connected to other representations within the Chocolate Algebra investigation, each new step in the linear modeling content was "built on a solid foundation and properly scaffolded" (Hyde 2006) by using a variety of manipulatives and questioning techniques that allowed my students to think about their understanding in a way that naturally enabled them to synthesize or pull it all together.

Where to next? Before I moved linear functions into strictly naked numbers and letters, I had my students work with linear function problems (My Old Kentucky Furniture Store and the Ballad of Buttons and Sleeves) in a variety of contexts, each with a similar mathematical structure.

My Old Kentucky Furniture Store

My students had previously completed a two-and-a-half-week investigation of Chocolate Algebra and had built a stable framework of linear modeling in the form of analyzing and making predictions with linear graphs, tables, and equations.

Day 1   As students entered the classroom, I handed them a small printout that contained their daily opening activity (or "sponge," as I call it) for the first five minutes of class:

> What are the three major representations of linear models that we used in Chocolate Algebra? How are they useful? Begin with a KWC.

Several moments passed and as the bell rang I noticed that most of my students were quickly writing down or roughly sketching pictures of tables, graphs, and functions. When the five minutes were up, I opened a whole-class discussion about their responses. As I predicted, most of the students suggested tables, graphs, and equations, but what was most interesting were their responses to the second question. One girl said, "Tables, graphs, and equations all represent the same relationship, they are just different pictures of the same data." Another boy stated, "I liked the tables the best for figuring out the patterns and equations, but I liked the graphs the best for making predictions." A short debate ensued about the best representation used in our Chocolate Algebra investigation.

Knowing my very real time constraints, I interrupted to announce that they would not have to make a decision over which representation was best because each situation that required analysis of the data presented might beg for a different representation—it all depended on the situation. I further calmed my students' unsettled opinions by stating that their choice in representation often varied and their ability to create and work flexibly with multiple representations would enable them to make informed decisions about which representation would be the best in a variety of contexts. This was a great segue into the first day of our dresser drawers investigation, an activity that provided a new context for the same concepts studied in Chocolate Algebra.

I organized the students into six small groups of four students each and then handed out the following My Old Kentucky Furniture Store problem on a sheet of paper to each group:

A small furniture store is about to close and the owners think they have enough wood to make many more dressers. However, they are bit a concerned that they have only a limited number of antique brass handles and knobs. Their model of the big dresser always has 8 large brass handles and 4 small brass knobs. Their model of the small dresser always has 4 large brass handles and 6 small brass knobs. After taking inventory the owner found they had 120 large brass handles and 132 small brass knobs. To use up all of their brass, how many dressers of each type should they make? Begin with a KWC.

After students shared their responses to the KWC (see Figure 5.18), I prompted them with the following question: "How would you set up a table to collect data?" This question was important for several reasons. First, I knew that once they figured out how the table should be organized, they could access their prior knowledge and use their patterning and insight to quickly complete the table. Second, because this problem involved two different variables, each with two different constraints—which added another dimension to the linear combinations problem-solving process—I knew it would be an excellent opportunity for them to construct the table themselves based on the information they had. I would argue that there have been many times that just setting up the table itself to organize data can be a daunting task, which is precisely why I did not want to rob my students of this authentic learning opportunity to use their KWCs by giving them a teacher-created table.

Immediately, hands shot up to answer my prompt. One girl stated, "Well we don't know how many dressers of each type we have total, because that's what we are trying to find out. This thing that we don't know

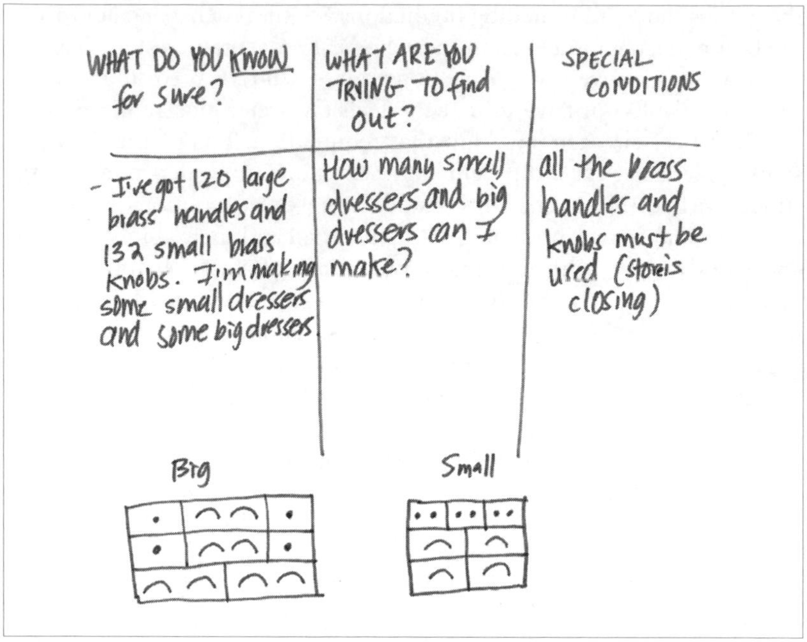

FIGURE 5.18

[the number of each type of dresser] is our variable and that means it's like the number of candy bars that changed a lot in chocolate algebra."

I knew she was on to something, but I demanded more: "What do you mean that it's like the number of candy bars?"

Another student interrupted, "We're gonna pick values of big dressers (B) and small dressers (S) and play around with their number of large brass handles and small brass knobs."

I responded, "This seems like a little more going here than what we did in chocolate algebra." The students agreed, but before I gave in to the desire to just give them the table with the proper headings, I decided to let them work in small groups for about five minutes to generate an effective way to organize their data.

To my surprise, several students dissected the problem deeply and created four individual tables. I asked them how would they ensure that the large brass handles always totaled 120 and the small brass knobs always totaled 132; the students responded that they would just keep totaling the B large brass handles and the S large brass handles to make sure they were 120 and then total the B small brass knobs and S small brass knobs to make sure they were 132. I nodded in approval, but I wanted to simplify this task for them. I positively acknowledged their insight and willingness to work, but I also asked if there was any way to condense the four tables into two. One student spoke up, "Yeah, just a table for large brass handles with Bs and Ss that always gotta equal one twenty, and then another table for small brass knobs with Bs and Ss too that always gotta equal one thirty-two." I agreed and I could tell that the students also thought their classmate's suggestion would be much more time effective.

Once the students had worked through and understood *how* to set up the tables, I gave them a blank template with the following headings:

LARGE BRASS HANDLES			120		SMALL BRASS KNOBS			132	
Big Dresser (B)	8	Small Dresser (S)	4		Big Dresser (B)	4	Small Dresser (S)	6	

The tables were equipped with empty total bubbles for students to fill in using what they read from the original problem. Because these students had successfully worked through two weeks of Chocolate Algebra, they were ready to work with the empty total bubbles. As I circulated, I noticed that many students quickly recognized the similar mathematical structure in this problem as they had seen in Chocolate Algebra. This was especially key for me to see and hear them make this math-to-math connection because the connection enabled them to use shortcuts while completing the tables. See Figure 5.19.

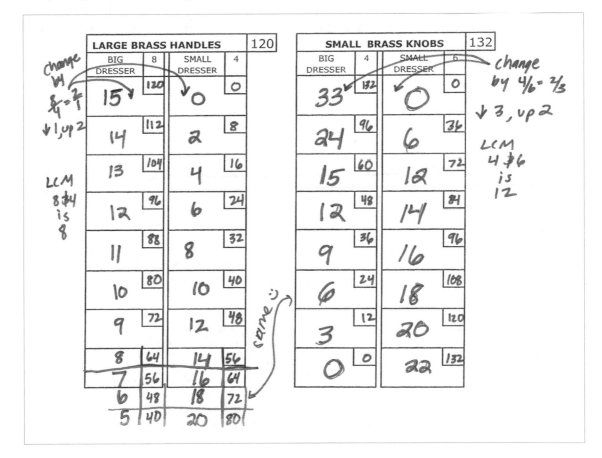

FIGURE 5.19

One of the first shortcuts I overheard a group mentioning was that the number of large brass handles for Bs (8 and 4) and Ss (4 and 6) were not relatively prime.

Acknowledging that they were not relatively prime enabled most groups to quickly conclude that the table for large brass handles would fluctuate by the simplified ratio (2 to 1). One girl was so excited about her revelation that when she proudly announced to her group that the large brass handles would fluctuate down by 1, up by 2, she bounced out of her chair and ran up to the board where she sketched a picture of what the graph would look like where the rate of change was a constant 2-by-1 fluctuation. The stair-like steps that she drew on the board enabled some of the students who hadn't readily connected the mathematical structure of this problem to Chocolate Algebra to see in picture form that this data would also make a picture whose graph is a straight line. For these students, the graphical representation of the same data, regardless of how roughly sketched, enabled them to make the math-to-math connection I was striving for.

Another shortcut that I observed, and had *not* planned for, was that many students remembered their discovery from Chocolate Algebra that related the top numbers and the total bubbles. One small group pointed out that in Chocolate Algebra the total bubbles would always fluctuate by the lcm of the number pairs. And so, their classmates were able to generate quickly the lengthy table by activating their prior knowledge from the Chocolate Algebra investigation.

Day 2   At the beginning of the second day of the dresser drawer investigation, my students received another sponge as they arrived to class:

> Look at the tables you finished yesterday. Why are there two tables in this investigation and only one table in Chocolate Algebra? I thought they were the *same!*

As the first five minutes of class concluded, I initiated a large-group discussion framed around the day's sponge. I generated a list of students' responses on large paper and planned to save it because I knew in the near future we'd be continuing to investigate linear models in yet another context, adding a few new concepts, and I wanted to be able to refer back to these valuable math-to-math connections I knew my students were making.

The sponge was another opportunity for my students to take a step back to analyze the mathematical structure of linear modeling in tabular representations without being confined to one specific context. They were able to solidify a more global interpretation and understanding of the multiple representations in multiple contexts, which is usually the *only* perspective that their textbook provides.

As the students checked their tables and graphs that they had completed for homework after the first day of My Old Kentucky Furniture Store, I overheard one student state, "On my graphs, the two lines intersect, but how do I *see* that in my tables?" The moment I heard that question, my heart fluttered and I paused all group work to allow the student and her group to ask their question out loud.

Initially, there was a silence in the classroom—a processing silence. After a few moments of paper shuffling, several hands shot up, including my usually quiet student who loves to teach or show his classmates the patterns when others don't get it right away. This student proceeded to take his paper up to the document camera (after I nodded in approval) and show the class what the intersection point meant on the graph and how it was possible to find it in the tables. I was so impressed not only by this student's explanation and demonstration but also by his ability to use the language of linear modeling *without* explicitly giving the answer to the class—I knew secretly that he loved his time playing teacher.

As the groups enthusiastically worked on the reflection questions (see Figure 5.20a) with their new level of understanding this linear modeling problem, I noticed that there was enough time for debriefing. See Figures 5.20b and 5.20c for student answers.

My Old Kentucky Furniture Store Reflection

1. In what ways was this investigation similar to Chocolate Algebra?
2. In what ways was this investigation different from Chocolate Algebra?
3. Look at the table for large brass handles. What did each of the total bubbles represent?
4. Did you notice any patterns in the total bubbles for the large brass handles table?
5. Explain how the number of large brass handles for big dressers and small dressers fluctuated (changed). Does this have anything to do with the 8 large brass handles for big dressers and 4 large brass handles for small dressers (the numbers 8 and 4) not being relatively prime? Why or why not?
6. Look at the table for small brass knobs. What did each of the total bubbles represent?
7. Did you notice any patterns in the total bubbles for the small brass knobs table?
8. Explain how the number of small brass knobs for big dressers and small dressers fluctuated (changed). Does this have anything to do with the 4 small brass knobs for big dressers and 6 small brass knobs for small dressers (the numbers 4 and 6) not being relatively prime? Why or why not?
9. Generate a rule that represents 120 total large brass handles, assuming I have x number of Bs and y number of Ss.

FIGURE 5.20a

10. Generate a rule that represents 132 total small brass knobs, assuming I have *x* number of Bs and *y* number of Ss.

11. Notice you have two different equations—one for large brass handles and one for small brass knobs, each of which both have *x* number of Bs and *y* number of Ss. We don't yet have the ability to solve for two variables at the same time, *however,* take a look at both of your tables. Find a common solution in both of the tables. What is this solution?

12. Plug in these values *x* number of Bs and *y* number of Ss first into the equation you generated for question 9. Does it make a true statement? How do you know?

13. Now plug in these values *x* number of Bs and *y* number of Ss first into the equation you generated for question 10. Does it make a true statement? How do you know?

14. So what's the answer? How many big dressers can the store make? How many small dressers can the store make? How do you know? Be *specific!*

FIGURE 5.20a *continued*

1. Chocolate Algebra & Dresser Drawers were similar, because the observations both fluctuated by the LCM. (for the total bubbles) and # each dresser type changed by constant ratio.

2. They were dressers. — and there were 2 different tables, one for large brass handles and one for small brass knobs.

3. they represented the total)

4. Yeah B's ↓ by 1 and S's ↑ by 2.

5. They fluctuated by LCM of the 2 #'s. They fluctuated by simp. fraction 8/4 = 2/1.

6. They represented the total.

7. Yeah B's ↓ by 3 and S's ↑ by 2.

FIGURE 5.20b

In our debriefing, we again discussed the many similarities and differences between this activity and Chocolate Algebra and how acknowledging this enabled them to problem solve with confidence. It was clear to me from the reflections submitted in class the next day that the students had developed an understanding of the mathematical structure of linear modeling in multiple representations, under the guise of multiple contexts.

Chocolate Algebra. Dresser Drawers. What linear modeling context could possibly be next? Psychedelic Buttons, of course! What materials do your students need for this strange, but similarly structured math problem? Why, we needed lots of chart paper for tables and samples of men's shirts to look at.

8. They fluctuated by LCM of the 2 #s. They fluctuated by simp. fraction 4/6 = 2/3.

9. $8x + 4y = 120$

10. $4x + 6y = 132$

11. $x = 6$ Big Dressers $y = 18$ small dressers

12. $8(6) + 4(18) = 120$
    $48 + 72 = 120$ ✓

13. $4(6) + 6(18) = 132$
    $24 + 108 = 132$ ✓

14. like #11
    6 Big Dressers ⇒ on data table, these are the only #s that are exactly the same!!!
    18 small Dressers
    Also on graph, this point in both lines (where they meet)

FIGURE 5.20c

The Ballad of Buttons and Sleeves

I typically have my students do the Ballad of Buttons and Sleeves investigation after they have had practice working with problems that have similar mathematical structures, which not only enables them to think increasingly more abstractly using more abstract representations but also allows them to take strategies—such as shortcuts to completing a table and identifying what it means to find a "common solution" among tables—and apply them in new contexts with ease.

The Ballad of Buttons and Sleeves

A mom-and-pop variety store sells psychedelic dress shirts (either long- or short-sleeved) from the 1960s onto which they sew mood-sensitive buttons (either large or small). Consider:

- Long sleeve shirts require 13 large buttons and 6 small ones. Large buttons are 7 up the front, 2 on each sleeve, and 2 sewn at the bottom for spares. The small buttons are 2 for the button collars, 1 on each sleeve, and 2 spares.
- Short sleeve shirts have only 7 larger buttons up the front and 2 small buttons for the collar.

Mom and Pop have a limited inventory after 40 years: only 235 large buttons and 90 small buttons and fewer than 20 of each kind of shirt. How can they use all of the buttons to make long-sleeved shirts and short-sleeved shirts? Begin with a KWC.

The first thing I had my students do was visualize these crazy shirts. There was a lot of information for them to digest. Before they proceeded to sink their teeth into this problem I wanted them to draw a picture of what they thought the shirts looked like. I did not have the luxury of owning such apparel, so to help my students sketch their pictures, I brought in a few of my husband's work shirts. See Figure 5.21. My students completed a KWC while reading through the problem in small groups. See Figure 5.22.

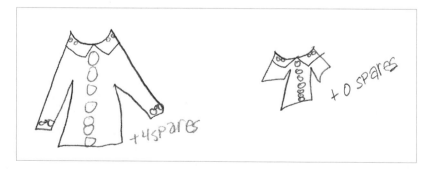

FIGURE 5.21

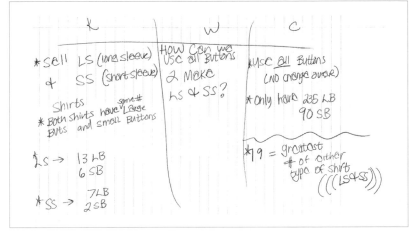

FIGURE 5.22

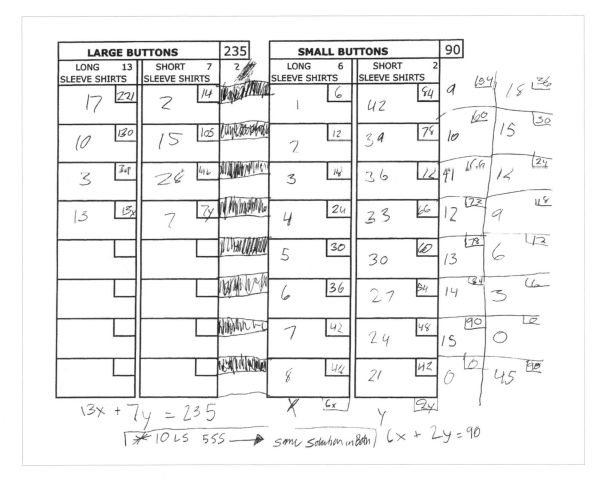

FIGURE 5.23

What was most interesting about the Ballad of Buttons and Sleeves problem was not only how extensive my students' KWCs were but also how students were able to use their prior knowledge of linear modeling, built from prior activities, to complete the table with ease. See Figure 5.23. Finally, I asked students to write a rule for each type of button and identify how it could be a solution to the problem. In our linear modeling activities, my students had exceeded my expectations.

FINITE DIFFERENCES: QUADRATIC, CUBIC, AND BEYOND

Finite differences is a powerful technique for analyzing functions to:

1. determine if the functions are based on polynomials; there are many functions that are not polynomial (for example, exponential $y = 2^x$);

2. determine what degree is involved if the function is polynomial (for example, *linear* functions are based on first-degree exponents, not higher than 1: $y = ax + b$; *quadratic* functions are based on second-degree exponents: $y = ax^2 + bx + c$; *cubic* functions are based on third-degree exponents: $y = ax^3 + bx^2 + cx + d$); and

3. create an equation that models the data using the proper degree, which involves a series of calculations (thanks to hand-held calculators, much of the tedium surrounding the calculations is removed).

Although the topic of finite differences is often found as only a page or two in an Algebra II textbook, to me the technique is a logical follow-up to Chocolate Algebra with students who are strong in eighth-grade algebra. In fact, some of what we did in Chocolate Algebra in the previous section is very similar.

It's important for teachers to assess their students' prior knowledge to determine readiness and understanding for finite differences—we don't want students to merely memorize the procedures. For example, in the Chocolate Algebra problem, when Susan's students had a $5 chocolate bar and a $2 chocolate bar and $40 to spend, they created a table that revealed five points with values that lay on a straight line when graphed. See Figure 5.24.

$5	$2
8	0
6	5
4	10
2	15
0	20

FIGURE 5.24

After creating the table, students looked for a pattern in the data and saw that one side went down and the other side went up. They calculated this pattern as *down by 2, up by 5*. Formally, students analyzed the difference in the $5 item (the x values) to see if it was constant through the column. It was, so we will call this difference "delta x" (symbolically, Δx). Similarly, we will call change in the $2 items (the y values) the first difference of y or just Δy. Figure 5.25 shows that these differences are down by 2 (–2) and up by 5 (+5). Because these two values are constant, their rate of change is constant. We know this must be a linear function and that $\Delta y / \Delta x$ is the slope of the line:

$$5x + 2y = 40$$
$$2y = -5x + 40$$
$$y = (-5/2)\, x + 20$$

Total $40			
Difference			**Difference**
	$5 item	$2 item	
–2	8	0	5
–2	6	5	5
–2	4	10	5
–2	2	15	5
	0	20	

FIGURE 5.25

In situations where $\Delta x = 1$ (for example, the x variable is time and you check the change in the y variable every hour), if Δy is constant, then Δy is the slope because $\Delta y / \Delta x = \Delta y / 1 = \Delta y$. It is a constant rate. How many bottles of Ginkojinkoba can the robotic assembly line fill per hour? It doesn't get tired; it runs at the same rate every hour.

Quadratic Equations

Next we move to quadratic equations using a version of the handshake problem.

High Fives All Around

The five starting players on the basketball team come out to center court one at a time as they are announced over the loudspeaker before the game begins. As each player comes out he high-fives (kind of like a handshake) each player who is already there. What are the number of high fives at the beginning of a game?

It's helpful for students to act out the problem and look for patterns. There is an obvious pattern that each successive player will high-five one more person than the player who came out just before him. The students' next step is to create a data table. See Figure 5.26.

Player	Cumulative High Fives
1	0
2	1
3	3
4	6
5	10

FIGURE 5.26

Obviously, $\Delta x = 1$ but Δy is not as easy to discern. Students must fill out the table to find the first difference for y. To do this they need to think about these questions:

- How do you get from 0 to 1?
- How do you get from 1 to 3?
- How do you get from 3 to 6?
- How do you get from 6 to 10?

See Figure 5.27.

Player	Cumulative High Fives	$\Delta 1$
1	0	1
2	1	2
3	3	3
4	6	4
5	10	

FIGURE 5.27

The students can see a pattern now and it makes sense, but they are not finished because the numbers in $\Delta 1$ are not constant. It is not a linear relationship. They must look at the second difference, the difference between connective data in the first column. See Figure 5.28.

Player	Cumulative High Fives	Δ1	Δ2
1	0	1	1
2	1	2	1
3	3	3	1
4	6	4	
5	10		

FIGURE 5.28

Now everyone can see the constant difference in Δ2, which means the function is *quadratic*. How do we figure out what that quadratic equation is? We take the function form of a quadratic $y = ax^2 + bx + c$, we use it to develop a general procedure that will always work, and we substitute consecutive values of x. See Figure 5.29.

Quadratic Equation	$y = ax^2 + bx + c$
x	y
0	c
1	$a + b + c$
2	$4a + 2b + c$
3	$9a + 3b + c$
4	$16a + 4b + c$

FIGURE 5.29

- Substituting 0 for x into the equation $y = ax^2 + bx + c$ shows that when $x = 0$, $y = c$;
- Substituting 1 for x into the equation $y = ax^2 + bx + c$ shows that when $x = 1$, $y = a + b + c$;
- And so forth, when $x = 2$, $y = 4a + 2b + c$; when $x = 3$, $y = 9a + 3b + c$; when $x = 4$, $y = 16a + 4b + c$.

See Figure 5.30.

Quadratic	Equation		
x	y	$\Delta 1$	$\Delta 2$
0	c	$a + b$	$2a$
1	$a + b + c$	$3a + b$	$2a$
2	$4a + 2b + c$	$5a + b$	$2a$
3	$9a + 3b + c$	$7a + b$	
4	$16a + 4b + c$		

FIGURE 5.30

When students are ready to expand the table to derive the values of the first difference, all we need to do is ask, "What would you have to combine with c to get $a + b + c$? Or, what is the difference between c and $a + b + c$?" Students would continue finding the first difference because they will need at least five examples to get three constant differences, assuming they're dealing with a quadratic.

Next, we derive the second difference in the same manner:

- When x is 0, then the value of y is equal to c.
- The constant second difference is equal to $2a$.
- When x is 0, then the value of $\Delta 1$ is equal to $a + b$.

For our High Fives All Around problem, students must take the table shown in Figure 5.28 and fill in the row when $x = 0$. See Figure 5.31.

Player	Cumulative High Fives	$\Delta 1$	$\Delta 2$
0	0	0	1 $\Leftarrow$
1	0	1	1
2	1	2	1
3	3	3	1
4	6	4	
5	10		

FIGURE 5.31

They start by filling in the constant second difference, which is 1. Working from right to left they determine what numbers must be in each cell in row 0 that fit with what is already in row 1. In this case we get only zeroes. Therefore, $c = 0$, $2a = 1$, and $a = \frac{1}{2}$; $a + b = 0$, $\frac{1}{2} + b = 0$, $b = -\frac{1}{2}$. The equation $y = ax^2 + bx + c$ becomes $y = \frac{1}{2}x^2 - \frac{1}{2}x + 0$, $y = \frac{1}{2}x(x - 1)$, or $y = x(x - 1)/2$.

Students can check the accuracy of $y = x(x - 1)/2$ by trying the following extension problem:

The Supremes

When the nine U.S. Supreme Court Justices meet for a session, each justice shakes the hand of all eight other justices. How many handshakes take place?

Students need to think through the mathematical structure of this problem in order to determine if the structure is the same as that in the High Fives All Around problem. For instance, nine baseball players who are the starting lineup for their team could shake hands with the opposing team's starting nine players, which would be a different structure.

Using the equation $y = x(x - 1)/2$ students would predict $y = 9 * 8/2 = 36$. Thirty-six handshakes by the nine "Supremes." Does the tabular solution agree? See Figure 5.32.

# of Justices	Cumulative Handshakes	Δ1	Δ2
1	0	1	1
2	1	2	1
3	3	3	1
4	6	4	1
5	10	5	1
6	15	6	1
7	21	7	1
8	28	8	
9	36		

FIGURE 5.32

Yes, it does. Students might recognize the triangle numbers 1, 3, 6, 10, 15, 21. . . .

Next, students work on a problem with seemingly similar mathematical structure in order to see how slight differences in tabular entries can amount to significant changes in graphical representations:

Stacking Boxes

The manager of the supermarket tells his ace stock boy, Rupert, to make a display for the new breakfast cereal, Crunchy Jalapenos. He wants the display to be about 7 feet tall and the boxes are about 10 inches tall. He wants the display to be triangular (see below). He figures Rupert will make 9 rows. How many cereal boxes will he need and how many would he start with on the bottom row?

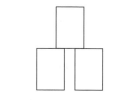

When the students create the table for the above problem, they get a slightly different table from the Supremes problem table. See Figure 5.33.

Rows	Cumulative Boxes	Δ1	Δ2
0	0	1	1
1	1	2	1
2	3	3	1
3	6	4	1
4	10	5	1
5	15	6	1
6	21	7	1
7	28	8	1
8	36	9	
9	45		

FIGURE 5.33

The difference is the first justice who enters the courtroom with no one there yet to shake his hand. Therefore $y = 0$ in row 1. But in the stack of boxes, the first (top) row has 1 box, so $y = 1$ in row 1. Using the finite difference values as before, students fill in row 0; they get: $c = 0$, $2a = 1$, $a = \frac{1}{2}$, and $a + b = 1$, therefore $b = \frac{1}{2}$. The equation for this problem becomes $y = \frac{1}{2}x^2 + \frac{1}{2}x = \frac{1}{2}x(x + 1) = x(x + 1)/2$, which differs from the equation in the Supremes problem by just one little sign that makes a big difference!

Some teachers may decide to ask students to progress their data from a tabular representation into a graphical representation. There are several routes to go here. Students could graph the data they collected; however, the concern would be that they would only see a portion of the graph and possibly assume that a quadratic equation creates a half *U* shape, similar to exponential equations.

Students could also play with the zoom function on their graphing calculators to see the whole graph. The advantages of this are that students can see what a typical quadratic equation looks like when graphed and they can understand which values on the graph are meaningful and work realistically with respect to the *context* of the problem and which values on the graph only work mathematically. This creates a great opportunity for teachers to discuss with students why endpoints are necessary on some graphs.

Finally, students could use paper and pencil and graphing calculators with adjusted windows (or one of the dozens of free graphing calculators online) to look at individual pieces in quadrants I and II and explain what is happening in each picture. This helps students really see how one little sign can make such a big difference. See Figures 5.34 and 5.35.

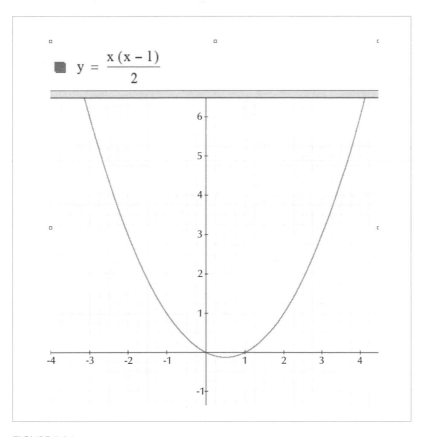

FIGURE 5.34

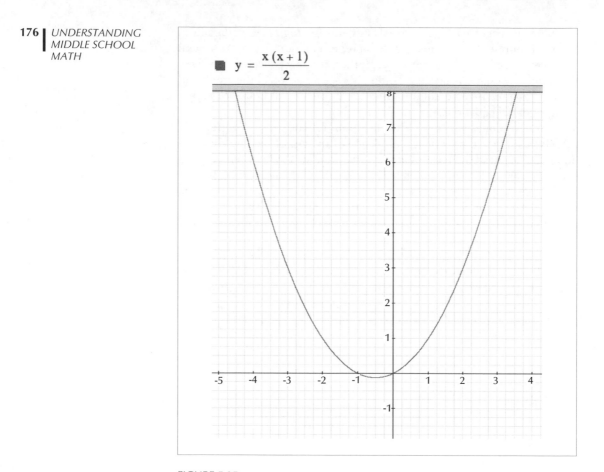

$$y = \frac{x(x+1)}{2}$$

FIGURE 5.35

Cubic Equations

Next, we follow the same line of reasoning with cubic equations. Figure 5.36 shows the cubic equation:

CUBIC EQUATION	$y = ax^3 + bx^2 + cx + d$
x	y
0	d
1	$a + b + c + d$
2	$8a + 4b + 2c + d$
3	$27a + 9b + 3c + d$
4	$64a + 16b + 4c + d$
5	$125a + 25b + 5c + d$

FIGURE 5.36

We can see what values of y are created when values for x are 0–5. See Figure 5.37.

CUBIC EQUATION	$y = ax^3 + bx^2 + cx + d$			
x	y	$\Delta 1$	$\Delta 2$	$\Delta 3$
0	d	$a + b + c$	$6a + 2b$	$6a$
1	$a + b + c + d$	$7a + 3b + c$	$12a + 2b$	$6a$
2	$8a + 4b + 2c + d$	$19a + 5b + c$	$18a + 2b$	$6a$
3	$27a + 9b + 3c + d$	$37a + 7b + c$	$24a + 2b$	
4	$64a + 16b + 4c + d$	$61a + 9b + c$		
5	$125a + 25b + 5c + d$			

FIGURE 5.37

From Figure 5.37 one can see how row 0 is created:

When x is 0, then the value of y is equal to d.
The constant third difference is equal to $6a$.
When x is 0, then the value of $\Delta 1$ is equal to $a + b + c$.
When x is 0, then the value of $\Delta 2$ is equal to $6a + 2b$.

Let's try it on a problem:

The Fold-Up Boxes

For Arts and Crafts some students are going to make boxes to hold 1-inch cubes of chocolate. The teacher has given them some thick and colorful 15-by-15-inch sheets of paper. To make a box for the chocolate, students must cut 1 square out of each corner:

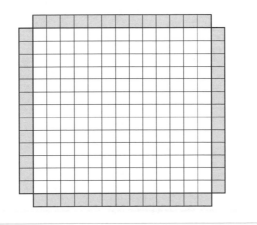

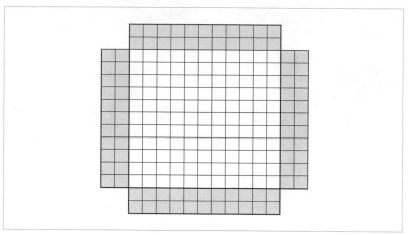

FIGURE 5.38

One square in each corner is cut out to allow the four sides to be folded up to make a box with a 13-by-13-inch base, a 1-inch height, and capacity to hold 169 1-inch cubes of chocolate. (The box on page 177 does not have a lid, although it would probably *make* a good one.)

A 2-by-2-inch square cut from a 15-by-15-inch sheet of paper produces an 11-by-11-inch base with 2 layers (a capacity of 242 cubes or cubic inches). See Figure 5.38.

If we continued cutting a square from each corner in this manner, 3-by-3, 4-by-4, etc., which box would hold the most chocolate cubes? The students' work on the data table produced some surprises. See Figure 5.39.

Square corner	Volume	Δ1	Δ2	Δ3
0	0	169	−96	24
1	169	73	−72	24
2	242	1	−48	24
3	243	−47	−24	24
4	196	−71	0	24
5	125	−71	+24	
6	54	−47		
7	7			

FIGURE 5.39

Students are always surprised when the volume goes up and then down. It looks like cutting a square of 3 inches will give the largest volume, 243 cubic inches, but the problem doesn't necessarily require that the square be a whole number. Maybe there is a value just above or just below 243 that will yield a greater volume. As much as I love tables, if we stay with integral values for x, we may miss the maximum volume (value of y). So let's find the general formula:

1. Looking at the differences, neither $\Delta 1$ nor $\Delta 2$ is constant. However, the third difference ($\Delta 3$) is constant. Therefore, the equation is cubic, which makes sense because the Fold-Up Boxes problem is about volume.
2. From the 0 rows in Figure 5.39 above, we can see that the constant third difference of $24 = 6a$.
3. Then $a = 4$, $6a + 2b = -96$, $24 + 2b = -96$, $2b = -120$, $b = -60$, $a + b + c = 169$, $4 - 60 + c = 169$, $c = 225$, and $d = 0$.
4. Therefore the equation for a 15-inch square is $y = 4x^3 - 60x^2 + 225x$.

Students can now enter the equation $y = 4x^3 - 60x^2 + 225x$ into their graphing calculators and set the increase on the x variable to .1 so that they can find the maximum y value. When they do, they'll then find that at $x = 2.5$, $y = 250$.

Some teachers may decide to go even further by having their students play around with the graphing function on their calculators. Again, there are several routes to take. Students could graph the data they've collected; however, the concern would be that they would see only a portion of the graph and possibly assume that a cubic equation creates a parabola, similar to quadratic equations. See Figure 5.40 for a spreadsheet program showing a virtual plateau between 242 and 243, where students could easily assume a cubic looked like a quadratic.

See Figure 5.41 for a graph of the function for quadrant I with positive values for both x and y. The graph nicely shows the curve rising above 242 and 243, up to 250 at $x = 2.5$. However, students could still be confused about what the cubic function looks like.

Students could also play with the zoom function to see the whole graph. The advantages are that students can see what a typical cubic equation looks like when graphed (the right tail shoots up to y values in the 2000s quite fast!) and they can understand which values on the graph are meaningful and work realistically with respect to the *context* of the problem and which values on the graph only work mathematically. Again, this creates a great opportunity to discuss why endpoints are necessary on some graphs. Figure 5.42 shows a bigger picture of the function, where the seemingly parabolic curve shown in Figure 5.41 is actually just a little characteristic "bump" in the cubic function, which goes from infinitely negative x and y to infinitely positive x and y.

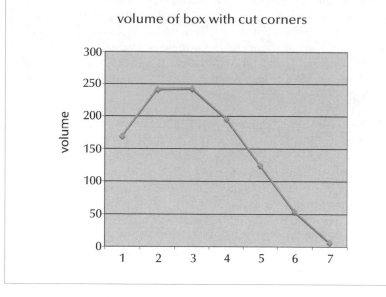

FIGURE 5.40

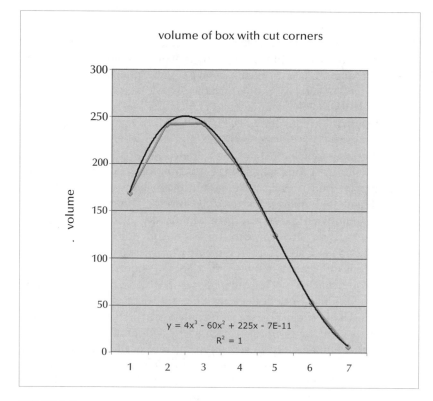

FIGURE 5.41

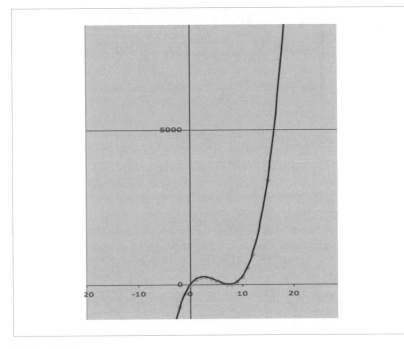

FIGURE 5.42

Finite difference is a powerful tool that can be used on many different kinds of data sets. See www.braidedmath.com for extension problems that have fourth-order equations (quartics) that generalize really simple and concrete phenomena.

CONCLUSION

In this chapter, we demonstrate three powerful approaches that will enrich any algebra curriculum, give meaning to procedures, and help students get into the real game of doing mathematics: line of best fit, linear combinations, and finite differences. I remember a class of ninth graders who had already completed their textbook's chapter on systems of equations. Their teacher allowed me to do some Chocolate Algebra with them as a kind of review. The students had no trouble with it but many looked surprised and some even stunned, and during our review of Chocolate Algebra several spoke out: "Why didn't the book show us this way?" "This way makes so much more sense." Their classmates exclaimed in agreement, "That's right!" One student, who had been quiet all during the lesson, raised his hand and simply said, "Now I understand this stuff."

6 | GEOMETRY AND MEASUREMENT

MULTIPLE REPRESENTATIONS FOR SOLVING A GEOMETRY PROBLEM

Ordering Shapes by Two-Dimensional Size

What follows is a tricky little problem in geometry that will present some surprises. I usually do this with students in grades 5, 6, and 7. Most elementary schools use pattern blocks, aptly named for the many patterns that can be made from them. They consist of six different shapes (see Figure 6.1) that have several powerful relationships that allow them to be combined on flat surfaces in many ways (e.g., tessellations).

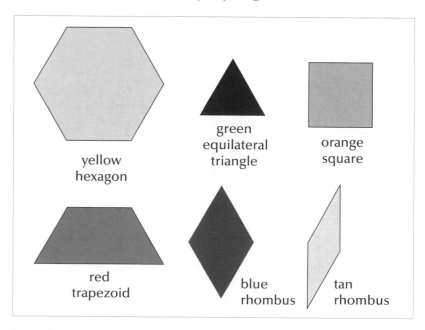

FIGURE 6.1

I ask the students, "*What do you know for sure* about these six shapes. What are their attributes?" They tell me their names, for example, diamonds or rhombus, or special parallelogram with all sides equal. The first and most obvious relationship that they see is the lengths of the sides. Someone usually blurts out, "All the sides are the same (or the same length)." Then other students chime in, "Not *all*. Look at the red one." I ask them to systematically compare all sides by placing them against one another. All are the same except the red trapezoid, which has three sides the same but one long side. I ask them, "How much bigger or how many times bigger?" They easily find that it is twice as big. All the sides are 1 inch, except the long side of the trapezoid, which is 2 inches. Therefore, they could tell me the perimeter of each shape (3, 4, 4, 4, 5, and 6 inches). I often ask because many of our middle school students do not know the difference between perimeter and area.

There are two "secrets" about the pattern blocks that create their incredible flexibility. I'll tell you one and the other will be revealed in this activity. The first secret, and a reason for their flexibility, is the relationships among the angles. When placing pattern blocks on top of one another, students can discover that all the angles are multiples of the acute angle of the tan rhombus, which is 30 degrees. Of course, this presupposes that they know what angle is. Nonetheless, a teacher can use pattern blocks to inductively derive a tremendous amount of information about angles. Here is the problem that leads to the other secret:

> Put the six shapes in order by two-dimensional size. You do not have to measure the area of each shape, but you should be able to demonstrate your solution.

This problem initially may appear simple. There are many relationships among these shapes of which kids are very much aware, from making shapes with them in earlier grades. They'd know that two green equilateral triangles can be put together to be the same shape and size (they are congruent) with the blue rhombus. Similarly, three of the equilateral triangles can be congruent with the red trapezoid. Two red trapezoids can be made congruent with the yellow hexagon. See Figures 6.2, 6.3, and 6.4.

Students immediately pull out the equilateral triangle, blue rhombus, red trapezoid, and yellow hexagon to show their order from smallest to largest. Ask them to explain their reasoning and they will tell you some of the size relationships like the ones I just mentioned. There are a dozen size relationships based on building up the large pieces from the smaller ones (for example, six triangles can make a hexagon). I do prefer that the students move toward more mathematically accurate and precise terminology, but I am not going to drive them crazy with it either. For instance, I would model for them, "Six equilateral triangles with a side length of

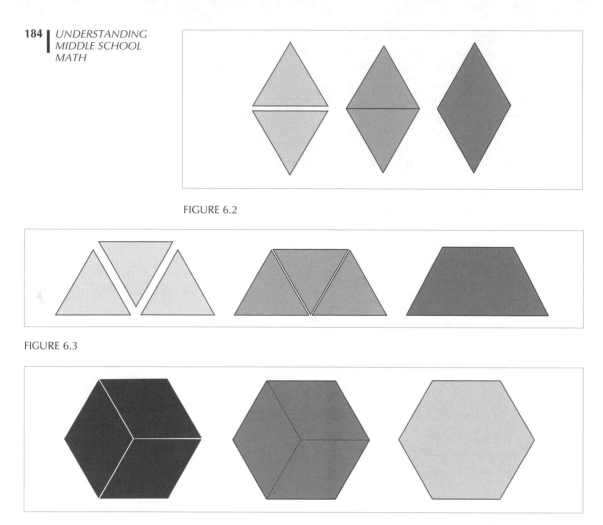

FIGURE 6.2

FIGURE 6.3

FIGURE 6.4

one inch can be made congruent to a regular hexagon that also has side length of one inch."

They easily discern the order of the four shapes that are based on multiples of the equilateral triangle. I suggest to the students that the equilateral triangle is the *basic building block* of this family (Figure 6.5).

But what about the square and the tan rhombus in Figure 6.6?

They start thinking of ways to compare two shapes, but I want to see a technique so I suggest, "Try comparing the square and the red trapezoid." On the overhead projector I place reds and oranges as in Figure 6.7.

I use the term *overhang* to get their focus on the "extra" red trapezoid that goes beyond the square on the left and the extra part of the orange square that goes over the top of the red trapezoid. I ask, "Which is greater, the red overhang (which is two right triangles) or the orange overhang (the thin rectangle)?" The red overhang is the unanimous winner. The trapezoid is bigger than the square.

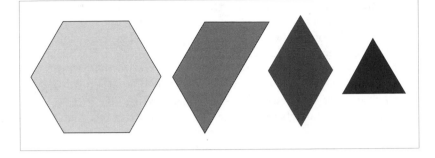

FIGURE 6.5

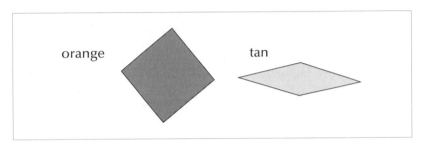

FIGURE 6.6

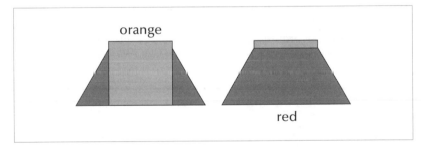

FIGURE 6.7

Frequently students will assert that the square and the blue rhombus are the same size. I ask, "What is it about these shapes that leads you to this *conclusion*?" "They look about the same size." I tell them that we're going to need more evidence than that. There is usually a lot of hemming and hawing, but eventually (although it occasionally comes quickly) someone says that they have the same perimeter. A key moment!

I turn to the class and say, "We have an interesting thesis being offered here. On the basis of your extensive work with geometric shapes in your life, would you infer that shapes that have the same perimeter also have the same area? Is that a pattern you have seen before now?" I want to assure you, there is no trace whatsoever of sarcasm in my voice. The students who have offered this idea are thinking. They have taken some risk. I want to make sure they know that making mistakes is a *natural* part of learning. Plus it can alert me to their misconceptions. In this case, we still have some work to do with area and perimeter.

Meanwhile some other students are reasoning that the tan rhombus also has the same perimeter but certainly does not have the same area as the square and blue rhombus. I ask, "What makes you say that? How would you convince me?" Three kids have put the blue rhombus on top of a tan rhombus and vice versa (see Figure 6.8). I ask, "What inferences can you draw now?" They talk about how the blue overhang is bigger than the tan overhang. The blue is larger in area despite the same perimeter.

At this point I bring out four yardsticks that I have bolted together at their ends to make a square yard. I ask the students if it looks like a square. I distribute four geostrips and four fasteners to each student and ask them to make a square. My yardsticks are really giant geostrips. I loosen the bolts on mine and ask them what happens to the shape in the center as they vary the angles of the geostrips? See Figure 6.9.

I ask the students to describe what they are seeing. What relationships or patterns can they infer about rhombuses (rhombi)? All of them have some sense that the square (a rhombus with four 90-degree angles) has the largest size (maximum area). When you push in or pull out on the corners (vertices), the angles change, making two acute and two obtuse angles opposite each other. The more acute and the more obtuse the angles, the smaller the area of the rhombus. The length of the sides and, thus, the perimeter of the rhombi do not change. Figure 6.9 shows four different rhombi with acute angles at the top and bottom, and obtuse angles on the left and right sides of each rhombus. To sum this up, I tell the students I am now going to ask them a question in the fancy mathematical way: *Can you hold the perimeter of a rhombus constant and still vary its area?* They think about it and then give a resounding YES!

I remind them that just because the geostrips make it look like the square is bigger than the blue rhombus doesn't prove that it actually is

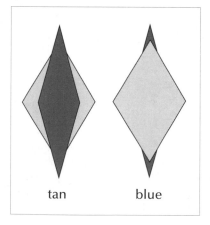

tan   blue

FIGURE 6.8

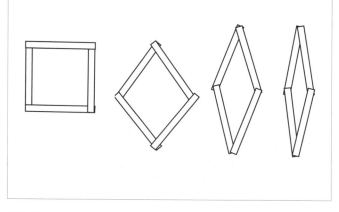

FIGURE 6.9

and it doesn't show us how much bigger it may be. We have to compare them more directly. Invariably, a student suggests that we lay them on top of one another and look at the overhang, the way we did before. They might see what is going on with these small pieces, one inch on a side. However, artists and billboard advertisers know that a bigger visual display makes it easier for the eye to see differences.

I have long held that a math teacher is like an artist who seeks the best medium to express the main ideas. I show the students on an overhead projector with overhead pattern blocks what the common area and the overhangs look like. But for them to be fully engaged in examining the relationship, they need to act on the objects themselves. They see a piece of the blue that they would love to cut off and place over with the other side (see Figure 6.10). But they can't cut the plastic pieces. So we change the medium.

I give each student a large orange square and a blue rhombus made of paper with side lengths of one decimeter. The critical math concept here is *similarity*. If the paper shapes are truly similar to the plastic pattern blocks, then any relationship we discover with the big paper shapes must apply also to the original small plastic pieces. All squares are similar because they all have four right angles and equal side lengths. The paper rhombus has four equal sides *and* they are the same length as the square, but are the angles the same between the paper and plastic version? We ask the students to slide the plastic blue rhombus on the blue paper rhombus to see if their acute angles are the same. *Yes*. Then they compare their obtuse angles. Both blue rhombi are 60 degrees and 120 degrees for the acute and obtuse angles.

The students place the paper rhombus on the square, as in the previous figure that still sits on the overhead projector. Next they place the square on the paper rhombus. They draw a line on the blue paper with the right side of the square and cut off what looks a lot like a blue right triangle. See Figure 6.11.

FIGURE 6.10

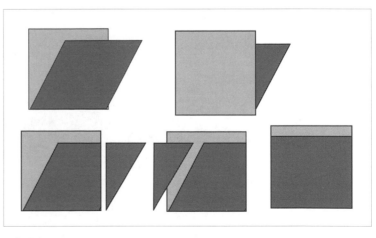

FIGURE 6.11

Students then place the blue triangle onto the orange square and slide it right up into the other part of the blue rhombus. Clearly the orange square is larger than the blue rhombus.

Often at this point some of the students will use their prior knowledge about shapes and place a green triangle onto an orange square. See Figure 6.12.

They state that the green is less than half of the square, and the blue must be less than the square because two greens make a blue. This is excellent reasoning if the original premise were true.

I ask if they are certain that the green is not half the square—students who are well acquainted with shapes readily say the top of the triangle does not come all the way up to the middle of the top side of the square.

That isosceles triangle (not equilateral) is half of the square. See Figure 6.13.

Other students in the class take a different approach. Realizing that the angle of an equilateral triangle is the same size as two of the tan acute angles—that is, 30 + 30 = 60 if they knew the angle measures—they place an equilateral on top of two tan rhombi. A wonderful bit of reasoning is made possible by the manipulatives. Some "saw" that the triangle must be smaller than the tan rhombus. Do you see what they saw? Although the top vertex of the triangle and its sides fit perfectly with the two rhombi, they do not go down enough to cover half of each rhombus (for example, down to the minor diagonal). See Figure 6.14.

I ask them, "Explain to us why you believe the green equilateral triangle is smaller than the tan rhombus?" They respond that if you draw a line on each tan rhombus (the minor diagonal), it separates each in half. See Figure 6.15. Therefore, if the green equilateral triangle *were* the same size as one tan rhombus, it would cover one-half of each of the two tan rhombi. (Actually, the kids did not use the subjunctive. So few people do.)

Sometimes we have to direct students' attention, such as compare the blue rhombus to the orange square. Sometimes when students are stuck,

FIGURE 6.12

FIGURE 6.13

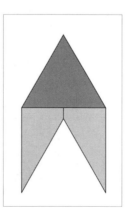

FIGURE 6.14

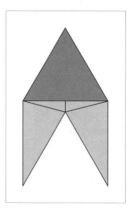

FIGURE 6.15

they might need a little prompting: take a square and a triangle and make a house. Then take a triangle and two rhombi and make a condo (we might also call it a chalet or a church.)

What do you see? See Figure 6.16.

The students place one on top of the other (usually the house on the condo) and verify that they are *congruent*. Then somewhere between "some" and "most" of the students can reason that if they took out the green equilateral triangle from each, what remains must be equivalent in size, even though the shapes are different. See Figure 6.17.

If this is true, then one tan rhombus is exactly one-half of the square. Now seriously, would Figure 6.18 lead anyone to think the rhombus is half the square? It is very counterintuitive. However, we tell the kids to place the tan paper rhombus on the orange square with vertex to vertex and one side against a side of the other. See Figure 6.19.

The students can see the tan rhombus overhang, imagine cutting it off, and sliding it onto the rest of the rhombus. So that is what they do. It *is* half. *This is one of the secrets.* Just to be sure, the students cut a second tan rhombus the same way and fill up the other half of the square.

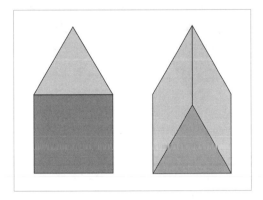

FIGURE 6.16

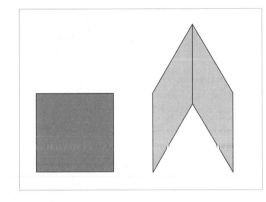

FIGURE 6.17

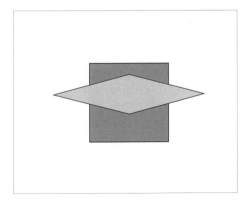

FIGURE 6.18

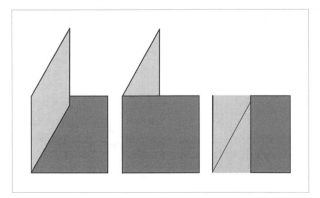

FIGURE 6.19

Now the students know how to order the shapes. See Figure 6.20.

What about the patterns in this problem? First, notice that there are three pairs where a 2-to-1 ratio exists. The hexagon is twice as big as the trapezoid, which is half the hexagon; the blue rhombus is twice the equilateral triangle; and the tan rhombus we found to be half of the square. See Figure 6.21.

We mentioned earlier that all angles present are multiples of 30 degrees. But the really amazing property to me was when we dissected the paper shapes. What we cut off in several cases was the same shape.

In Figure 6.19 the students cut off a right triangle, as they did in Figure 6.11. In Figure 6.7 they could see the overhang on either side of the square was a right triangle. When they compare these paper pieces they cut off, all the right triangles are congruent and they are each half of the equilateral triangle!

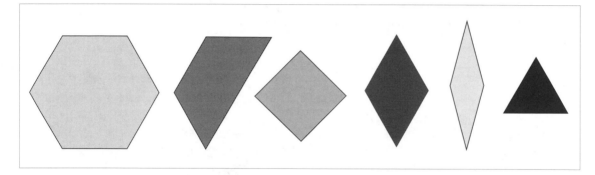

FIGURE 6.20

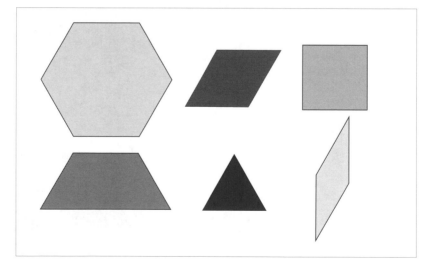

FIGURE 6.21

The students are now in the position to formally measure the area of each of the six shapes. The orange paper square is one square decimeter or 100 square centimeters (ten centimeters on each side), which is the same as the Base Ten Hundred. The orange square of the smaller plastic pattern blocks is one square inch. You have the option of pursuing area in decimeter and centimeters or in decimal parts of an inch. Let's see how the small plastic inch pieces go. The orange square is 1.00 sq. in. and tan rhombus is ½ or .50 sq. inches.

I give the students a handout of a square with one square decimeter or one hundred square centimeter cells. See Figure 6.22. It is congruent to the paper orange square. (Recall that all the paper figures were similar to the plastic shapes [10 cm for each inch—a scale factor of 3.94], if you want to explore that concept.)

I ask the students to determine what part of the square is the blue rhombus. They know the blue rhombus is smaller than a square of same side length. I try to hold back and not give them too much structure; the question certainly is sufficiently focused. Some grab centimeter rulers, some chatter away with their group members about how to do this, and a few go for the paper versions to find what is left of their blue. They move blue pieces on top of the 100 grid. See Figure 6.23. They repeat, making a blue rectangle fit on the square as they did in Figure 6. 11.

They can see in Figure 6.23 that the blue rhombus, now a rectangle, definitely covers eighty of the one hundred square centimeters, maybe eighty-five, but not ninety. To find the exact decimal part that the blue covers requires trigonometry. The area of the blue rhombus is .866 of the square. The area of a rhombus is given by Area = Sine ø * S^2 where ø is 60 degrees and S is the side length. Sine 60° = .8660 and S = 1. Therefore the area of the blue rhombus is .866 of the square.

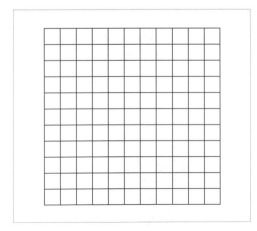

FIGURE 6.22

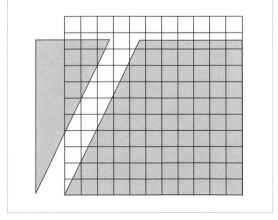

FIGURE 6.23

I ask the students what part of the square is the green equilateral triangle. They readily respond .433 because the blue rhombus can be congruent to two green equilateral triangles, an equilateral triangle must be half of .866. Another good validation of .433 is the formula for the area of a triangle, $A = \frac{1}{2}$ base $*$ height. The equilateral triangle has a base of 1.00, but what is its height? Its angles are all 60°, but when you cut it in half, you get two 30°, 60°, 90° right triangles with sides in proportion 1, $\sqrt{3}$, 2. Therefore, the area of an equilateral triangle is $A = (\sqrt{3} * S^2)/4 = (1.7320 ^ 1)/4 = .443$.

I ask about the red trapezoid and the yellow hexagon. Again they can readily see that trapezoid and the hexagon are made from three and six equilateral triangles, 1.299 and 2.598 square inches, respectively. Note specifically that four of the shapes are multiples of the equilateral triangle. It is as if they are all from the same family. The square does not easily measure with this family as can be seen in Figures 6.7, 6.10, 6.11, and 6.12; neither does the tan rhombus. With some effort we determined that the tan rhombus is half the square. So, we might consider the square and the tan rhombus to be from the same family, a dysfunctional family perhaps—because they don't play well with the members of the other family, but still a family. To summarize:

The regular hexagon has side length 1.00 units (e.g., inches, decimeters) with   Area = 2.598 sq. units

The red trapezoid is half of the hexagon with Area = 1.299 sq. units

The square of side length 1.00 has   Area = 1.000 sq. units

The blue rhombus of side length 1.00 has   Area = .866 sq. units

The tan rhombus of side length 1.00 has   Area = .500 sq. units

The equilateral triangle of side length 1.00 has Area = .433 sq. units.

Have you grasped the awesome significance of this information? Think of what your students can do now as they make various shapes from these six polygons. Not only can students describe and analyze shapes, they can figure out their perimeters and also their area. For example, Figure 6.24 shows the regular hexagon and a second hexagon. Compare their areas. The regular hexagon has an area 2.598 square inches. And the other? Simply 1.000 + .500 + .866 = 2.366 square inches.

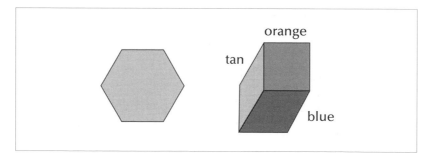

FIGURE 6.24

Make My Polygon

We can also play a little game of "Make My Polygon" where I give students several pieces of information about a convex polygon I have made and they try to recreate it or make one that fits.

> I am thinking of a convex polygon: It is an octagon with perimeter of 12 inches and area of 10.428 square inches made with 12 shapes. Begin with a KWC.

This is challenging because it is not your usual stop-sign regular octagon, which cannot be made with pattern blocks because its angles are multiples of 45° (45°, 90°, 135°). Also, this octagon has perimeter of 12 inches and is made with pattern blocks, so it is not regular. These ideas will come out in a KWC.

So you thought Sudoku was challenging! If you have some pattern blocks, try it but don't look at the next page. If your students get stuck, you can scaffold by providing a border. See Figure 6.25. On challenging problems like this one you might want to break out a table of the multiples for them. It can help decipher what combination of decimals from the two families would ever get .428 in the decimal places.

TABLE OF MULTIPLES

Square	Tan Rhombus	Hexagon	Trapezoid	Blue Rhombus	Triangle
1	0.5	2.589	1.299	0.866	0.433
2	1	5.178	2.598	1.732	0.866
3	1.5	7.767	3.897	2.598	1.299
4	2	10.356	5.196	3.464	1.732
5	2.5	12.945	6.495	4.33	2.165
6	3	15.534	7.794	5.196	2.598

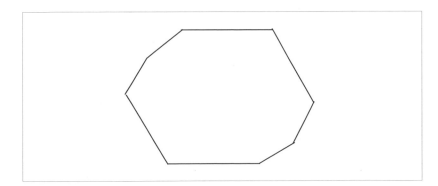

FIGURE 6.25

With smaller areas the students can find solutions by adding different combinations of multiples of .5 and .433. For larger shapes, a good strategy would be to see if the total area (10.428 square inches) is divisible by .433. If so, then you are just dealing with the green family. If not, you could subtract multiples of .5 until you got a number that as divisible by .433.

Why would that work? We did that in Chocolate Algebra. Some .5s and some .433s make 10.428. $10.428 - 3.5 = 6.928$ and $6.928/.433 = 16$. Now we know there must be seven tans or a mix of tans and squares and also the equivalent of sixteen triangles from the green family.

TANS & SQUARES	0.5	GREEN FAMILY	0.433	AREA 10.428
20	10		0.428	no
18	9	3.297921478	1.428	no
15	7.5	6.762124711	2.928	no
7	3.5	16	6.928	yes
	2.634	18	7.794	no
	0.902	22	9.526	no

Another way to figure out as difficult a one as this is to go to the equation in standard form which would be:

$$.5x + .433y = 10.428 \qquad x + .866y = 20.856$$
$$.866y = -x + 20.856 \qquad y = -1.154734411x + 24.08314088$$
$$\text{or round it to } -1.1547x + 24.083$$

Enter this yucky equation into a graphing calculator. Set x to 1 start at = 0 and the xs will all be whole numbers. Scroll until you find y value that is also a positive integer. You will find only (7, 16)! So the area is correct although twenty-three pieces are too many. The next task is to consolidate the tan rhombi and green equilateral triangles into big pieces so that there are only 12.

There are only four ways to get 3.5 units of area from squares and tan rhombi and they would use four, five, six, or seven pieces.

	1	TAN RHOMBUS	0.5	AREA
SQUARES				3.5
3	3	1	0.5	
2	2	3	1.5	
1	1	5	2.5	
0		7	3.5	

Of course there are many more than four options with the green family. And their are multiple solutions. Figure 6.26 gives one.

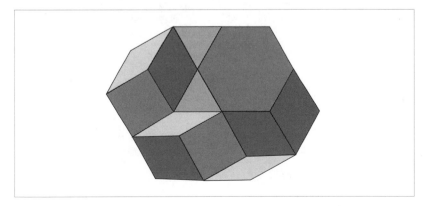

FIGURE 6.26

A Great Extension: Making Dodecagons

A great problem for students and teachers (even high school teachers) is to find the area in square inches that makes up the regular dodecagon of side length 1 inch (a 12-sided polygon.). We give the students the border of the polygon and ask them to find several ways to make/fill the dodecagon with pattern blocks. If they know the area of each pattern block, they will be able to calculate the area. You may download a blackline master of Figure 6.27 from www.braidedmath.com. All the figures in this chapter using pattern blocks are on the website in color.

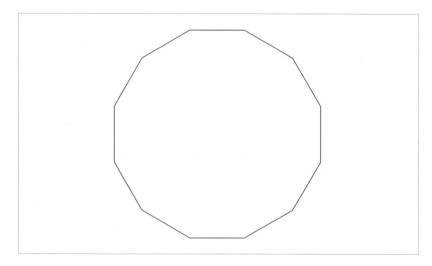

FIGURE 6.27

Here are some solutions, with analysis on the next page.

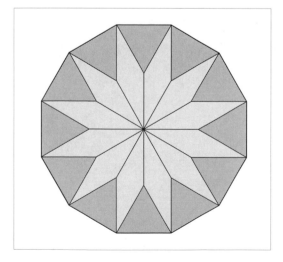

FIGURE 6.28

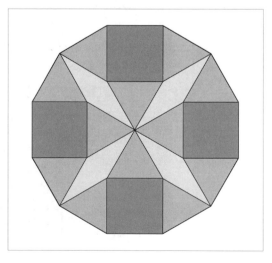

FIGURE 6.29

12 small rhombi @ .5 square inches = 6.00 square inches	4 small rhombi @ .5 square inches = 2.00 square inches 4 squares = 4.00 square inches
12 equilateral triangles @ .433 square inches = 5.196 square inches	12 equilateral triangles @ .433 square inches = 5.196 square inches
area of dodecagon = 11.196 square inches	area of dodecagon = 11.196 square inches

Does a pattern begin to emerge? Let's add two more examples (Figures 6.30 and 6.31) and set up a table like we do for Chocolate Algebra.

TAN RHOMBI 0.5		SQUARE 1		HEXAGON 2.598		TRAPEZOID 1.299		BLUE RHOMBI 0.866		TRIANGLE 0.433	
6	12									5.196	12
2	4	4	4	4						5.196	12
6	12							3.464	4	1.732	4
4	8	2	2	2		2.598	2	1.732	2	0.866	2

The pattern is: 6 square inches of area come from the small rhombi and square; 5.196 square inches of area come from the equilateral triangle family.

FIGURE 6.30   FIGURE 6.31

I love this activity. Everybody wins. Everyone finds at least two ways to fill a dodecagon with pattern blocks. Many of my teacher friends use this dodecagon investigation to create a classroom bulletin board—students color the solutions they find and may put them up on the bulletin board *if* it is a new solution. It cannot be a rotation nor a reflection of one that is already on the board. It is really cool to see a sixth or seventh grader standing in front of a bulletin board scanning the patterns already found, taking her recent solution, turning it around, and then flipping the paper over to the other side to see the reflection (mirror image). Because she has colored one side of the paper with magic markers so that they bleed through, she can quickly see the mirror image. Some of the solutions are very hard to discern (see Figure 6.31), others very easy (see Figure 6.28).

What's Your Angle?

Angular measure and, in fact, the concept of angles is generally poorly done in the elementary curriculum. Many students don't really know what an angle is when they are given a protractor in fourth grade and told to measure. I have run into many middle schoolers who are baffled by a protractor. They don't have a clue where to put the protractor to measure a specific angle. Some don't really know what a degree is or what angle is. How can they measure if they don't know what they are measuring?

Angle is a geometric attribute that is measured with specific standard units called *degrees*. (Actually an unfortunate choice of words considering this context has nothing to do with temperature.) The most common way students are taught to conceive of what an angle is involves the scissors metaphor (line segments, rays, the hands of a clock): The key question is, *How open are they?* Compelling as that language may sound to a teacher, it doesn't grab all the students. See Figure 6.32.

For instance, students often tell me that the angle on the right is bigger. Although some mistakenly look at the length of the rays in the picture, others look at the distance between the arrow heads, which they thought was the end of the rays.

Many of us have found that angles can be explored with the *wedge* metaphor: slices of pie, corners of polygons. The key question is: *How big*

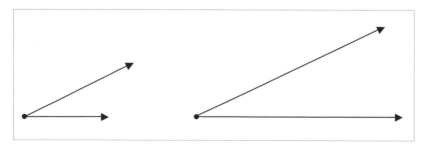

FIGURE 6.32

is the wedge? Personally, I like *How SHARP is the point created by the two sides of the wedge?*

In our earlier examples using pattern blocks, I spoke of their angles. One of the reasons pattern blocks fit so well together is that every angle at the vertex of each of the six shapes is a multiple of 30 degrees. For this problem, What's Your Angle?, I made giant pattern blocks out of high-density foam board with their sides one foot in length. While students work with their one inch on a side plastic pattern blocks and the one decimeter paper versions, I put overhead manipulatives on the screen and also use the giant-sized foam version while I interact with them. I ask them to tell me what corner or vertex of what shape has the smallest angle and what shape has the largest. I ask them to compare all the angles to a corner of the big square by placing a vertex from each against the square corner. Smaller than a square corner would be: *A cute little angle (acute)*; larger would be just a big *obtuse angle*. We go through each angle to compare and order them.

I'm not presenting a random set of actions or questions; I am walking my students through a developmental sequence for measurement that humans must do in order to truly understand the concepts:

1. Discern the attribute.
2. Order two.
3. Order three or more.
4. Use a familiar nonstandard unit of measurement or use a reference (e.g., a square corner).
5. Use a standard unit of measurement.
6. Use a calibrated instrument.

Once the students appear to be getting it, I use my giant-size pattern blocks and give them plastic strips with holes punched at the ends so they can fasten two strips together and then open them like scissors. I hold up one of my big shapes, and they must open their strips to the same angle that I indicate on my shape. Then I insert the vertex indicated into the students' strips to see how close to my shape's angle they have estimated. The two metaphors (scissors and wedge) reinforce one another and build a solid understanding of what an angle is.

The final stage you may have seen before, but is an important step. Don't skip it. Each student has a big sheet of paper and puts a big dot in the center. I ask them to slide an equilateral triangle up until a vertex touches the dot, then slide up another. Their task: Completely encircle the dot. It takes six equilateral triangles to go all the way around. Then I ask them to slide some hexagons one at a time to encircle the dot. I ask them why they only have to use three hexagons and six triangles. Most students simply reach the conclusion that the angles of the hexagon are bigger than those of the triangle. Occasionally, a student will realize the reason and blurt out, "The hexagon's angles were twice as big, so it only took half as many."

While the students slide each of the six shapes up to the dot, I am usually at the overhead projector putting up what they have found and

Shape	Obtuse Angles	Acute Angles	Right Angles	Angles Around the Dot
hexagon	6	0	0	3
square	0	0	4	4
equi. triangle	0	3	0	6
blue rhombus	2	2	0	3 obtuse 6 acute
trapezoid	2	2	0	3 obtuse 6 acute
tan rhombus	2	2	0	12 acute

FIGURE 6.33

ensuring that they don't mix angles (for example, rhombus two acute and two obtuse). If they do, it gives you an opportunity to help them see a key attribute of rhombuses and all parallelograms: adjacent angles are supplementary (they sum to 180°). All of this sliding up can be done fairly quickly and kids record what they find. See Figure 6.33.

Now we return to the paper versions of the shapes and I tell them a little story.

Some history of mathematics books will tell you that the Babylonians started all this—they had a number system that was based on sixty, not ten. They loved sixty and multiples of sixty (120, 180, 240, 300, 360, and so on). They thought of a year as 360 days and threw in some special feast days. They looked at the stars in the sky and divided the sky up into the signs of the zodiac (constellations). And they used their love of sixty to do so. They imagined that there was a great circle all around the earth, and they cut the sky into twelve zodiac signs and into 360 chunks coming from the 360 days in the year. The twelve signs each had thirty chunks and each of the 360 chunks became a degree. Therefore it takes 360 degrees to go all around a point in the center of a circle. I have photocopied a circular protractor so students can see all 360 degrees. (See www.braidedmath.com for a larger version of the protractor.) See Figure 6.34.

Notice the single degree on this protractor. Students need to see and feel the units of measure they are supposed to use. Do you have a good feel for 1 liquid ounce? For a foot? For a meter? For a pound?

If the protractor is 360° all the way around a point, and it took 4 squares, they each must take up 90 of those chunks. And six equilateral triangles each must take up 60 of those degrees. We ask the students to take their paper one decimeter pattern blocks and slide one vertex up to the point and mark where its sides cross the protractors hash marks. Check to see if the square takes up 90 of those chunks. The students should in this way measure each of the paper angles and connect the measures to the number of that angle it took to encircle the dot in Figure 6.28.

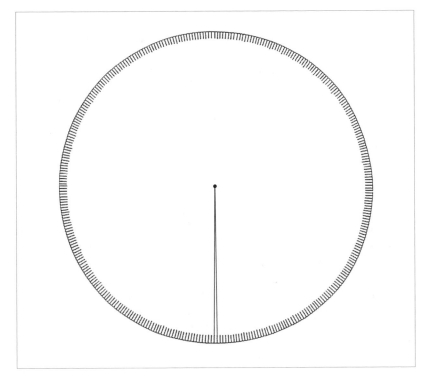

FIGURE 6.34

The Babylonians put all this into play about four thousand years ago. Why do we still have this system? Why did the Egyptians, the Greeks, the Romans, and so on keep it? Why didn't somebody go to one hundred clicks around a circle (essentially the metric system)? I think I know why. Most of these people talked about fractions as "a fifth part" or a "fourth part" so if you had 100 degrees in a circle, then halfway around (a half part) would be 50 degrees. Okay, but a third of the way around (a third part) would be a messy 33.33333. Now let's try parts of 360:

- A half of 360 is 180.
- A third of 360 is 120.
- A fourth of 360 is 90.
- A fifth of 360 is 72.
- A sixth of 360 is 60.
- A seventh is not even.
- An eighth of 360 is 45.
- A ninth of 360 is 40.
- A tenth of 360 is 36.
- An eleventh is not even.
- A twelfth of 360 is 30.

So 360 is the smallest number that is evenly divisible by every number from 2 to 12, except 7 and 11—which is why there are no 7-11s in Babylon.

Tessellations: A Different Way

Tessellation is the forming of images into a mosaic pattern. There are a great many resources for middle school teachers and their students on tessellations. Most resources emphasize the visual beauty of the geometric display and generate a lot of artwork for classroom bulletin boards and school hallways. Whether multiculturally or Escher-inspired, tessellations catch the eyes of the beholders. Rather than trying to round up the best activities in this genre that I have presented to my students in the past, I'll explore a more analytical direction.

I usually start a tessellation project with pattern blocks. I have them tessellate with squares, leaving no gaps or overlaps. Then they tessellate with equilateral triangles, then hexagons. In almost every class someone asks about using pentagons in tessellations, so I hand out some regular pentagons made from oak tag. However, regular pentagons do not tessellate by themselves—there are gaps that can be filled by other polygons . There are also a number of nonregular pentagons that will tessellate; see Figure 6.35 for my personal favorite.

A really great combination for tessellating two different polygons is the blue and the tan rhombi. They give the students plenty to work with—four different angles. I ask the students to take out only the blue and tan shapes, take out a clean piece of paper and put a dot in the middle, then slide vertices from the rhombi up on the dots and keep adding rhombi until they have encircled the dot. I refer to this group of shapes around the dot as a *seed* and I ask the students to focus on the *common vertex* of these shapes. Can they grow out from that initial seed by placing rhombi so that every common vertex is identical? Figure 6.36 shows a personal favorite.

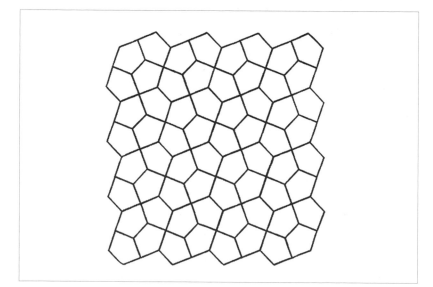

FIGURE 6.35

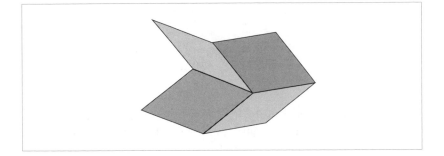

FIGURE 6.36

Then I ask:

- How would you describe the seed [in Figure 6.36]?
- What is happening at the common vertex?
- Can this seed be repeated? Infinitely?
- If you have some pattern blocks handy, try to answers these questions empirically, concretely.

You might say the common vertex contains one of each of the four angles. You might add that the acute angle of each rhombus is opposite its obtuse angle. You also might say that if we listed the angles clockwise from about one o'clock, we'd have 120°, 150°, 60°, 30°. This seed can be repeated indefinitely. See Figure 6.37.

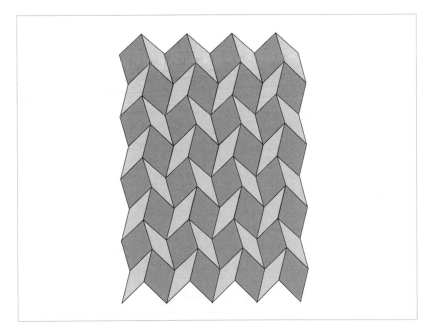

FIGURE 6.37

I pose to the students a problem.

> How many different seeds are possible with these two shapes? Begin with a KWC.

With a good KWC and a lively discussion in small groups and then the whole class, they usually recognize this is a combinations problem: What are the combinations of 30, 60, 120, and 150 that will make 360? And there are four critical questions I ask them:

1. How many ways have you found?
2. Did you check for duplicates?
3. Have you found them all?
4. And the most important question: How do you know when you have found them all?

Everyone agrees to try the kind of table they've done on prior problems. They start out recording the seed in Figure 6.36 with four rhombi, two of each, with the common vertex having one of each angle. See Figure 6.38. Rarely does anyone in the class realize that there is more here than meets the eye.

TAN	BLUE	BLUE	TAN
150°	120°	60°	30°
1	1	1	1

FIGURE 6.38

In Figure 6.39, we can see what most of the small groups have done. They would likely proceed on through finding all twenty-four rows for this table. However, when they have about a dozen of each rhombus and make the arrangement, they discover that there is often more than one way to arrange the numerical solutions. If they simply create the table by working the numbers, they might miss the many possibilities.

	TAN 150°	BLUE 120°	BLUE 60°	TAN 30°
A	2	0	1	0
B	2	0	0	2
C	1	1	1	1
D	1	1	0	3
E	1	0	3	1
F	1	0	2	3
G	1	0	1	5

FIGURE 6.39

Nothing happens on row A's solution, but on row B most of the students, while in the process of making a solution concretely with the pattern blocks, realized that there was more than one way to make a seed that used two 150-degree and two 30-degree angles. See Figure 6.40.

Once students realize the complexity of the problem, some are freaked out, saying that there must be hundreds of them and that they'll never find them all. Others are more confident, saying that they can find them, they just have to be systematic. I ask the students how they would record the *positions* of the angles at the common vertex, and we begin to talk about lists and pictures of shapes. One student mentions that there are patterns we could use, so I suggest that everyone start finding numerical solutions while I get a special recording device ready that will allow them to record the different ways a particular numerical solution can be done. See Figure 6.41.

The left side shows the 30-degree increments around the circle made easy to sketch by using isometric dot paper. Figure 6.42 shows a quick way of recording the two different ways to do 2-0-0-2 from row B in the table in Figure 6.39 (and pictured in Figure 6.40).

I then list the twenty-four numerical solutions for possible seeds and the different ways or arrangements for each, for a total of seventy-eight different seeds (all of which are on www.braidedmath.com). See Figure 6.43.

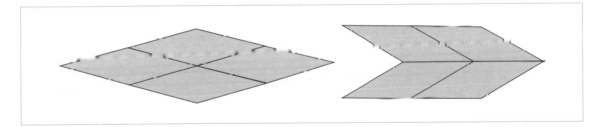

FIGURE 6.40

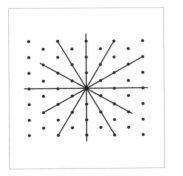

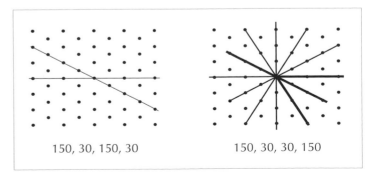

150, 30, 150, 30   150, 30, 30, 150

FIGURE 6.41   FIGURE 6.42

	TAN	BLUE	BLUE	TAN	
	150°	120°	60°	30°	Ways
A	2	0	1	0	1
B	2	0	0	2	2
C	1	1	1	1	3
D	1	1	0	3	2
E	1	0	3	1	2
F	1	0	2	3	6
G	1	0	1	5	3
H	1	0	0	7	1
I	0	3	0	0	1
J	0	2	2	0	2
K	0	2	1	2	5
L	0	2	0	4	3
M	0	1	4	0	1
N	0	1	3	2	6
O	0	1	2	4	9
P	0	1	1	6	4
Q	0	1	0	8	1
R	0	0	6	0	1
S	0	0	5	2	3
T	0	0	4	4	8
U	0	0	3	6	7
V	0	0	2	8	5
W	0	0	1	10	1
X	0	0	0	12	1

SEEDS FOR TESSELLATIONS

78

FIGURE 6.43

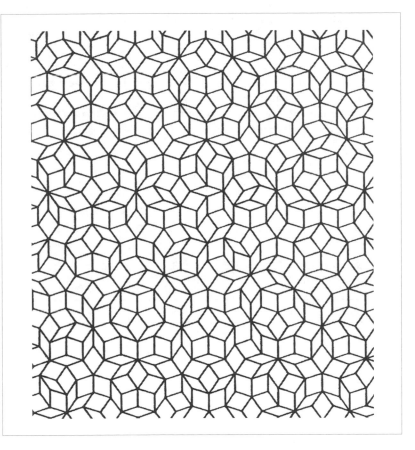

FIGURE 6.44

Extension

I give the students a tessellation (see Figure 6.44) and ask them a series
of questions:

1. What shapes do you see that are made up of a bunch of polygons? The two most likely are different balls; actually they are
   two-dimensional decagons and a five-pointed star fish.
2. There are two rhombi in this tessellation. What are their angles?
   How do you know?
3. Give a numerical analysis for these two rhombi of all the possible seeds or angles at a common vertex. Which are present in
   this tessellation and which are not?

The answer to question 2 is given below and the answer to question 3 is
given in Figure 6.45.

The tessellation in Figure 6.44 is an example of tiling with Penrose
Tiles. Created by Sir Roger Penrose in the 1980s, these two rhombi (72,

108) and (36, 144), when certain constraints are placed on how they may be joined, will not tile periodically in a regular repeating fashion like the tessellation in Figure 6.37. They will tile *aperiodically* in what appears to be random and *chaotic*. It is an example of chaos theory. It is not random; there is a pattern, it just does not repeat in the way we are used to. You cannot predict that the next starfish will appear twelve inches to the north of the one you are looking at, but you can say the ratio of starfish inside decagons to decagons without starfish will approach 1 to 5 over a given area.

THE PENROSE 5 TESSELLATION

144°	108°	72°	36°	Present
2	0	1	0	x
2	0	0	2	
1	2	0	0	x
1	1	1	1	x
1	1	0	3	
1	0	3	0	x
1	0	2	2	x
1	0	1	4	
1	0	0	6	
0	3	0	1	x
0	2	2	0	
0	2	1	2	x
0	2	0	4	
0	1	3	1	
0	1	2	3	
0	1	1	5	
0	1	0	7	
0	0	5	0	x
0	0	4	2	x
0	0	3	4	x
0	0	2	6	x
0	0	1	8	
0	0	0	10	

FIGURE 6.45

Pythagoras 'R' Us

If you ask ten people at random on a sidewalk in Chicago who was Pythagoras and for what is he famous, seven people will say he owned a restaurant on Halsted Street in Greektown. Everyone had some brief encounter with Pythagoras in school. Probably all they heard and saw was:

> The sum of the squares of the lengths of the two legs of a right triangle are equal to the square of the hypotenuse.

It might have been accompanied by a drawing in the textbook or on the board of a 3, 4, 5 right triangle with squares coming off the sides. See Figure 6.46.

I recall in my first year of teaching saying some version of those words and trying to draw something reasonable on the board. One of my ninth graders lived for the chance to tease me: "Hey, Mr. Jekyll, I don't see no legs on the Hippopotamoose. Where is they?" Half the class is rolling on the floor laughing. The other half is saying over and over "Hip-po-pota-moose! Hip-po-pota-moose!"

I got them to quiet down and I went ahead with what I realized I should have done first. I passed out to each person four congruent quadrilaterals. (See www.braidedmath.com for reproducibles for all the shapes in this activity.) Their task was to put these shapes together to form a square—not so easy because each piece had two right angles. It appears that these shapes do not have a special name, they are simply quadrilaterals. See Figure 6.47.

When students had made the square from the four quadrilaterals they recorded it on graph paper. It looked like Figure 6.48.

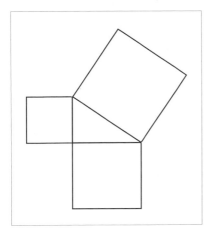

FIGURE 6.46

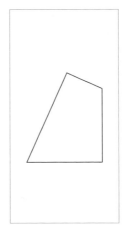

FIGURE 6.47

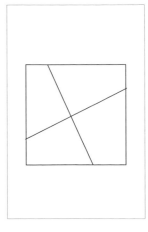

FIGURE 6.48

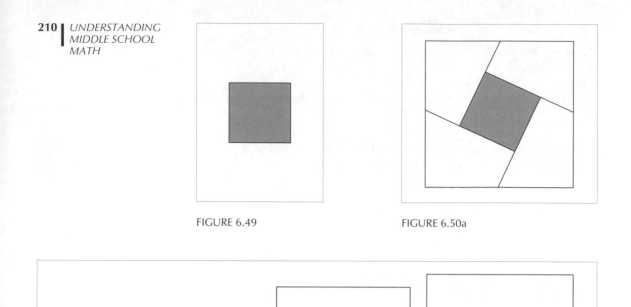

FIGURE 6.49   FIGURE 6.50a

FIGURE 6.50b

Next, I gave them a small square and asked them to combine the small square (see Figure 6.49) with the four quadrilaterals to make another square. This square proved to be even more difficult than the first one. See Figure 6.50a.

Next, I gave students a right triangle and three squares that were congruent with Figures 6.48, 6.49, and 6.50a. See Figure 6.50b.

I asked them to arrange three squares flat against the triangle so matching sides (congruent) were stuck together. See Figure 6.50c.

In the debriefing portion of this activity, I asked the students to write in their math journals what was unusual about all these shapes. They got together in small groups and shared ideas. I asked another open-ended question:

How would you describe the relationship among the three squares? What is the relationship among the sides and the squares?

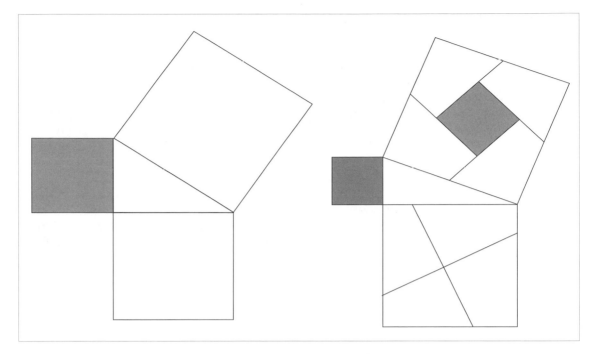

FIGURE 6.50c

The students were able to see that the big square could be made by dissecting the middle square and adding it to the small square.

The set of shapes discussed above illustrated the Pythagorean Theorem; we should encourage tactile and visual experiences with shapes to help our students grasp the relationships. However, this was just the start of our exploration—next I gave students a sheet of square centimeter graph paper glued to oak tag (I reuse old file folders). I asked them to cut out a right triangle that had the 90-degree angle between the two smaller sides, six and eight centimeters. Then they were to cut out three squares: (6×6) (8×8) (10×10).

I asked students to fit the squares around the right triangle, side to side. I hadn't yet said anything about the length of the long side (the hypotenuse—or *hippopotamoose*, if you prefer). As they slid the squares up alongside the triangle, many students caught on and saw that the two shorter sides (6 and 8) had areas of 36 and 64 and were equal in area to the 10-by-10 square. The symbolic representation for this would be $6^2 + 8^2 = 10^2$.

I used to be surprised that my students had no idea where the term *squaring a number* originated. The terms, as well as their meaning, had never been connected—*squaring, raising to the second power, perfect square, square numbers, an exponent of 2, completing the square* are all connected. Therefore, for the sake of simplicity, I will refer to the three squares as

A, B, and C going from smallest to largest. They have side lengths of a, b, and c. It is not a coincidence that these are also the side lengths of the triangle. So, in general, we can see and say $a^2 + b^2 = c^2$ for any and all right triangles. Conversely, if I tell you that I have a triangle with sides 65, 72, and 97, is it a right triangle? Is the following true? $a^2 + b^2 = c^2$? Does $65^2 + 72^2 = 97^2$? Does $4225 + 5184 = 9409$? Yes.

The task for the students now would be to take the middle square B, and figure out where to draw the lines of dissection (see Figure 6.51) so they will fit perfectly around square A and fill square C. See Figure 6.52 Then they must draw (not cut) square B on a new single sheet of graph paper. I warn them that this is challenging!

I ask them to do a KWC incorporating all the features and attributes they know from the immediately preceding activity. I add one other bit of scaffolding, suggesting that they label the lengths as they worked on their KWCs in small groups. When we get back together to talk as a whole class, they have a great deal of information to share.

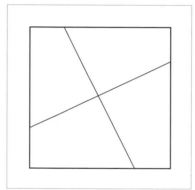

FIGURE 6.51

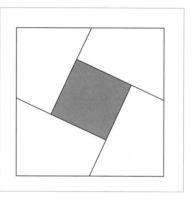

FIGURE 6.52

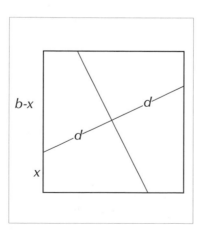

FIGURE 6.53

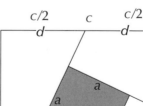
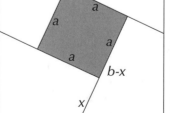

FIGURE 6.54

One of the great aspects of this problem is that the students must make assumptions—and realize they are making them. Likewise they must make inferences and, finally, conjectures. They reasoned that in dissecting square B, the lines cross in the center of square B perpendicular to one another because they must form the corners of square C. These lines cut side b into two parts, x and b − x, which is true for all four sides of square B. See Figure 6.53. They reasoned that length d had to be half of c (or c/2) because the four congruent quadrilaterals created in the dissection consisted of lengths d, d, x, and b − x.

The major insight that has to happen is the relationship shown in Figure 6.54. The side of the quadrilateral with length b − x is matched with x from another version of itself and a from square A. Some of the students really get it, but others can't make the connection. The ones who can say and write $a + x = b − x$, which is easily transformed into $2x = b − a$ and therefore $x = \frac{1}{2}(b − a)$. So what looked like a complicated bunch of non sequiturs has been reduced to two variables, a and b. All students need to know is two lengths and their desire to have them be the two "legs" of a right triangle. For instance, we asked students to try this with 6 and 8; then from $a^2 + b^2 = c^2$ we knew c = 10. Therefore, students could draw on graph paper a 10-by-10 square then an 8-by-8 square, which they then dissected using $x = \frac{1}{2}(b − a)$ and found x = 1. See Figure 6.55.

That's all they need to do. They could then cut them out, and they have a puzzle and a proof (proof lite).

Misconception

Most students think that the basic principle behind the Pythagorean Theorem applies only to squares because that is the only shape they've ever seen associated with the theorem. Also, the equation is all about squaring: $a^2 + b^2 = c^2$. But when you raise something to the second power, you multiply two numbers together—recall the partial products. This can be conceived of as area. In fact, the theorem of Pythagoras applies to any set of *similar* shapes.

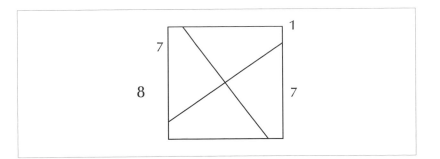

FIGURE 6.55

Pythagoras and Similarity

The unusual numerical relationship that exists when $a^2 + b^2 = c^2$ allows the teacher a lot of latitude in what shapes to use. Triangles, hexagons, and semicircles are frequent selections in textbooks. In each case, when the three shapes are *similar*—same shape, different size, in proportion to each other—the area of the two smaller shapes will sum to be the area of the largest shape. See two examples in Figure 6.56.

I hope you found this interlude interesting. If so, check out www.braidedmath.com for more on this topic.

Primitive Pythagorean Triples (PPT)

Of course we never really left Pythagoras. Did you wonder why I chose the 6, 8, 10 right triangle for our earlier example? They are three even numbers—in fact, each side is simply double the 3, 4, 5 right triangle, which would make it similar to the 3, 4, 5 with 4 times the area. I chose the 6, 8, 10 because I knew we were heading for finding x in the equation $x = \frac{1}{2}(b - a)$, and I wanted x to be a whole number. Both of these triangles are based on a set of numbers called Pythagorean triples, but though similar, 3, 4, 5 has no common factor and is called a *primitive Pythagorean triple (PPT)*.

PPTs are a vast topic in the number theory branch of mathematics. As you may have guessed, 3, 4, 5 is the smallest PPT. They are very cool numbers and some very interesting problems can be done with them. Note that there are only five PPTs whose three numbers (side lengths) are each less than thirty. Why do I mention thirty? Because if you were to make manipulatives of PPTs and you wanted to use 1 centimeter scale, then thirty centimeters would be your limit on an 8½-by-11-inch piece of paper. If you allow PPTs up to one hundred, you'll get the five under thirty and only eleven more with side lengths less than one hundred or sixteen altogether.

The task I gave my students was to find these sixteen PPTs, which could be difficult without some more information about PPTs' properties beyond $a^2 + b^2 = c^2$. In our problems, c stands for the hypotenuse, the longest side; b may be greater or smaller than a. Here are some properties of PPTs, which you can write on index cards. Arrange the students in small groups and each person gets one card.

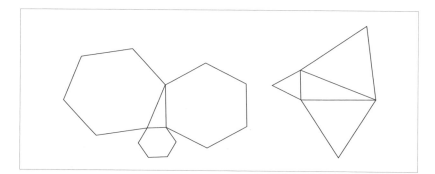

FIGURE 6.56

- Of the two legs, one is even and the other odd; we will designate side *b* as the even leg.
- Hypotenuses are always odd.
- One of the two legs is always divisible by 3.
- One of the two legs is always divisible by 4.
- One of the three sides is always divisible by 5.
- The hypotenuse minus the even leg is always a square.
- The hypotenuse plus the even leg is always a square.
- The sum of the hypotenuse and the odd leg divided by 2 is always a square.
- The difference of the hypotenuse and the odd leg divided by 2 is always a square.

I had given the students two of the three numbers and they had to figure out the third.

Examples are: (12, 37) (11, 60) (20, 21) (7, 25) (15,17). They can then generate Pythagorean triples—both primitive and nonprimitive—by setting $a = m^2 - n^2$, $b = 2mn$, $c = m^2 + n^2$ with *m* and *n* being whole numbers ($m > n$), one odd and the other even. Note that only certain values of *m* and *n* will generate PPTs. Can students discern them? (They must be relatively prime.)

Sometimes the Pythagorean Triples are given as an ordered triplet. The five less than thirty are : (3, 4, 5) (5, 12, 13) (8, 15, 17) (7, 24, 25) (20, 21, 29). The other eleven under one hundred are (12, 35, 37) (9, 40, 41) (28, 45, 53) (11, 60, 61) (16, 63, 65) (33, 56, 65) (48, 55, 73) (13, 84, 85) (36, 77, 85) (39, 80, 89) (65, 72, 97). See the table below.

m	n	a	b	c
2	1	3	4	5
4	1	15	8	17
6	1	35	12	37
8	1	63	16	65
3	2	5	12	13
5	2	21	20	29
7	2	45	28	53
9	2	77	36	85
4	3	7	24	25
8	3	55	48	73
7	4	33	56	65
7	6	13	84	85
9	4	65	72	97
6	5	11	60	61
5	4	9	40	41
8	5	39	80	89

Silent Snow, Secret Snow

No geometry chapter would be complete without some problem that involved the metric system. No geometry chapter of mine would be complete without my favorite snow activity. A few years ago in Chicago—February 2, 2002 to be exact—we awoke to the sound of. . . . Actually, there was no sound. I pulled back the curtain on a window and everything outside was white. Those big old fumbulo-numbulo clouds had unceremoniously discarded their cargo of snow one foot deep all over Chicago. Page 1 of the *Chicago Tribune* newspaper carried the follow item. See Figure 6.57.

I read the item and immediately began collecting material for the snow activity. As you can see, there is quite a bit of information, which I assume to be factual. One key piece for me was *one cubic foot*—not

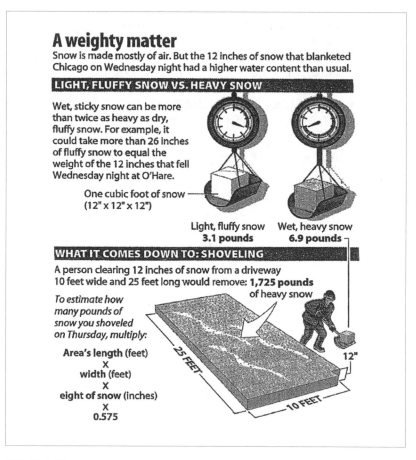

FIGURE 6.57

something you see every day. I found some fairly big cardboard boxes and cut out two strips, each 1 foot by 3 feet. I folded each one into three 1-by-1-foot squares. I folded each of these into a three-dimensional *U* and slid the two together to make a perfect cube—in fact, a cubic foot. It looked good and was sturdy so I made six of them for the students.

There were so many questions that could be asked about the information but most were just one-step translations or conversions. I wanted something bigger with more connections and opportunities for reconceptualizion. I asked the students two questions. The first question was:

> Estimate the pounds shoveled by multiplying four things: length, width, height, and .575. Where does .575 come from? Begin with a KWC.

The class did a KWC and some focused their attention on how the newspaper actually calculated the 1,725 pounds of snow. They multiplied 25 feet by 10 feet, which would be the surface area of the driveway, or 250 square feet. But then the instructions say to multiply by the height of the snow in inches. "Why not feet?" I asked. Then we'd know the volume of the snow one foot deep would give us 250 cubic feet of snow. Long pause. One student offered an interesting idea, "Maybe it didn't drop twelve inches of snow everywhere. Maybe this is some kind of general formula for what happens usually, like three or four inches." So we took the 250 square feet for the surface area of the driveway and multiplied it by 12 inches and got 3000. But 3000 what? We should be getting the volume of the snow. If we had used one foot for height of the snow our three measures would all be in feet and we'd have a volume of 250 cubic feet. The newspaper says this would weigh 1,725 pounds. How much would one cubic foot weigh? $1725 \div 250 = 6.9$, which means that the snow was the heavy wet kind. But the newspaper's general formula doesn't mention pounds. It just says multiply by .575. At this point several students realized that the 6.9 pounds must somehow be built into the .575, so that .575 is $(6.9x)$. *Okay!* So $6.9x = .575$ then $x = .575/6.9 = .08333$—which is $^1/_{12}$, so that inches get changed into feet.

Now we have two ways to calculate the weight of the snow to be removed. For the first, let's say we have the same driveway 10-by-25 feet, 250 square feet, and it snowed 6 inches of heavy wet snow. The newspaper would have us multiply by 6 and then again by .575. So $250 * 6 * .575 = 862.5$ pounds.

The other approach would be to multiply 250 square feet by $^6/_{12}$ of a foot ($^1/_2$ foot), multiplied by 6.9 pounds of heavy wet snow per cubic foot, which would give the total weight. So $250 * ^1/_2 * 6.9 = 862.5$ pounds.. Not only do the two methods agree, the answer makes sense because snowing six inches is half as deep as the newspaper example and 862.5 pounds is half the weight of 1,725 pounds. That was the warm-up.

The second problem I give students is from the top section of the newspaper article.

> Light, fluffy snow weighs 3.1 pounds and heavy, wet snow weighs 6.9 pounds because of the higher water content. Snow is mostly air, so a little water can make a big difference. What does a cubic foot of water weigh? Begin with a KWC.

A lot of info is already on the board from the previous KWC, but this is a new question and maybe some new knowledge needs to appear. And any time there is a new problem, there will be new constraints or conditions. I bring out the cubic foot again, and the only other scaffolding I do early is to remind students that we have a volume measure and weight (or mass) measure. How can we establish a relation between them?

The students start brainstorming math-to-world connections. That cubic foot looks smaller than the big water jugs carted in to office buildings. When we buy gas for our lawn mower, we fill up a five-gallon gas can, it is pretty heavy. How many gallons would be in a cubic foot? Here I intervene and I ask, "How would that help you?"

Several chime in. If we knew how many gallons in a cubic foot, then we'd only need to know what a gallon of water weighs. Could we just weigh a gallon of water? But then we still wouldn't know how many gallons in a cubic foot. I intervene again, and remind them that they are still dealing with relating volume to weight. The customary English system does not advertise this relationship, but there is one and I'll explain it shortly.

The metric system *does* show how to equate attributes very well. For instance, the most familiar measures they might know are:

Length: centimeters, meters
Area: square centimeter, square meter
Volume: cubic centimeter (cm^3), cubic meter
Capacity: milliliter (mL), liter (L)
Mass: gram, kilogram

The most curious and wonderful feature for me is the relationship that 1 cm^3 = 1 mL and 1 cm^3 of water has a mass of 1 gram. It does not take long for some of the students to realize how they could use this info to help them with the current problem. They see that they are starting with a cubic foot, a volume measure that if converted to metric volume can be easily equated with both metric capacity and metric mass. Then to get an answer in pounds, they'd have to convert from metric mass to pounds.

So I pull out the cardboard cubic foot and they think about how to convert this to metric. I give each table a pile of base ten blocks (ten sticks, one hundred squares, and one thousand cubes). The students try to get a feel for how these manipulatives could measure the cubic foot. Each of these base ten block sticks and square is actually a decimeter long. The decimeter is 10 centimeters long and three of them line up with one foot. Therefore we can use thirty centimeters for one foot. Nine (3 * 3) of the one hundred squares fill the bottom layer of the cubic foot. The thousand cubes fit nicely into the bottom of the cubic foot. These cubes, which are also cubic decimeters, also fit 3 * 3 on the bottom and two additional layers. Therefore, twenty-seven of the thousand cubes fill the cubic foot. Each of these thousand cubes is 1000 cm³ or mL and each weighs one thousand grams or one kilogram. Therefore, the weight of the cubic foot of water is twenty-seven kilograms. If we need that in pounds, we'd need the conversion factor of 2.2 pounds per kilogram. We'd estimate 59.4 pounds for the cubic foot. If we had been exact in measuring the foot, we would have said 30.48 cm in a foot: 2.54 cm/in. * 12 in. = 30.48 cm. The exact cubic inches would be $(30.48)^3$ = 28,316.85 cm³ or 28.31685 cubic decimeters, which would weigh 28.31685 kilograms or 62.297 pounds.

It is a curious and little known fact that we can equate mass and volume in the English system. The British Parliament, in the nineteenth century, declared that one gallon must equal 231 cubic inches (interestingly, the product of three prime numbers 3 * 7 * 11) so that merchants would not regularly cheat people—visualize a cereal box. Therefore, a gallon, or 128 ounces, would be 231 cubic inches or 1.804 cubic inches per ounce.

CONCLUSION

This chapter has examined the connections between geometry and measurement, algebra and geometry, number properties and geometry concepts. The activities are sufficiently rich that they could be modified for any grade in middle school or junior high, essentially fifth through eighth grades.

7 | Data Analysis and Probability

Any time students work on a probability experiment, they have the opportunity to learn or practice significant computation with data. In this chapter we create authentic environments for our students to use multiple data analysis and probability representations, in a variety of contexts, to inspire our students to build meaningful connections and models. In the first four problems, Chevalier de Mere's Game of Chance, Probability Bags, A Plethora of Pigs, and Montana Red Dog, we explore different aspects of experimental probability. In the last set of story problems, Combination Pizzas and Permutation Locks, Product Versus Square, Montana Red Dog Follow-Up, and De Mere's Bets Follow-Up, we examine *possible outcomes*, which is critically important in understanding theoretical probability.

EXPLORING EXPERIMENTAL PROBABILITY

Chevalier de Mere's Game of Chance

What comes to mind when someone mentions gambling or gamblers? Do you think of Las Vegas, Monte Carlo, James Bond playing Baccarat Chemin de Fer? Professional poker players in the World Series of Poker playing Texas Hold'em? A hoodlum with a handful of greenbacks at the back of a dark alley tossing dice against a wall?

If we were to go back to the gambling salons of Paris around the year 1650, we might see the infamous gambler Chevalier de Mere, noted rake and bon vivant. In those days in the salons, a gentleman might offer a wager to other gentlemen, and de Mere made a fortune by betting all takers that he could roll a single die no more than four times and get at least one six. De Mere fancied himself a bit of a mathematician and reasoned (incorrectly) that the chance of getting a six in a single throw was one out of six. Therefore, the chance of de Mers getting a six in four rolls was four times one out of six—in other words, two out of three. His reasoning was flawed, but the bet was in his favor and he made a fortune.

After a time, no one would take that bet with him, so de Mere came up with a new wager to tantalize the gentlemen. He bet that he could roll two dice and get a double six at least once in twenty-four rolls. He reasoned that the chance of getting a double six in one roll was one out of thirty-six. Therefore, his chance of getting a double six in twenty-four rolls was twenty-four times one out of thirty-six—in other words, two out of three.

But this time de Mere's erroneous reasoning caught up with him. More often than not, he lost this bet, and he was on his way to bankruptcy. He could not understand why, over the long run, he lost money on this wager; so, de Mere consulted Blaise Pascal. Pascal, noted mathematician, pondered the question and wrote to another luminary, Pierre de Fermat. The extensive correspondence between these two mathematical giants that began with de Mere's errant wager gave birth to a new branch of mathematics: probability.

In Chapter 1 we stated that teachers must lay a solid foundation of concrete probability experiments to build up to the more abstract concepts of theoretical probability. With the story of de Mere's two bets, teachers have two options. The first is describing the two bets, requiring the students to replay de Mere, then focusing their attention on the analysis of the data they collected. The second option is calculating the theoretical probabilities, which requires a strong foundation. We will work through the theoretical probability calculations for de Mere's two bets at the end of the chapter.

We begin by giving students a brief history of the games of chance de Mere played, but we wait until after they have played before revealing what actually happened. The students pair up; one keeps score as the other rolls the dice, then they switch roles. Each student should get two chances at playing both of de Mere's wagers. Then they should look at the aggregated data from the class. Are these fair games? Let the students think about it for a while.

Extension

Propose an advanced thinking question: How different in either direction from 50 percent wins would there have to be for students to believe the game was not fair?

Inference and Prediction: Probability Bags

This problem illustrates how patterns in sampling data may be inferred and used in prediction. I divide the class into eight lettered groups of three or four students and ask them to choose one student from each group to be a "supplier."

Then I hold up a brown paper bag. "The suppliers will come to me and get a bag labeled with the letter of their group," I begin. "They are responsible for making sure no one looks inside the bags. Inside the bags are ten cubes, some red, some blue, some yellow." I pull out one of each color and drop it back in the bag. Another person in the group is designated as the *grabber*. "You are *not* to look in the bag. Instead, you must take out one cube and drop it back in the bag. This is called *a sample of one, with replacement.* Another group member is the *recorder*, and this student records its color. Do this sampling twenty-five times, then analyze your data and predict how many of each color are in the bag. Each student should write an individual report about his or her group's reasoning, from data to prediction."

Suppliers get the bags and the groups begin sampling. When a group has finished, I collect its bag. I usually let students do any analysis they want to make the prediction; on other occasions I require them to use a particular procedure, such as represent the number of cubes as a fractional part of the total of twenty-five. When each group has completed its prediction, I ask them to go up to the board or a poster that I have prepared to enter their data and prediction in table form. See Figure 7.1.

Using the table, we explore how each group made its prediction. Each group explains their reasoning for going from data to prediction. There are always two approaches; the first is that students play with possibilities by using their number sense and the data. For instance, group W reasons:

> We got 13 blue, which is a little more than half, so we should say 5 or 6 blues. Red and yellow were both 6 so they should be the same, like 2, 2 or 3, 3. If we do 3, 3 then that leaves only 4 for blue, which does not seem right. So, we went with 2, 2, 6.

In the second approach, students use some kind of procedure that will always work regardless of the actual data. This approach must be ac-

GROUP	DATA				PREDICTION		
	R	Y	B		R	Y	B
Z	6	4	15	>>	2	2	6
Y	7	2	16	>>	3	1	6
X	8	5	12	>>	3	2	5
W	6	6	13	>>	2	2	6
V	7	5	13	>>	3	2	5
U	7	4	14	>>	3	1	6
T	5	6	14	>>	2	2	6
S	9	5	11	>>	4	2	4

FIGURE 7.1

companied by thinking to make sure students are using a good procedure and using it accurately. For example, group Z reasons:

> There were 15 blue (which is $^{15}/_{25}$ or $^3/_5$ or 60 percent). Red was $^6/_{25}$, so 6 divided by 25 is .24, or 24 percent, and $^4/_{25}$ is 4 divided by 25, or .16 or 16 percent. Then we took 60 percent of 10 and got 6 for blue, 24 percent of 10 is 2.4 red, which we rounded down to 2 red. And we took 16 percent of 10 for yellow, which is 1.6 yellow. We rounded that up to 2. So our prediction is 2 red, 2 yellow, and 6 blue.

Note that even with a good procedure, students still must use number sense and round.

Somewhere during our discussion, a student will ask, "Can we collect more data?" or "Can we do it over again to see if we get the same thing?" I seize the opportunity to engage the class in two conversations:

1. the law of large numbers, where increasing the samples will give us a more stable statistics; and
2. a little workout with proportional reasoning.

I ask the class, "If your data today gave you fourteen out of twenty-five blue, how many blues would you expect to get if you did it again seventy-five times, so that you had a sample of one hundred?"

A couple of students blurt out, "fifty-six!"

"What reasoning brought you that insight?"

They fumble around trying to explain that "everything is four times bigger"; I may have to summarize for them that if we can assume that, in general, the balance or ratio of blue to the total will remain the same, fourteen out of twenty-five times, then the three additional samples of twenty-five (to get seventy-five more) will each have fourteen blues (maybe). I then require each group to report on how they came up with their prediction.

One particular question typically always comes up during sampling: "Are the contents of all eight bags the same?" Up until now I've deflected the questions with "Let's wait and see." Now that we're exploring the groups' sampling results, I ask them to look at the table of data they've created (Figure 7.1). The class invariably is divided into three camps: The largest group thinks the bags are all the same; the smallest group says some are different; and in between are those who say, "We can't tell. There is no way to tell. You are playing a trick on us."

I ask the class to look at the data for each color. "How spread out is it?" They tell me that red goes from five to nine, yellow from two to six, and blue from eleven to sixteen. "If the bags are all the same, why are there differences among data?" They say things like, "chance," "random," "they cheated." I ask, "If one of the bags were different, but the other seven the same, which would you think is the different one?" Students nominate group S and group Y. I ask them to explain their reasoning. They tell me that group S had the lowest blue (eleven) and the highest red (nine). Group Y had the lowest yellow.

For those who are not sure what can be said, I ask, "How different would the data in one bag have to be before you were fairly certain that the contents of the bag were really different and that the data could not reasonably have happened by chance?" Pause.

"How about one red, one yellow, and twenty-three blue? Do you think that could happen by chance?" Yes, but it is *very* unlikely.

Then I tell them the truth. "*All the bags are the same!* These differences in the data happened by chance—S and Z are just random fluctuations that are to be expected. Now what do you think about the data? Do you want more data?"

Some students think of another possibility: If the bags are all the same, the eight groups give us two hundred samples of one. More often than not, I have to suggest the idea of summing the data for each color. See Figure 7.2.

I assign eight groups of 25 in order to have a base of 200, which allows percents to easily be calculated—just divide by 2. Therefore, 55, 37, and 108 become 27.5 percent, 18.5 percent, and 54 percent. I ask students if they want to change their predictions: "Let's think of some possibilities. Is 2, 2, 6 *possible*? Is 3, 1, 6 *possible*?" They have not caught on yet to what I'm asking. "Is 1, 0, 9 *possible*?" Finally, they get it. They tell me that 1, 0, 9 is *impossible* because there must be some yellow.

GROUP	DATA		
	R	Y	B
Z	6	4	15
Y	7	2	16
	8	5	12
W	6	6	13
V	7	5	13
U	7	4	14
T	5	6	14
S	9	5	11
TOTAL	55	37	108
percent	27.5	18.5	54
decimal	0.275	0.185	0.54

FIGURE 7.2

"Did you do a KWC?" I ask. Some did; some didn't. "Let me change the question, "Is 2,2, 6 *probable*? Which is more probable, 1, 1, 8 or 2, 2, 6? Another way to ask this question is, which is the more *likely*?"

I then ask students to nominate the three *most likely* combinations, which generates a lively discussion. They decide to go with 2, 2, 6; 3, 2, 5; and 3, 1, 6. Recall that the total data showed 27.5 percent, 18.5 percent, and 54 percent.

Finally, I ask each student to vote for his or her personal prediction of the most likely combination. With data we had, about nineteen students (two-thirds of the class) went with three red, two yellow, and five blue; four students went with two red, two yellow, and six blue; and five students went with three red, one yellow, and six blue. I handed back each bag to the team with the letter that corresponded to the bag. The teams fairly tore their bags open to reveal three red, two yellow, and five blue.

Some teachers will have one or more bags with varying numbers of cubes, but I have found it unnecessary. There is a enough random variation so at least one group is a little divergent, and teachers can get to what is perhaps the most important point in the activity: the basis of inferential statistics and a cornerstone of probability theory.

How different does the data have to be among groups for us to think that there is something other than chance operating to create the differences? There are only two possibilities: either the differences are random, chance variations or something is causing a difference; in this case, perhaps the contents could be different. The Probability Bags activity illustrates these possibilities based on patterns in the data in a fabulous way.

A Plethora of Pigs

About twenty years ago, I was looking for some fresh probability activities, alternatives to the familiar dice and spinners. I encountered Pigmania, still marketed as Pass the Pigs, a clever game that consists of two rubber pigs that are tossed like a pair of dice. The pigs are approximately one inch long, half an inch high when standing on all four feet, and three-eighths of an inch wide. See Figure 7.3.

In this game, students collect data on the outcomes from their tosses of a single pig. The frequency data are used to estimate the probability of the outcomes. We like that the six different outcomes of tossing a pig are not equally likely and that the theoretical probabilities are unknown. In

FIGURE 7.3

the following pages, Susan describes how she teaches A Plethora of Pigs to her students.

I begin by telling my students that I am planning a family party where I wish to play a game that I recently lost the rules to, and that the game involves tossing a tiny pale pink piglet with pointy ears, a small snout, and a curly tale. I also tell them that the object of the game is for my guests to earn the greatest number of points after each subsequent toss. At this point I stop and I say that this is all I can remember and I need their help to create a reasonable set of rules for the game.

I organize my students into small groups of three or four and give each group a KWC chart and a tiny piglet. I provide them with some guiding questions that enable them to dig a bit deeper. I ask them questions like:

- What's the object of the game?
- How could players earn points?
- What would a reasonable game look like?

Rephrasing these questions to look more like statements helps students develop the special circumstances of this problem. What usually happens next is that while I have been asking these questions, one student who has been busy fiddling with the piglet exclaims, "We gotta look at how it lands!" I respond by saying, "What do you mean, 'how it lands'?" The class as a whole then begins to gently toss their piglets and quickly identify the different ways the piglet could land.

On the board I record all the different ways the piglets could land that my students can think of. As they give me common names for landing positions, I inform them that the special names in this game are starting to come back to me. That is, on its side—*sider*, legs—*trotter*, back—*razorback*, nose—*snouter*, and side of mouth—*leaning jowler*. As we generate the list of possible outcomes, I hear several students mention that they can't get their own little piglet to land in the way another student has suggested. Aha! Key moment! I stop the piglet tossing and ask the students to repeat their concern.

Some students are actually quite surprised, and usually one student always suggests, "What if all the piglets are not the same?"

"That's a great suspicion," I respond, "but as far as the piglets themselves go they were all created in the same likeness at the factory."

This leads some students to continue tossing their piglets. Eventually someone says, "Wait a minute! These pigs can't land easily on everything!"

I respond, "But I thought we all agreed that we had generated an accurate list of all the possible outcomes! Does that mean that possible outcomes are just that—possibilities, not certainties?"

The students shake their heads and show me with their piglets that while it is possible for the pig to land in all the ways observed, some positions are just easier for it to land on. I ask, "If some positions are easier than others, how can we decide reasonable point values for each outcome?"

	Sider	Trotter	Razorback	Snouter	Leaning Jowler
A	34	4	10	1	1
B	30	9	9	1	1
C	28	4	15	2	1
D	36	5	8	1	0
E	28	3	16	2	1
F	28	6	14	1	1
Frac	$\frac{184}{300}$	$\frac{31}{300}$	$\frac{72}{300}$	$\frac{8}{300}$	$\frac{5}{300}$
Deci	.613	.103	.24	0.026 0.026	0.016
%	61.3%	10.3%	24%	2.6%	1.1%

FIGURE 7.4

Several hands shoot up and almost in unison they reply, "We've got to take it to the lab!" (My students have gotten quite used to me saying this in class whenever we need to collect data to draw conclusions.) I respond excitedly, "To the lab we go!"

In the lab, which is just our usual classroom, except now I'm wearing an old white lab coat for emphasis, we decide that we should toss our piglets to figure out which outcomes are easiest for them to land on. I have each group toss their piglet fifty times and record how their piglets land each time. I use fifty for several reasons: First, it's a reasonable number of trials to collect in about seven minutes of class time; second, fifty is a great number with which students can easily use proportional reasoning to predict what their data would look like in one hundred tosses, two hundred tosses, and so on; and last, but not least, all of the results can convert very nicely into fractions, percents, and decimals.

Once the students have generated their data, I record each team's data on large chart paper. See Figure 7.4.

After recording the data, we discuss as a class what that data implies as a reasonable point value system for the game I wish to play with my family. For homework that night, their job is to use mathematical evidence and sufficient support to respond to the following question:

> What point value system would you assign to each outcome? Be sure to explain your answer and support your reasoning with mathematical evidence.

What's really interesting is not only do most students assign the most point value to the most difficult landing positions (the snouter and the leaning jowler) but also they do so in a roughly proportional manner that reflects the data they collected. Additionally, I have even seen some groups actually assign negative point values to the easiest landing position (arguably the sider, which one class calculated to occur roughly 61 percent of the time in three hundred trials).

After the class shares their conclusions and debate with one another, I let them play the actual game once they agree on the best point value system. At the end of the period, to their surprise, I usually shout "Eureka! I've found the directions!" Students can compare and contrast the manufacturer's game rules with the ones they already created.

Model Building with Montana Red Dog

Montana Red Dog is another example of experimental probability that relies on data collection rather than on theoretical probability formulas. It exemplifies the cycles of rethinking, reinterpreting, and reconceptualizing that students go through, individually and in small groups. Note how their thinking changes with each successive data-gathering experience.

The card game of Montana Red Dog originated in the Old West and is rarely played today. We use a standard deck of fifty-two cards, with four suits and aces high. I arrange the students into ten groups of two or three per group. I am the dealer and I give each group four cards, leaving twelve cards for me. I discard the two bottom cards leaving me, the dealer, with ten cards. I turn over the top card of the ten in my hand and each group tries to beat me. A group wins if one of their four cards is higher in number than mine, but it must be in the same suit.

Students must answer this question: Is Montana Red Dog a *fair game*? They may say things such as:

- It is fair because it is just dumb luck what cards you get.
- It is not fair because you have twelve cards and we have only four. You are going to win.
- It is fair because you shuffled and everybody got random cards.
- We will win more because we gave four cards against your one card.

I ask them, "What does *fair* mean? How would I know?" Older students pick that up quickly and say, "We win half the time" or "We both have an equally likely chance of winning." Younger students might say "fifty-fifty." I ask them what that means, but some do not know.

Playing the First Game

I show students my top card. "Can you beat this? Show me *one* card in your hand that can beat me; hold it up." On the board I make a two column T-table with the headings *Dealer Loses* and *Dealer Wins* to help us keep track of data. I play my top card against all ten groups at once, which generates a lot of data quickly. See Figure 7.5.

Dealer's Cards	Z	Y	X	W	V	U	T	S	R	Q	Dealer Loses	Dealer Wins
A♦											0	10
6♠					7♠		J♠	A♠			3	7
9♥	Q♥		J♥						A♥		3	7
Q♠								A♠			1	9
9♣			Q♣		A♣		10♣		J♣		4	6
8♣			Q♣		A♣		10♣		J♣		4	6
4♦	5♦		6♦	K♦		J♦		Q♦		10♦	6	4
9♠							J♠	A♠			2	8
7♦			K♦			J♦		Q♦		10♦	4	6
6♣			Q♣		A♣		10♣		J♣		4	6
Player wins	2	0	5	2	4	2	5	5	4	2	31	69

FIGURE 7.5

I turn over each of my ten dealer cards one at a time, and each group that had a winning card holds it up. We can see that the dealer won 69 percent of the time. Only groups X, T, and S won five times by beating five of the dealer's ten cards. Once again I ask, "Do you think the game is fair?"

More Games, More Data

We play two or three games in which each group gets a new hand. I ask students to look for patterns in the data. Even in a single game of 10 groups and 10 rounds (as in Figure 7.5), we often see the dealer win 60 percent or more of the time. The dealer does not necessarily have an abundance of high cards (A, K, Q, J, 10), however; as shown in Figure 7.5, the dealer had only two of these high cards, yet still won 69 percent of the time. Of the ten competitions of the dealer's one card against each group, on only one occasion did the dealer lose more than win (with his lowest card, the 4 of Diamonds (4♦). With every other card—even with 6s—the dealer beat six or more of the ten groups. Even his 4 of Diamonds (4♦) beat four groups!

"Is the game fair or does someone have an advantage?" I ask. "What would fair look like as data?" Now the meaning of *fifty-fifty* becomes very clear to the students. Just about everybody says that if the data showed close to 50 percent for each, the game would probably be fair. However, there are always other students who cling to the phrases *dumb luck*, *chance*, and *random*, and say the game is always fair.

I pose some hypothetical data to the class: "If the dealer won 90 percent of the time on every game of one hundred we did, week after week, what would you think?" Some quickly respond, "I'd think he was cheating."

"So you would think it was not pure luck, but rather something is going on?" I reply. Some agree. "What if he were definitely *not* cheating?"I ask. Some say, "He had a lucky streak."

I counter, "What if this happened all year long? Is something in the game of Montana Red Dog that *makes* it more likely for the dealer to win?"

Comparing to a Different Probability Situation

Some students still think that the data is just chance or a lucky streak, so I show them a spinner with two colors, about three-fourth red and one fourth blue. "Two people play a game with the spinner," I tell them. "Each has one of the colors. Which color would you rather be? Which color will win more often if we play many times? What percent of the time will the red win? Would you think this game is fair?"

Everybody agrees that red would win more times, but some students are not sure how that applies to Montana Red Dog. That is, in Montana Red Dog, what represents the spinner? I have my students discuss this question in small groups. Some try to explain the connection as they see it:

> The spinner is rigged so that if you played a lot of times, the dealer would win most of them. Like at some of those carnival games, they look so easy, but the guy running the booth always has some angle. Sometimes people win, but mostly they lose. It is the same thing with this card game.

Another kid wisecracked, "Somehow the dealer has 65 percent of the spinner marked for him, but we don't see the spinner."

Analyzing a Hand

On the third or fourth deal, I ask the class, "Who has a good hand now? Show us your cards." One group thinks it does. They show the class and I ask:

- Is this a good hand?
- Why or why not?
- What makes a good hand?

This last question is key. Many students initially say "high cards," so I ask, "If turned up a two of clubs, who could beat me?" Typically six of the ten groups could, to which I respond, "Do you mean four of your ten groups cannot beat even the smallest club?" The students all begin to see that this can definitely happen when the dealer's card is from a suit they do not have. I try to crystallize their understanding by explaining that no matter how high the cards are, if they are missing a suit, right off the bat they will not beat one-fourth of the cards I could have. They realize a really good hand has high cards in all four suits.

Protests return from the proponents of the dumb luck theory: "But you don't know how many of your twelve cards are from that suit, maybe none, maybe all twelve."

Misconception

Students are focusing on individual hands and trials, and not thinking about what happens in the long run—they need to appreciate concepts such as the law of large numbers, sample size, and "the long run." I ask them about the spinner where three-fourths of the face is red: "If I spun this four times, will it definitely land on the red three of the four times?" Some say yes, some say maybe, some say not necessarily. We can see the movement across these three responses and a steady dwindling of the "yes" response across grades 3, 4, 5, and 6.

Using a handout I've prepared to help students analyze their hands, students circle the four cards in their hands. See Figure 7.6. Then they count how many cards are above the highest card they have in a suit and enter that number in the box under the suit in the *Cannot Beat* row.

SPADES♠	HEARTS♥	CLUBS♣	DIAMONDS♦	
Cannot Beat [0]	[8]	[13]	[2]	Total Cannot Beat [23]
Ⓐ	A	A	A	
K	K	K	K	
Q	Q	Q	Ⓠ	
J	J	J	J	
10	10	10	10	
9	9	9	9	
8	8	8	8	
7	7	7	7	
6	Ⓖ	6	6	
Ⓢ	5	5	5	
4	4	4	4	
3	3	3	3	
2	2	2	2	
Can Beat [11]	[4]	[0]	[10]	Total Can Beat [25]

FIGURE 7.6

In Figure 7.6 we have the example of the analysis of the four-card hand from group S in Figure 7.5. They see four cards in their hand. That leaves forty-eight cards they don't see: twelve are with the dealer and the remaining thirty-six cards are with the other nine groups.

Then students fill in the boxes by counting how many of the forty-eight cards are higher than the cards they have. Figure 7.6 shows no Spade cards above the Ace of Spades, so zero (0) goes in the *Cannot Beat* box on top of the Spades. There are eight Hearts that are higher than six, so eight (8) goes in the Cannot beat box on top of the Hearts. This hand has no Clubs, and therefore cannot beat any of the thirteen Clubs. Only the Ace and King of Diamonds can beat the Queen that they have, so two (2) goes in the box. Add those numbers across and they get a total of twenty-three cards that this hand cannot beat. The good news is that this means out of the forty-eight that cannot be seen, this hand can beat twenty-five.

A really important idea now is how do students *interpret* the number of cards in the *Total Can Beat* box? They definitely could see that if one had Ace, King, Ace, King in only two suits (for example, A♠ K♠, A♥, K♥), they could not beat half the cards in the deck (Clubs and Diamonds). In fact, they would be able to beat *less than half* of the forty-eight cards out there. How can this be true? They'd beat that half of the deck that were Spades and Hearts. Right? Not quite—they would lose to the twenty-six Clubs and Diamonds, and their two Spades and two Hearts would beat the eleven Spades and eleven Hearts still out there. They can beat only twenty-two out of forty-eight cards.

Calculating the Probability

If one group has twenty-four cards that *can* beat and twenty-four cards that *cannot* beat, it is easy to help students see that means beating twenty-four of the forty-eight, or 24/48, or half the cards out there. Then all groups can represent their hands as fractions with forty-eight as the denominator, allowing students to get good experience with equivalent fractions. There is logical reasoning aplenty about part-whole relationships that form the basis for fractions, decimals, and percents. Teachers can use Montana Red Dog as a vehicle for investigating any of these representations and their interrelations.

How do these representations influence students' conceptions of probability? Most of them can see $^{16}/_{48}$ as equivalent to $^1/_3$ and to .33 or 33.33 percent, but only some of them see that these statistics could mean this hand should beat the dealer's card 33 percent of the time in the long run or has a *probability of winning* equal to .33. Every time I play this game with older students, a discussion ensues in which some students argue with that statement and say, "You can't say that. It is just random, just chance" or "It depends on what cards the dealer gets and that is just chance." This is essentially the same conception that we saw earlier. Even some students who were able to see how the dealer appears to have

Groups' Hands

	Z	Y	X	W	V	U	T	S	R	Q
	Q♥10♥	2♠5♥	J♥3♥	K♦9♦	A♣K♣	8♥J♦	10♣J♠	A♠5♠	A♥4♥	5♣3♠
	7♥5♦	3♦2♣	6♦Q♣	3♣6♦	2♦7♠	4♣4♠	10♠8♠	Q♦6♥	J♣7♣	2♥10♦
wins	2	0	5	2	4	2	5	5	4	2
	.200	.000	.500	.200	.400	.200	.500	.500	.400	.200
can beat	11	5	22	11	16	19	15	25	19	
	$\frac{11}{48}$	$\frac{5}{48}$	$\frac{22}{48}$	$\frac{11}{48}$	$\frac{16}{48}$	$\frac{19}{48}$	$\frac{15}{48}$	$\frac{25}{48}$	$\frac{19}{48}$	$\frac{15}{48}$
p =	.229	.104	.458	.229	.333	.396	.313	.521	.396	.313

FIGURE 7.7

an advantage built into the game *in the long run* do not conceive of this statistic in the long run.

The students learn quite a bit from analyzing their hands and looking at who has good hands in the class. Figure 7.7 supplements what we saw previously in Figure 7.5. At the top of the table in Figure 7.7 we can see the four cards that each group had. The wins directly under the ten group columns are the number of times out of ten that a particular group won. The bottom two rows in Figure 7.7 give the number that each group can beat, this number as the numerator of a fraction with denominator of 48, this value as a decimal (you could readily use percent instead of decimal). These statistics are the probability of winning that each group has.

The students who have an initial, reasonable interpretation of these percents are quite surprised. I'd even say some are stunned. Their threshold understanding of the fraction and the decimal told them, "In the long run, regardless of which particular cards the dealer has in any one game (or many games), if you decided to keep this hand, that is the fraction or decimal part the times that you would win."

Only one of the ten groups—group S—had more than a .500 probability of winning. Nine of the ten hands have less than .500 chance of winning. Furthermore, even in one game (the short run), the probability of winning is close to what actually happened. Each group compared the number of wins they actually had as a decimal—wins divided by ten—to their probability of winning. For instance, group S had a probability of .521 and actually beat five out of ten, or .500, of the dealer's cards. The next highest probability was group X with .458, and they also won .500. Only group T did much better than would have been predicted from analyzing their hand (probability .313 versus actually won .500).

The first time students analyze their hands in a game this way, they are surprised. When they get similar probabilities upon analyzing the hands in three other games, most decide that the game is not fair. Some have even been known to say, "We have found the spinner!"

But have they? What causes the probabilities of the hands to be relatively low?

Do I Have a Suit for You!

Most of the time, somewhere along the way, one or more of the students will go back to the idea that good hands are not just high cards, they are also suits. When they look at the ten hands in any game, they are surprised. From Figure 7.7 they see the following information:

- Only three hands had a card from each of the four suits (groups Y, U, and Q). Together those groups only won four trials. What happened? They only had two high cards, the Jack and the 10 of Diamonds.
- How many groups had three suits covered? Only three groups, and they generated fourteen wins.
- Two suits? Four groups, and they generated thirteen wins.
- That's it. No one-suit hands.

I ask the class, "Why is having all four suits advantageous?" Eventually, students say things like, "The dealer does not have to worry about suits" and "The dealer determines the suit. He's got it and you'd better have one."

Although it is too difficult for middle school students to follow an analysis of the theoretical probabilities of Montana Red Dog, I do tell them that the dealer will win about 62 percent of the time. The groups will have cards in all four suits only 10 percent of the time. (See page 245 at the end of this chapter for the calculation shown in a way that students can follow.) Students can figure out that when having two suits, which is fairly frequent, even the best hand—two aces—only gets you a .458 probability of winning.

What a Fair Game Looks Like

I end Montana Red Dog with a twist. I have a new game for them to play, Illinois Blue Dog. The students get in to their ten groups again. I have prepared a deck of card with the four suits separated. I ask four students to shuffle them and I put the cards into four piles. Then I deal out one pile (one suit, one card) to each group. I repeat this with each pile so that each group has one card from each of the four suits. The twelve cards I have left must be three cards from each suit. I shuffle my twelve cards, then turn them over one at a time, as in Red Dog, each time asking, "Can you beat this card with a higher card in its suit?" I also ask, "Is this a fair game?"

The students think about it and most say, "It is fair, because in the long run it will be my spade and your spade, so it is really only the numbers that matter. That is like the card game War, and that is fair. Except in this game there would be no ties." If they wrote that in their math journals, I'd be happy.

EXPLORING POSSIBLE OUTCOMES IN THEORETICAL PROBABILITY

After students have completed the activities described so far in this chapter and built a foundation in probability, they can move toward more abstract representations and theoretical probability. Being able to determine all the possible outcomes of a situation is valuable in life. The activities in this section, Combination Pizzas and Permutation Locks, Product Versus Square, Montana Red Dog Follow-Up, and De Mere's Bets Follow-Up, creatively develop that capability.

Combination Pizzas and Permutation Locks

Some Background About the Activity

I have no data to support my contentions, but I believe that the incidence of food allergies in this country, especially peanuts and chocolate, has risen dramatically in the past ten or so years. In our probability activity Combination Pizzas and Permutation Locks, M&Ms play a major role. It is possible to substitute other items for the chocolate, such as Skittles or even colored cubes or tiles, as long as six different colors are available.

I was teaming a week-long workshop with Meg Ormiston many years ago when she did this activity with teachers. I think I've done it at least three times a year since then. The first part is largely motivational; I know this because when I leave it out, the students do not respond as well as usual. The major purposes of Combination Pizzas and Permutation Locks are to help students understand the Fundamental Counting Principle (FCP) and to make sure they understand what combinations and permutations are and how they are critical to theoretical probability. Therefore, this activity and Product Versus Square (see page 242) are bridges from experimental to theoretical probability.

A few days prior to this activity, the teachers talked about when order matters and when it doesn't. We all brainstormed a number of ways we could help students connect permutations and combinations to the world around them so that they could understand the difference between the two different types of arrangements.

1. When making change, only the total matters. The order in which one gives back the coins is unimportant, unless specific coins are needed (or you hate pennies).
2. The order of the letters used is very important. For example, I have a three letter nickname, *ART*. But those three letters could also be *TAR, RAT, TRA, RTA,* or *ATR*; therefore, these are the six different permutations of those three letters.

3. Some pizza parlors refer to *combination pizza*, which of course means that there are different toppings available. Ordering a pizza with onions, green peppers, and sausage would be the same if you ordered one with green peppers, onions, and sausage. The order is irrelevant.

4. People routinely refer to the locks on the junior high school lockers as *combination locks* and need to know the combination and enter the combination in the correct sequence, or order, to access the lockers. Wait a minute, then it's not a combination—the school is filled with *permutation locks*.

The M&Ms Game

To begin the game, I separate the class into four roughly equal teams, for example, four teams of seven. We arrange seven chairs in a circle with their backs touching so that those sitting in them are facing outward with their teammates. Through a random process we determine the order of the teams (first, second, third, and fourth). I explain to the teams that they will each get a turn at playing the game. The first team will sit in the chairs with the second team members each standing in front of one who is sitting. I hold up a basket of M&Ms with six colors: red, yellow, green, blue, orange, and brown. Each person sitting will have to pick a combination of three different colors. They are true combinations because order does not matter; that is, red, blue, green is the same combination as green, red, blue. To help illustrate this concept, I show three transparent bingo chips on the overhead and explain that even if I say the names of the three colors in a different order, it is still the same combination.

The tasks for the two playing teams are as follows:

Team 1 (Sitting Team)

1. The starting seated player pulls out one combination of three different colors from the basket.
2. That player says aloud the names of the three colors so everyone can hear what he or she picked.
3. The seated person to that player's *left* is the next one to choose from the basket. He or she must choose a different combination.
4. Each successive player repeats these actions so no talking is allowed except repeating the three colors.

Team 2 (Standing Team)

1. The members of the standing team pass the basket and hold it down so that the sitting team can easily see into the basket and select three colors.
2. No talking by the standing team is allowed.
3. The standing team player should look at the seated player's hand to see if the combination just chosen and spoken by a player is in the hand of the sitting team player in front of her.

I send the four teams to different parts of the room where they are given three to five minutes to plan. However, they may not take any paper, pens, or pencils. The seven players in each team must quickly agree on a strategy.

The first team sits and the second team stands in front of them. The other two teams stand nearby, quietly observing. The play begins with the first person choosing three colors, placing them in her open hand so the other team's watcher can see. The next person chooses two colors the same as the first, but the third color is different. It appears that their strategy is to hold two constant and vary the third. The strategy works fine until the fifth student forgets that he is supposed to switch over to a new pair. He repeats the third combination. His watcher says stop. I announce they got four combinations.

The watchers and sitters trade places and the second team plays. They actually get all the way around and back to the starting person, who now holds up one palm with two combinations. The second team was able to chose twelve different combinations before repeating. I tell them that they did very well—there are perhaps only twelve combinations and they found them all.

Several students from the third and fourth teams say there are more than twelve, so I say, "Show me!" Teams 3 and 4 switch with Teams 1 and 2. One gets ten and the other eight. I tell them maybe there *are* only twelve combinations.

I ask all the students to go back to their seats and get set up with a partner. I give each pair two strips of paper with rows of three circles, big enough to accommodate a single M&M or Skittle and a bowl filled with M&Ms. I tell them I do not want any lists, no letters, and in fact I don't want to see any pencils or pens at all. Just use the M&Ms in combinations of three. Find as many combinations as you can. Be sure to check for duplicates.

For most of the students, there is an intense motivation, piqued by the introductory game, to find all the combinations. The students place their six colors of three at a time onto the recording sheet. They very quickly see why I didn't want to see pens or pencils. With these colorful objects there is no scratching out, no erasing when they find a duplicate. The objects can be moved easily. Many times students create permutations of the three colors and don't immediately see that they are of the same combination, so simply removing the candies or tiles is a distinct asset. In addition, some students tell me that the color circles make it much easier to spot the duplicates than a list would.

Three or four approaches come from the students themselves and often reflect what their group of seven tried. The two most popular approaches have been:

- Hold one constant and vary the other two in some order.
- Hold two constant and vary the third. In both cases the students could keep the pattern going for ten or twelve combinations.

As I circulate among the groups I try to discern the pattern they are creating. Sometimes I have to ask them to describe to me how they are doing because it is not obvious. They always check with me to see if they have found all the combinations. I have a list of standard responses that I use for every combination problem:

- I am not going to say how many there are and my recording sheets always have more slots than there are solutions.
- Did any of the solutions seem unusual in some way?
- Did you check for duplicates? How?
- Is there a pattern in your solution?
- Did you find them all?
- How do you *know* when you found them all?

The last question is the really crucial one. What I hope to hear is, "I systematically, in order, went through every possibility." Of course, I always ask them to describe *systematic*. See Figure 7.8 for an example of a systematic approach that some students use.

There are twenty possible combinations. When the students find all of them, they carefully remove the candy and color in the circle with colored pencils. They eat the candy. Then we analyze the patterns together.

Notice that the students who made the example in Figure 7.8 started with red and tried to make every combination that involved red. They intentionally used blue as the next color and made all four combinations that go with red and blue. There can be only four because there are only six colors. Can you see the triangle numbers? Follow the number of each color in the left column of the recording sheet: 10 red, 6 blue, 3 green, 1 yellow. Then the middle column shows consecutive numbers: 4 blue, 3 green, 2 yellow, 1 orange (to get full power of color in the table, please visit www.braidedmath.com).

Formulas for Combinations and Permutations

Of course, most students want to know if there is a formula to tell you how many combinations there could be in the Combination Pizzas and Permutation Locks problem. There are actually two—one is a formula, the other is more a theorem. The well-known formula for combinations is:

$$C_r^n = \frac{n!}{r!(n-r)!}$$

Its companion formula for permutations is:

$$P_r^n = \frac{n!}{r!(n-r)!}$$

The two are related:

$$C_r^n = \frac{P_r^n}{r!}$$

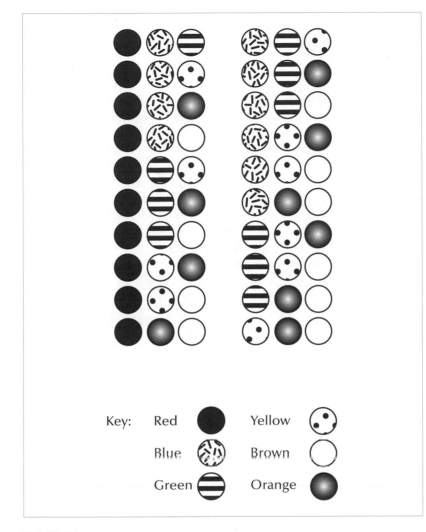

FIGURE 7.8

This is the kind of math that scares children and small animals. But using M&Ms in this activity provides a gentle way to help students understand the symbols shown in the formulas.

First, the factorial symbol *!* is an exclamation mark and I have been known to tell students when they see it they may pronounce it "eeek!" About the only places they'll ever see that symbol is in combinatorics and probability. I tell the students that mathematicians are always looking for shortcuts—for example, if they had to multiply 9 ∗ 9 ∗ 9 ∗ 9, they do shorthand to go with their shortcuts and they write 9^4 instead. So, if they had to multiply 1 ∗ 2 ∗ 3 ∗ 4 ∗ 5 or 5 ∗ 4 ∗ 3 ∗ 2 ∗ 1 they'd write *5!* and they'd say, "five factorial" (or "five eeek!").

Where did this strange shorthand come from? I'm not sure, but I have students play a little game with me that connects a lot of this. I ask five students to stand up in the back of the room in a row. I write down the order in which I want them to stand left to right. I tell them no one is now in his or her right place. I let them change places and then I'll tell them how many of them (but not who) are in the right place. If you want to do this faster, have four students stand up. If you are doing five and are running out of time tell them who's in the right place.

Now the key question: *How many different ways could the five students arrange themselves?* The Fundamental Counting Principle (FCP) theorem states that if you can choose one item from a group of *m* items and a second item from a group of *n* items, then the total number of two-item choices is *m* * *n*. The FCP is a powerful and general principle that can be extended to many different situations.

Students can now answer the key question asked above. The five students who are standing can act this out.

1. I like to think of *slots*. Five people have to fit into five slots:
   [left]   [left center]   [center]   [right center]   [right]
2. If we fill the slots left to right, we can have any one of the five go into the left slot:
   [5]   [left center]   [center]   [right center]   [right]
3. Once we choose that person, there are only four choices for the left center:
   [5]   *   [4]   [center]   [right center]   [right]
4. Once we choose *that* person, there are only three choices for the center:
   [5]   *   [4]   *   [3]   [right center]   [right]
5. Once we choose *that* person, there are only two choices for the right center:
   [5]   *   [4]   *   [3]   *   [2]   [right]
6. Once we choose *that* person, there is only one person for the right:
   [5]   *   [4]   *   [3]   *   [2]   *   [1]

This all means that there are 5 * 4 * 3 * 2 * 1 = 5! or 5 factorial (okay, 5 eeek!) ways to arrange those five students—120 ways.

Now here is the crucial connection: This same situation can be mathematically represented by the permutation of five things taken five at a time:

$$P_5^5 = 120$$

Because the order was essential, the arrangement is a permutation. In general:

$$P_n^n = \frac{n!}{(n-n)!}$$

Eeek! This looks bad! What is $(n - n)!$? $(0)!$, or zero factorial. $(0)! = 1$. Therefore:

$$P_n^n = n!$$

Now recall that:

$$C_r^n = \frac{P_r^n}{r!} \quad \text{or} \quad C_n^n = \frac{P_r^n}{n!} = \frac{n!}{n!} = 1$$

This relationship is just like when I sent five students at random to the back of the room. No order, just a single combination of five students taken five at a time:

$$C_5^5 = 1$$

Those 120 got divided out into one.

The students can apply these ideas to the six different colors of M&M's. Their task, reworded slightly, was to find all the combinations of six things taken three at a time:

$$C_3^6$$

Using FCP would give us $6 * 5 * 4$, or 120, in those slots. However, each of the 120 is a permutation (for example, Yellow, Red, Green—YRG) and there are always six that are all the same combination: YRG, YGR, RYG, RGY, GRY, and GYR. These are the duplicates we pull off the M&Ms circles on our chart. Therefore, we must divide 120 by 6:

$$C_r^n = \frac{P_r^n}{r!} \quad P_r^n = \frac{n!}{(n-r)!} \quad C_3^6 = \frac{P_3^6}{3!} \quad P_3^6 = \frac{6!}{(6-3)!} = \frac{6!}{3!}$$

Note how dividing by 3! which is 6 cuts down the 6! (720) to 120. Remember, there are only three slots, not six. Therefore:

$$P_3^6 = \frac{6!}{3!} = \frac{6 * 5 * 4 * 3 * 2 * 1}{3 * 2 * 1}$$

We have $3 * 2 * 1$ in the numerator and denominator, leaving $6 * 5 * 4$ for the three slots—which is what the FCP said we'd have. *So . . .*

$$P_3^6 = 6 * 5 * 4 = 120$$

Recall that those 120 permutations must be cut by $r!$ to eliminate the duplications as we switch from permutations to combinations $r! = 3! = 6$. Therefore:

$$C_3^6 = \frac{P_3^6}{3!} = \frac{120}{6} = 120$$

Being able to flexibly move back and forth among these concepts and their representations with understanding is essential to success in theoretical probability.

Product Versus Square

This activity can be an excellent bridge between experimental and theoretical probability.

I put the students in pairs. One student gets a pair of dice, one red and one white, and the other gets a single green die. They will play against each other rolling the dice for twenty-five trials, recording their own results. The numbers on the pair of dice are multiplied and those on the single die are squared. The higher value wins the trial.

I ask the class if they think this is a fair game. Most students are uncertain; some do say the square will win more because it has an exponent. Why would that matter, I ask, since both players multiply two numbers together? No one is sure why, so I say, "Let's play!"

Pairs begin rolling dice and recording data. A fairly typical result for the Product Versus Square activity is eight or nine squares versus five or six, an indication of an advantage, but not a certainty. Instead of collecting more data or aggregating the class as we have done in previous problems, I tell the students that we are going to go right for that *spinner* and see how it is painted!

I ask the class, "What are all the different outcomes of the square person throwing the die?" They all agree 1, 2, 3, 4, 5, 6, which would give point values respectively of 1, 4, 9, 16, 25, or 36. Now what about the person with the two dice? I ask them to list all the outcomes that could happen when she throws two dice. In a prior activity in which they found all thirty-six ways for the sum of two dice, we established that a red 2 and white 4 are not the same as white 2 and red 4. There are also thirty-six ways that one can multiply two dice together. See Figure 7.9.

To summarize: The single die is thrown and its number squared, making for six separate events. Completely independent of the single die, the pair of dice can generate thirty-six different outcomes. By the FCP,

	red die					
	1	*2*	*3*	*4*	*5*	*6*
1	1	2	3	4	5	6
2	2	4	6	8	10	12
3	3	6	9	12	15	18
4	4	8	12	16	20	24
5	5	10	15	20	25	30
6	6	12	18	24	30	36

white die

FIGURE 7.9

there must be 6 * 36 or 216 possible outcomes. Is this a fair game or does one of the players have an advantage? This must be answered empirically, not intuitively. We must examine each of the 216 outcomes using a powerful analytical device. See Figure 7.10.

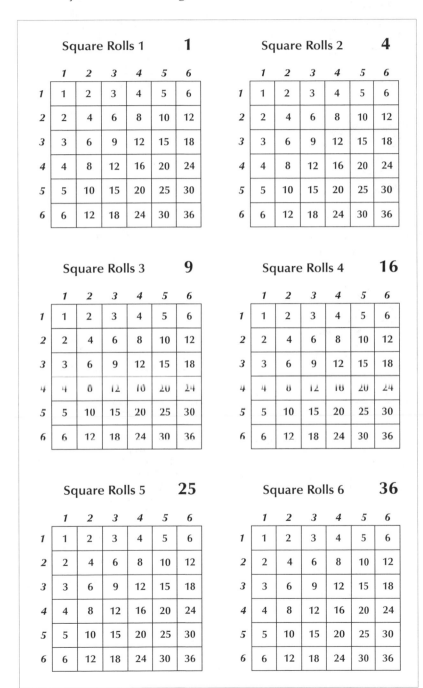

FIGURE 7.10

Square Rolls 1 — 1

SQUARE

WINS 0
LOSES 35
TIES 1

SQUARE	1	2	3	4	5	6
1	1	2	3	4	5	6
2	2	4	6	8	10	12
3	3	6	9	12	15	18
4	4	8	12	16	20	24
5	5	10	15	20	25	30
6	6	12	18	24	30	36

Square Rolls 2 — 4

SQUARE

WINS 5
LOSES 28
TIES 3

SQUARE	1	2	3	4	5	6
1	1	2	3	4	5	6
2	2	4	6	8	10	12
3	3	6	9	12	15	18
4	4	8	12	16	20	24
5	5	10	15	20	25	30
6	6	12	18	24	30	36

Square Rolls 3 — 9

SQUARE

WINS 16
LOSES 19
TIES 1

SQUARE	1	2	3	4	5	6
1	1	2	3	4	5	6
2	2	4	6	8	10	12
3	3	6	9	12	15	18
4	4	8	12	16	20	24
5	5	10	15	20	25	30
6	6	12	18	24	30	36

Square Rolls 4 — 16

SQUARE

WINS 25
LOSES 10
TIES 1

SQUARE	1	2	3	4	5	6
1	1	2	3	4	5	6
2	2	4	6	8	10	12
3	3	6	9	12	15	18
4	4	8	12	16	20	24
5	5	10	15	20	25	30
6	6	12	18	24	30	36

Square Rolls 5 — 25

SQUARE

WINS 32
LOSES 3
TIES 1

SQUARE	1	2	3	4	5	6
1	1	2	3	4	5	6
2	2	4	6	8	10	12
3	3	6	9	12	15	18
4	4	8	12	16	20	24
5	5	10	15	20	25	30
6	6	12	18	24	30	36

Square Rolls 6 — 36

SQUARE

WINS 35
LOSES 0
TIES 1

SQUARE	1	2	3	4	5	6
1	1	2	3	4	5	6
2	2	4	6	8	10	12
3	3	6	9	12	15	18
4	4	8	12	16	20	24
5	5	10	15	20	25	30
6	6	12	18	24	30	36

SQUARE WINS 113/216 EVENTS OR 52.33 percent
SQUARE LOSES 95/216 EVENTS OR 43.98 percent
TIES OCCUR 8/216 EVENTS OR 3.7 percent

FIGURE 7.11

All 216 outcomes are contained in Figure 7.10. For each of the six tables, students must color code the ties, wins, and losses for square. I usually show them an example with square rolling 1, then I ask them to do square rolls 6. There is beautiful symmetry in the two—what could that symmetry mean? Students may say, "They are going to balance each other and the game will be fair." Then they work on the other four tables on their own. Figure 7.11 clearly shows the advantage for the square.

Montana Red Dog Follow-Up

In Montana Red dog, we figured out that it was advantageous to have a card (preferably a high card) in every suit. If not, then you'll lose every time that your missing suit is pulled by the dealer. How likely is a hand with all four suits?

We know there are four slots this time. We want to know the *circumstances* under which the four slots are filled with each of the different suits.

The actual probability of having all four suits covered is .1055.

The first card has the probability of one that it matches nothing.	The second card can be any of the thirty-nine that do not match the suit of the first card.	The third card can be any of the twenty-six that do not match the suits of cards 1 or 2.	The fourth card can be any of thirteen cards that do not match the suits of cards 1, 2, or 3.
p = 1	* 39/51	* 26/50	* 13/49 = .1055

We can see that there are four slots, but we are not interested in getting the same kind of result—we only want to know the *circumstances* under which the four slots are filled with four different suits. For example:

- The first card did not match anything: It has a probability of 1.00 (a certainty).
- The second card is pulled out of the fifty-one cards left and there are thirty-nine that are from the other three suits. Thirty-nine out of fifty-one times (76.47 percent of the time) the second card will be a different suit.
- The third card is pulled out of fifty, and there are twenty-six cards from the two suits not in the hand. Twenty-six out of fifty means that 52 percent of the time the third card will be different from the first two cards.

The probability of someone getting these first three different would be .7647 ∗.52 = .3976 or only about 40 percent of the time.

Like the fundamental counting principle (FCP), the probabilities are multiplied together to determine how likely both events occurring might be. In this case, the fourth card is pulled from forty-nine cards; we are trying to get one of the thirteen cards from the one suit we don't have. Thirteen out of forty-nine is 26.53 percent. The joint occurrence and joint probabilities would be .7647 ∗ .52 ∗ .2653 = .1054. Only 10.54 percent of the time would we expect to see a hand with all four suits.

De Mere's Bets Follow-Up

De Mere reasoned incorrectly on both bets. His winnings on the first bet probably assured him that his reasoning was accurate. De Mere reasoned that the probability (p) of getting a six on a single throw is $1/6$, but we will reason conversely that p of *not* getting a six is $5/6$ ($1 - 1/6$). If you throw a second die, p that both throws did not yield a six would be $5/6 * 5/6$. For three throws, not getting a six is $5/6 * 5/6 * 5/6$. For four throws the probability of not getting a six is $5/6 * 5/6 * 5/6 * 5/6 = (5/6)^4$. Reasoning conversely again, if p of *not* getting six in four rolls is $(5/6)^4$, then the p of getting at least one six in four rolls is $1 - (5/6)^4 = 1 - {}^{625}/_{1296} = {}^{671}/_{1296} = .5177$. Therefore, de Mere had a definite advantage 51.77 percent versus 48.23 percent over his opponent, clearly not a fair game.

But why must we use the converse? We don't have to, but it makes the reasoning much easier. If we set out directly to determine p for *at least one six* we'd have to account for not just getting one six, which could happen on any of the four throws, but also two sixes, which could happen any one of six ways. And we'd have to account or possibly, although unlikely, getting three or even four sixes. It is much easier to calculate the p of not getting a six at all.

De Mere's second bet was that he could get a double six by throwing a pair of dice twenty-four times. There are thirty-six different outcomes when throwing a pair of dice. The p of getting double six from a throw is $1/36$. Therefore the p of not getting double sixes in a single row is $35/36$ (.9722). De Mere threw twenty-four times and didn't get double sixes. The probability of not getting any is $(.9722)^{24} = .508596$ and the p of getting at least one double six is $1 - .5086 = .4914$, meaning de Mere gave the advantage to his opponents. In one more roll, the advantage flips over the fifty-fifty line:

- $1 - (.9722)^{24} = 1 - .50896 = .4914$: With twenty-four throws de Mere wins less than half the time.
- $1 - (.9722)^{25} = 1 - .494468 = .5055$: With twenty-five throws de Mere wins more than half the time.

CONCLUDING THOUGHTS

In many ways this chapter epitomizes the approach we advocate throughout this book. Activities start out real and tangible, and as different representations are used, students' thinking becomes increasingly abstract. They develop many kinds of connections, especially math to math. Integrating data work with probability makes good sense. In addition, any probability experiment can be a meaningful opportunity for computational work.

In Chapter 2 we explained six major ideas and wove them throughout this book. To recap, we advocate:

1. Broadening our view of *problem solving*—moving beyond the traditional story problem to building mathematical models of situations and phenomena.

2. Students making *connections* between the problem they are working on and their lives, the world around them, and the mathematical concepts they know (tapping into their prior knowledge).

3. Students creating their own *representations* of increasing abstraction: creating their own meaningful representations of language, objects, pictures, actions, lists, tables, graphs, and equations.

4. Students solving problems involving the same concept in multiple, different *contexts* to build a generalized understanding of the concept.

5. Cognitively based *planning* for teaching: planning for language, connections, contexts, and representations.

6. Putting it all together in the *Braid Model* of problem solving.

We hope to inspire other teachers to adapt their curricula to a broader sense of what problem solving can be, including the mathematical models that we describe students creating. We have seen firsthand our students creating multiple representations and reconceptualizing problems, interpreting, refining, connecting to what they know, and then going way beyond.

Last year, a popular educational journal published an article I wrote, originally entitled "The Missing Ingredients in Math Teaching: Language and Thinking." Some people thought I was being too judgmental. I thought that I was being very fair-minded and based any critique of current practice on the Third International Math and Science Study, especially their analysis of videos of about one hundred eighth-grade math teachers from the United States compared to about one hundred math teachers from six other countries.

The major finding that stood out on the videos was that in the six countries where eighth graders scored higher than U.S. students, when their students were supposed to tackle problems intended to build conceptual understanding by making connections among concepts, teachers—through various means of questioning and dialogue—actively tried to facilitate students making connections.

In stark contrast, *none* of the U.S. teachers implemented the conceptual understanding problems the way they were intended. Instead, teachers turned *all* of these problems, rich in mathematical concepts, into procedural exercises—for example, by giving the students a formula and telling them to plug in the numbers. On some occasions, the teachers just gave the students the answers. In U.S. classrooms, *none* of the problems, each designed for serious discussion of the connections of mathematical concepts, provoked conceptual dialogue.

We hope *Understanding Middle School Math* will stimulate dialogue among teachers and provoke mathematical dialogue in their classrooms.

APPENDIX

PLANNING CONSIDERATIONS

Big Ideas, Enduring Understandings, and Essential Concepts

What is the concept that I want students to understand?

To what prior knowledge should we try to connect?

Are there different *models* of the concept?

Should I break down the concept into its underlying ideas?

Is there a sequence of understandings that students need to have?

What additional mathematical concepts are related?

Authentic Experiences

What are the real-life situations or contexts in which students would encounter the concept?

Will they see the concept in their science or social studies classes?

How can I vary contexts to build up a more generalized understanding?

What version of this situation can I present to start students thinking about the concept?

What questions can I ask to intrigue students and initiate problem solving?

Cognitive Processes in the Context

How do I scaffold students' experiences for progressive development, from concrete to the abstract?

How concretely should I start?

How can I encourage initial play and exploration with the materials or ideas?

How can I make experiences challenging but not overwhelming?

What questions can I ask or terms could I use to help students visualize or imagine the context, situation, or problem?

Should students work in small groups to discuss the problem or concept in the specific context?

Grouping Structures to Encourage the Social Construction of Meaning

How can I vary grouping structures—whole class, small group, or individuals—with attention to small groups of two to five students?

How can I enhance small-group discussions to enable students to develop, refine, and elaborate their thinking?

Language Representations

How do I talk about the concept or ask questions to reveal connections or promote reflection?

How can I model thought processes, strategies, and practices to encourage both cognitive and metacognitive thinking?

How can I incorporate reading, writing, speaking, and listening into activities?

How can I help students use journals to document, reflect upon, and refine their thinking?

How can I help students explain their representations orally or in writing?

Other Representations

How do I scaffold experiences so that the representations students create are increasingly more abstract?

What manipulatives or physical objects help students see what is going on?

Should students draw pictures of objects, situations, or problems as they imagine them?

Does the situation contain a sequence of actions that students could act out?

Should students record information in a list and later organize it into a table?

What symbols—n, objects, or pictures, for example—are essential for students to understand?

How does each symbol specifically relate to the situation?

What patterns—visual, spatial, or numerical—do I want students to see?

What questions do I ask to help students see patterns?

What questions do I ask to build bridges and help students make connections?

How do I talk about other mathematical concepts that are related to patterns?

What terms or language could I use? What metaphors or analogies could I make?

What connections are important for students to make as we debrief the activity?

How do I help students move from natural language to more precise mathematical terms?

How do I help students communicate their solutions and understandings orally and in writing?

REFERENCES

Ausubel, D. P. 1978. *Educational Psychology: A Cognitive View.* 2nd ed. New York: Holt, Rinehart, and Winston.

Blachowicz, C., and D. Ogle. 2001. *Reading Comprehension: Strategies for Independent Learners.* New York: Guilford.

Bransford, J. D., A. Brown, and R. R. Cocking, eds. 2000. *How People Learn: Brain, Mind, Experience, and School.* Expanded ed. Washington, DC: National Academy Press.

Bruner, J. 1977. *The Process of Education.* 2nd ed. Cambridge, MA: Harvard University Press.

Carroll, Lewis. 1936. "The Mock Turtle's Story." In *Alice's Adventures in Wonderland.* New York: Crown.

Donovan, M. S., and J. D. Bransford. 2005. *How Students Learn: History, Mathematics, and Science in the Classroom.* Washington, DC: National Academy Press.

Harvey, S., and A. Goudvis. 2007. *Strategies That Work: Teaching Comprehension for Understanding and Engagement.* 2nd ed. York, ME: Stenhouse.

Hiebert, J., R. Gallimore, H. Garnier, K. Bogard Givvin, H. Hollingsworth, J. Jacobs, and A. M. Y. Chui. 2003. *Teaching Mathematics in Seven Countries: Results from the TIMSS 1999 Video Study.* Washington, DC: US Department of Education, National Center for Educational Statistics.

Hyde, A. 2006. *Comprehending Math: Adapting Reading Strategies to Teach Mathematics, K–6.* Portsmouth, NH: Heinemann.

Hyde, A. 2007. "Mathematics and Cognition." In *Educational Leadership* 65 (1). Alexandria, VA: Association for Supervision and Curriculum Development.

Keene, E. O., and S. Zimmermann. 2007. *Mosaic of Thought: The Power of Comprehension Strategy Instruction.* 2nd ed. Portsmouth, NH: Heinemann.

Kline, M. 1964. *Why Johnny Can't Add: The Failure of the New Math*. New York: St. Martin's Press.

Lamon, S. J. 2005. *Teaching Fractions and Ratios for Understanding*. 2nd ed. Mahwah, NJ: Lawrence Erlbaum.

Lesh, R., and H. Doerr, eds. 2003. *Beyond Constructivism: Models and Modeling Perspectives on Mathematics Problem Solving, Learning, and Teaching*. Mahwah, NJ: Lawrence Erlbaum.

Lesh, R., and J. S. Zawojewski. 2006. "Problem Solving and Modeling." In *The Handbook of Research on Mathematics Education*. Reston, VA: National Council of Teachers of Mathematics.

Miller, D. 2002. *Reading with Meaning: Teaching Comprehension in the Primary Grades*. York, ME: Stenhouse.

National Council of Teachers of Mathematics. 2000. *Principles and Standards for School Mathematics*. Reston, VA: National Council of Teachers of Mathematics.

Sarason, S. 1971. *The Culture of the School and the Problem of Change*. 1st ed. New York: Allyn and Bacon.

Zawojewski, J. S., and R. Lesh. 2003. "A Models and Modeling Perspective on Problem Solving." In *Beyond Constructivism*, edited by Richard Lesh and Helen Doerr. Mahwah, NJ: Lawrence Erlbaum.

PROBLEM INDEX

There are more than fifty problems or activities in this book and we want to help readers quickly find them. We have included with each problem the mathematical concepts that can be connected to it. Almost all problems require some computation, however; therefore we include computational concepts only when they are specially emphasized. Similarly, process standards abound in these problems and activities, especially multiple representations; if a process standard is cited, it is especially important.

Chapter 3

Chapter 4

INDEX